Medieval
Studies
Library

THE STRUCTURE OF THE CANTERBURY TALES

The Structure of
The Canterbury Tales

Helen Cooper

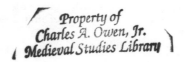

Duckworth

First published in 1983 by
Gerald Duckworth & Co. Ltd.
The Old Piano Factory
43 Gloucester Crescent, London NW1

ISBN 0 7156 1718 4 (cased)

British Library Cataloguing in Publication Data

Cooper, Helen
  The structure of the Canterbury Tales.
  1. Chaucer, Geoffrey—Canterbury Tales
  I. Title
  821′.1   PR1874

  ISBN 0–7156–1718–4

Typeset by Input Typesetting Limited, London
and printed by
Unwin Brothers Limited, Old Woking

Preface

The justification for a new book on the *Canterbury Tales* must lie in the text, so I shall not attempt to give one here. I have tried to write the kind of book I always wanted to read about the *Tales* but which no one else appeared to have produced. I hope other readers will find it satisfying.

With a subject of such general interest as Chaucer, I have run up an especially large number of debts. Foremost among those to whom I owe thanks are the many students I have taught, at Cambridge and Oxford, whose ideas, enthusiasm and bewilderment have helped me to formulate my own thoughts. A number of people have answered specific queries or discussed particular matters with me: Dr Malcolm Parkes and Miss Kate Harris on textual traditions, Miss Beryl Smalley on Ovid and his commentators, Dr Colin Day on alchemy. Dr Ruth Morse commented on the first draft of the book with her usual generosity of time and trouble, and Dr Peter Godman and Mr Nick Joint also contributed invaluable criticisms. The errors and infelicities that remain are largely due to my ignoring their advice. The script benefited further from the skilled and critical typing of Miss Vivian Cadbury.

I must also acknowledge two more general debts. One is to my husband, for chasing me away from domestic distractions to the pursuit of scholarship. The second is to University College, Oxford, both for the grant of a term's sabbatical leave, and for its interest in all matters intellectual.

H.C.

Contents

Introduction

Chaucer was the best story-teller in an age renowned for its skill in narrative. In the *Canterbury Tales* he wrote some of the finest stories ever produced, in poetry of a quality unmatched in that golden age of the late fourteenth century.

It is necessary to stress those two very obvious facts – that the *Canterbury Tales* is a series of stories, and that they are brilliantly written – since criticism on them has tended to focus on other issues. The relationship of the tales to their tellers has been endlessly analysed, often with the assumption that the stories only exist to illustrate the psychology of the various pilgrims. The links between the tales have been sieved for references to time and place so that the stories can be fitted into a coherent itinerary of an actual pilgrimage from London to Canterbury. There is even a plaque on the site of the old Tabard Inn in Southwark that declares with bureaucratic assurance,

> This building stands on the site of the old Tabard Inn whence Chaucer and the Pilgrims set out for Canterbury 1383 A.D.[1]

Alternatively, the pilgrimage has been seen as primarily an allegorical rather than a literal journey, describing the pilgrimage of man's life with not Canterbury but the celestial city as its goal. Other readings would find a consistent moral meaning, *sentence* or *doctryne*, across the whole range of tales.

The trouble with all such readings is that they do not square with what Chaucer wrote. Concentration on the framework leaves the tales

[1] The opening footnote is an illustration of the hazards of scholarship. A long search of the Borough High Street, Southwark, failed to produce any sign of the plaque I had seen a few years ago. I owe the wording to the records in the Local Collections section of the John Harvard Library, Southwark, which also noted that the plaque itself was 'temporarily removed' and subsequently lost. I leave the reference in the present tense in the trust that it will soon be replaced.

as something of an embarrassment. Attempts to impose a rigid scheme of meaning recoil before the multifariousness of the work. Focus on a single aspect, such as the psychological, can result in the writing of a *Canterbury Tales* parallel to Chaucer's but with a different, and narrower, set of interests. When Chaucer has long been admired for such immediately attractive attributes as clarity, humanity, sharpness of perception, and humour, it is alarming to discover that there is probably less of a critical consensus on what he was doing in his poetry than for any other English writer.

Textual studies often offer a haven of refuge from the storms of critical opinion, but the text of the *Canterbury Tales* is one of the least certain things about the work. It is self-evident that Chaucer never completed it. The pilgrims do not tell even one tale each, let alone the four that the Host suggests, and many of the narrative links are missing. We cannot be certain that he did not envisage a return to the Tabard at the end; the work would then have finished with a supper at the inn, and not with the austerity of the Parson's Tale, told at a 'thropes ende' which is usually understood (though Chaucer does not say so) to mean the approach to Canterbury itself. If our knowledge of the shape Chaucer may have intended to give the work is so scanty, our understanding of his intentions in the parts we do have is little better. The work consists of a number of groups of linked tales, and it was believed until recently that Chaucer never put these completed groups into any final order; but this too has now become a matter of dispute. If the text as we possess it may be in some respects a scribal or editorial accident, then it is dangerous to build hypotheses on it that assume its fixity. It is even more dangerous for a critic to assume its fluidity and to re-arrange the building blocks into an edifice proclaimed as representing Chaucer's original intentions.

The problem, then, is to find some way of approaching the *Tales* that takes full account of their richness and yet can do justice to the sense one gets that Chaucer knows precisely where he is going, even if we don't know where that is. It must be a principle rooted in the text; it is too easy to construct theories on the *Tales* by turning one's back on the work and looking instead at various kinds of allegorical exegesis or whatever else suggests itself. It must also be an idea that allows for the uncertainties of the text as we have it – it should, indeed, profit from the nature of the uncertainties, as showing at times where Chaucer was still looking for final answers. It must be central enough to be obvious to the work's original audience, and not merely one of a range available to them; and central enough too to make sense of the work in modern terms as well, for the *Canterbury Tales* is obviously a work of far more than historical interest.

It might seem that the way out of this dilemma would be to look at the individual stories in isolation, since they, at least, are more or less fixed entities, regardless of who tells them or where in the sequence they might be supposed to come. Clearly, however, this will not do. Chaucer emphatically does care about relating his stories in some way to their tellers, as the reassignment of tales from one pilgrim to another paradoxically confirms: if there were no relation between tale and teller, there would be no need for change. Sequence is clearly important for similar reasons. If any arrangement were equally suitable, there need be no confusion: the tales could follow each other in the order he wrote them. In his earlier story-collection *The Legend of Good Women* (in which the heroines are actually noted more for being deserted than for being good), there is no logical internal development from story to story and no signs of doubt as to arrangement. In the *Canterbury Tales*, by contrast, Chaucer seems to have taken considerable thought and effort over arranging the tales in the fragments we now possess. It is as if they were pieces of a jigsaw, some still looking for a place in the pattern, some for which the right place has been found. The tales firmly joined in the separate fragments make recognisably coherent patterns, even though it may still be obscure as to how they might all eventually fit together and what the finished jigsaw would look like. And the pieces do join together, as much recent criticism has stressed: the *Canterbury Tales* is not a ragbag of unrelated narratives. One still cannot construct the final picture when so many pieces are missing, but one can get a better idea of the work from looking at the sections Chaucer completed, where the pieces are fitted together, than from the stories in isolation from each other.

The analogy with the jigsaw would seem to break down over the fact that the stories are clearly not going to form any kind of single picture, and they are much too highly individualised to fit together in any predictable way. The variety of the tales in the Canterbury series is one of the most extraordinary things about it. There were plenty of other mediaeval story-collections, but none of them is remotely like Chaucer's; and that is itself remarkable, for the nature of a genre is to conform to a pattern – genres *are* patterns, in fact, and that is how one recognises them, distinguishing tragic patterns of form and content from those of the novel or the epic or the romance. The story-collection was familiar enough in the fourteenth century to be a genre to itself; but the *Canterbury Tales* does not fit.

The story-collection is none the less the obvious place to start. As a recognised genre, it would raise certain expectations in the audience. One can discover a great deal about the *Canterbury Tales* from seeing how far Chaucer fulfils these expectations, and, even more important, where he departs from the generic conventions. Perhaps the single most important fact about literary conventions is that variations on them are immediately significant: mediaeval readers were in the habit of reading intertextually. Gawain's comparative failure on his quest for the Green Knight is all the more striking when the knights errant of romance so consistently achieve their quests, just as the Dark Lady of Shakespeare's sonnets acquires most of her literary point through her distance from the Petrarchan ideal. If Gawain or Shakespeare's mistress had fulfilled the conventions, they would have been interesting in an entirely different way – but little literature is written simply within a convention, least of all Chaucer's.

'Convention' means, in essence, a thing agreed – agreed between author and audience. It is a familiar and expected way of doing something, and it becomes conventional in the first instance because it represents a truth. In size a convention can range from a few formulaic words of description to patterns of behaviour or to the associations of an entire literary genre. Mediaeval literature is conventional in the richest sense: it works within or through or against traditional expectations. In modern usage the word can sometimes become almost synonymous with 'cliché', but there is a crucial difference between them. Cliché is dead convention – truism rather than truth. The profound attractiveness of beauty, handled as cliché, will produce yet another wearisomely beautiful lady to serve for every incidental female character. Chaucer gives us the Emily of the Knight's Tale, beautiful indeed, and with all the standard attributes of beauty, but through imagery and her association with the spring she is given a quality far surpassing cliché. The very familiarity of the details of her beauty recalls all the other beautiful ladies of lyric and heroines of romance; so precisely because of their conventionality, her attributes give a resonance to the whole passage, making her the embodiment of all the other lovely women poets have ever desired. It is this kind of resonance that makes conventions live, and this kind of convention that Chaucer is supremely good at manipulating. The description of Emily itself takes on additional resonances in the course of the *Canterbury Tales*, as later heroines recall her in varying ways, for better or for worse, as they fulfil the conventions or contradict them. It is Chaucer's brilliant handling of convention that makes his poetry so striking – not, as we tend to think, complete originality. Originality cut off from its informing sources is limited to what it says; conventions and their variations work through association and resonance to achieve something greater than themselves.[2]

The *Canterbury Tales* is a particularly fascinating example of how conventions work, for Chaucer is able to set up multiple layers of reference. Every genre he uses – and he uses just about every one

---

[2] There is an interesting discussion of the need to read Chaucer 'vertically', in terms of literary tradition as well as internal sequence, in Derek Brewer, *Towards a Chaucerian Poetic* (Sir Israel Gollancz Memorial Lecture, British Academy, London, 1974), esp. pp. 22–4.

available to him – brings its own associations and traditions; and in addition, by bringing together so many stories of so many different kinds, he is able to play off associations between the tales within the work. The richness of literary kinds in the Middle Ages is remarkable by comparison with the twentieth century, and Chaucer exploits it to the full. The multiplicity of readings of the world enshrined in the various tales is drawn primarily not from the different tellers but from traditional generic distinctions.

The *Canterbury Tales* is written with an unusually high degree of poetic self-consciousness. This is shown not only in the quality of the writing and the manipulation of convention and genre, but in Chaucer's handling of fiction. The story-collection gives unusually rich opportunities for exploring the nature of narrative. Most writers made little of this potential: the average story-collection is a collection of stories, and no more. Some of the older oriental collections are much more sophisticated in their handling of story. The *Thousand and One Nights* works by starting the next story before the previous one has finished, or by setting one story within another; and if that collection was unknown in the west in the Middle Ages, the same technique is used in parts of the *Fables of Bidpai*, which was widely available in a Latin version, and also occasionally in the *Metamorphoses*. Tale is placed within tale in a *mise-en-abîme* effect – the effect of the story-book cover that shows a child reading the same story-book, with the same picture on its cover of a child reading the book, and so on. The term itself has a venerable history, being heraldic in origin. Such a technique used in narrative demands a high degree of literary awareness. The *Canterbury Tales*, at first glance, belongs with the simpler kind of story-collection; a second glance shows that there is more to it than that.

For a start, all the tales are set within the larger story of the pilgrimage. This serves as more than a functional connecting device, however brilliant. It provides a way of making the tales lead out of one another, dramatically and thematically; and very often, the setting serves to alter the stories told. A tale that would mean one thing in isolation can be given a very different meaning, running in parallel or on a collision course with the first, when it is put in the mouth of a particular teller or juxtaposed with certain other tales. The Pardoner's Tale is thus at once moral (as inveighing against avarice) and flagrantly immoral (as serving to line the Pardoner's pockets); Chaucer's tale of *Sir Thopas* is either appallingly or brilliantly written, or both.

Furthermore, not all the stories are told sequentially. In the most poetically self-aware of them all, the Nun's Priest's Tale, Chaucer gives a kind of story-collection in miniature that works through receding layers of narrative. In the oriental story-collections, each successive story moves to the foreground while it is being told. This also happens in modern works that deliberately set out to play with the nature of fiction by similar methods, such as Italo Calvino's recent *If on a Winter's Night a Traveller* (of which the dust-jacket of the English edition portrays a series of miniatures of itself). The stories of the outermost layers of the Nun's Priest's Tale move to the foreground in this way, but as Chaucer moves further in he manages to keep the sense of recession, of progressive miniaturisation, which is much harder to achieve in narrative than pictorially. The outermost storyteller (number one) is the author, Chaucer himself, who tells of his pilgrim persona (number two) reporting the tale told by his fictional narrator, the Nun's Priest (three). The Priest tells the story of the cock Chauntecleer; and from this point on the levels of narration no longer rise to the surface but move inwards. Chauntecleer in his turn tells a number of stories (the fourth level of narration). The simplest is his account of a dream he has had. Dreamers must always tell their own dreams since the experience is entirely within the mind: that is why all dream-poems must have first-person narrators. Beyond that, Chauntecleer cites the stories he has read in an 'auctor' (a fifth teller) of men whose dreams are in turn recounted, and who therefore in a sense add a further layer of narration (six). The second of these dreams, a prophetic one warning a traveller not to sail the next day, is indeed 'tolde' by the dreamer to his companion. His account contains yet another layer (the seventh and last) to add to the receding narratives:

> Hym thoughte a man stood by his beddes syde,
> And hym comanded that he sholde abyde,
> And seyde hym thus: 'If thou tomorwe wende,
> Thow shalt be dreynt; *my tale is at an ende.*'[3]

'Tale' by this time obviously means 'speech' rather than a full-scale narrative, but then at this stage the picture of the picture is getting very small indeed.

It is interesting that the *sentence*, the meaning, of these successive tales becomes less clear as they move outwards. At the centre, the speech of the figure in the dream is unequivocal in meaning, and accepted as such by the dreamer. When he tells the dream to his companion, however, it is not believed: the true *doctryne* it gives is not accepted. Rather the same happens with the *auctor* who recounts the story: Chauntecleer accepts his argument 'douteless' for the moment, but a few lines later he is just as prepared as the traveller's

---

[3] VII 3079–82. All quotations from Chaucer are taken from *The Works of Geoffrey Chaucer* ed. F. N. Robinson (2nd ed., London, 1957).

companion to deny any credit to dreams. As far as the tale proper is
concerned, the argument for the truth of dreams is validated by the
narrative – Chauntecleer's own dream is prophetic – but the tale itself
calls attention to just how fictional it is, being set in a time when
'beestes and briddes koude speke and synge', and as true as the story
of Lancelot. The balance between truth and fiction is finely equivocal.
Dreams held a special place in Chaucer's ideas about the nature of
literature: they offer a 'fictional' world where real life is suspended
and the creative imagination can rule undisturbed by empirical fact,
but they also have the potential for containing a higher truth than
normal waking life can perceive. It is hardly surprising, then, that the
meaning of the Nun's Priest's Tale as a whole is impossible to disen-
tangle. The Priest himself gives altogether too many hints as to what
the *sentence* of his tale may be for any definitive interpretation to be
extracted. The pilgrim Chaucer does not help, merely recording that
sir John promises to be 'myrie'; and this bare commitment to *murthe*
does not help in defining *doctryne*. On the outside is the poet who
invents everything, who manipulates all these multiple stories within
stories and dictates what their tellers should say; and if the dream
guide was a model of clarity, Chauntecleer confused and the Nun's
Priest enigmatic, Chaucer himself is totally inscrutable.

The Nun's Priest's Tale brilliantly displays Chaucer's self-consciousness as a teller of tales. Because of its small scale, it also demonstrates
clearly many features of the whole *Canterbury Tales* that can become
blurred when enlarged. The insistence that everything is relative is
one of these; so is Chaucer's refusal to declare a single meaning, even
though the Nun's Priest insists that surface narrative is not enough
and meaning must be sought for too. Its non-sequential arrangement
of stories is also suggestive. The stories of the entire work have to be
told as a sequence; but they do not have to be understood as separate
items in a series. The Nun's Priest's Tale is in a sense the model for
the whole collection. Thematically and poetically all the tales are
inter-related. To study them in isolation from each other is almost as
sterile an exercise as to extract a play within a play from its frame
and look at the tedious brief scene of young Pyramus and his love
Thisbe while ignoring that other study of the nature of fiction and the
imagination in which it is set, *A Midsummer Night's Dream*.

The *Canterbury Tales*, then, must be read as a story-collection in a
more significant sense than the term might suggest. To discover just
what Chaucer is doing with the form, one must start by looking at the
conventions of the genre, at how other people were writing story-
collections. Chaucer's audience will have come to his work with certain
generic expectations in mind; whether Chaucer fulfils these or frustrates them is the clearest indication of how he conceived of his own
work. Story-collections must be the point of departure.

1

The Genre of the Story-Collection

Story-collections had been in existence for some three thousand years before Chaucer. The form had a venerable history, and it was given new life in the Middle Ages. Oriental and classical collections were translated, adapted and widely disseminated, and there was a large output of new collections of all kinds. The process culminated in the fourteenth century, when the production of handbooks of moral tales for preachers reached a peak, when Ovid's *Metamorphoses* were read and glossed and re-written with a new pitch of enthusiasm, when collections of legends and miracles and pseudo-historical legendary stories abounded. The same century was the great age of artistically self-conscious story-collections compiled by great authors: Boccaccio and his lesser followers in Italy, Gower and Chaucer in England.

In the fourteenth century the story-collection reached maturity. One can distinguish certain characteristics of the form and trace them in earlier story-collections – the use or lack of use of a frame, for instance, or the degree of concern for making the moral of a story explicit – but they are not apparently treated with any measure of fresh thinking. These earlier story-collections establish a series of conventions: the fourteenth-century collections can build on these conventions, use them and exploit them. By the time Chaucer wrote the *Canterbury Tales*, the form was so familiar – even fashionable – and its conventions so clearly understood that he could treat it with great sophistication and rely on an informed appreciation from his audience.

The story-collection never acquired a single set of rigid conventions. The very fact of gathering things together implies a miscellany, even a jumble. The various conventions of structural organisation are largely aimed at overcoming this problem, of imposing some kind of coherence or order, or both, on a mass of disparate material. The other major concern of the compilers was with morals. It was rarely sufficient for a story to exist solely for its entertainment value – a number of authors, indeed, go out of their way to say that their own compilations are designed as a godly answer to the rhymes and stories of the

world, the flesh and the devil. Mediaeval story-collections range over
the whole spectrum of possible relationships of tale to meaning, from
those where the narrative is all to those where the story is a functional
wire coat-hanger from which to hang an elaborate allegory. The range
of answers to the problem of balancing tale and moral was enormous,
but awareness of the problem was unavoidable.

In this chapter I shall outline the variety of story-collections in the
Middle Ages, culminating in separate discussions of the works of
Boccaccio, Gower and Chaucer. The point of such a survey is not to
make a census – there are far too many for that – nor even a history,
but to indicate the different ways taken by different authors to solve
those key problems of structure and morality. There are no clear lines
of chronological development here: the most elaborate frame-stories
belong to the very oldest and the very latest collections; stories are
most fully allegorised in the *Gesta Romanorum*, and their potential
for moral didacticism totally ignored by Boccaccio when he borrows
some of the same stories half a generation later. If historical development will not serve as a framework for discussion, neither will the
question of origin: some of the collections are of oriental or classical
derivation in their entirety, but many borrow their stories from any
source available to them and present a complete mixture of eastern
and western folk-tale, history and pseudo-history, myth, legend and
fable. A discussion of story-collections therefore threatens to be as
much a miscellany as the collections themselves. I shall follow the
example they set, and use the question of ordering as the basis for
ordering the discussion that follows. This has the added advantage of
bearing directly or indirectly on the *Canterbury Tales* itself and the
principles of ordering that Chaucer uses there – the subject, indeed,
of the rest of the book.

First, for a definition – a working definition, that is designed to
avoid problems, not invite them. A story-collection is a collection of
separable tales compiled and written, or more probably re-written,
essentially by a single author; and it circulates in a recognisably
coherent form. It is different, therefore, from an anthology or a manuscript miscellany, or from a collection of separate works by a single
man, where the different items do not necessarily belong together; and
it is different from works such as interlaced romances, where there
may be a number of stories but they are not at all easily extractable. The stories must be essential to the work, not incidental, and so
a sermon with a generous use of story *exempla* is not in itself a story-
collection, though a preacher with sufficient enthusiasm for narrative
can turn a moral treatise into something indistinguishable from one.

Story-collections can be divided very simply into three kinds in
terms of their structural ordering. There are those that consist simply
of tales, with no enclosing material at all; there are those that have

But you decided C's ordering of the CT was not recoverable

a prologue and sometimes an epilogue but no linking matter between the tales; and there are some that have a fully-developed framework enclosing and connecting the stories. I shall discuss each kind in turn; and in order to try to re-create some sense of the knowledge of the form such as Chaucer, and his audience, might have had, I shall concentrate on collections either that were widely disseminated throughout Europe and could have been known, or in some cases were certainly known, to Chaucer, or else that were compiled in England or by Englishmen, whether in Latin, Anglo-Norman or English.

To start with the simplest, the unframed tales. The most famous collection of these was unquestionably the *Gesta Romanorum*, which was compiled early in the fourteenth century, almost certainly in England.[1] This consists of some hundred and eighty tales of very variable length, generally told with the minimum of amplification, and each with a moralisation attached, which can be longer than the story itself. It was presumably intended, as many of these unframed collections were, as a sourcebook for sermon *exempla*. Its method can be illustrated by a single story, number 33, *De jactantia*, which is of particular relevance since Chaucer also used the story in the Wife of Bath's Prologue. Chaucer and the compiler of the *Gesta* derive the tale from the same source, the *Epistola Valerii ad Rufinum de Non Ducenda Uxore* ('On Not Getting Married'), doubtfully ascribed to Walter Map. The story in the *Gesta* runs as follows:

> Valerius tells us that a man named Paletinus one day burst into a flood of tears, and calling his son and his neighbours around him, said, 'Alas! Alas! I have now growing in my garden a fatal tree, on which my first poor wife hung herself, then my second, and after that my third. Have I not therefore cause for the wretchedness I exhibit?' 'Truly,' said one who was called Arrius, "I marvel that you should weep at such an unusual instance of good fortune! Give me, I pray you, two or three sprigs of that gentle tree, which I will divide with my neighbours, and thereby afford every man an opportunity of indulging the laudable wishes of his spouse.' Paletinus complied with his friend's request, and ever after found this remarkable tree the most productive part of his estate.[2]

[1] Ed. Hermann Oesterley (Berlin, 1872); on the provenance see pp. 256–66. There is a modern translation by Rev. Charles Swan, revised by Wynnard Hooper (London, 1905). The shorter Middle English version is edited by Sidney J. H. Herrtage, *Gesta Romanorum* (EETS E.S. 33, 1879).

[2] Trans. Swan, tale XXXIII; 'Refert Valerius, quod homo quidam nomine Peratinus flens dixit filio suo et omnibus vicinis suis: Heu, heu michi! habeo in orto meo arborem infelicem, qua uxor mea prima se suspendit, postmodum secunda, modo tercia, et ideo dolor est michi miserabilis. Ait unus, cui nomen Arrius: Miror, te in tantis successibus lacrimas emisisse. Da michi, rogo te, tres surculos illius arboris, quia intendo inter vicinos dividere, ut quilibet arborem habeat ad uxorem suam suspendendam. Et sic factum est' (ed. Oesterley pp. 330–1). Swan gives only a summary of the long moralisation. The tale goes back to Cicero, *De Oratore* II.

Chaucer, not surprisingly, uses this story as an anti-feminist *exemplum*, which is the force it has in the *Epistola Valerii*. The *Gesta* version, however, offers an allegorical interpretation considerably longer than the story itself and by all normal standards of literary decorum highly inappropriate. The tree is the Cross; the garden is the soul of man, who should be thinking on the Passion; the three wives are pride of life, lust of the flesh and lust of the eyes; the man who solicited slips of the tree is the good Christian, *bonus Christianus*. The most impressive thing about such an interpretation is less its eccentricity (it is indeed typical of a widespread form of allegorical reading) than its irrelevance to the story. There is no necessary, or even logical, connection between the tale and the meaning that can be extracted from it.

This particular story is an extreme case, but there are many like it in the *Gesta*. It demonstrates in miniature the lack of structural coherence in the work: not only is there no logical connection or ordering between stories, there is minimal internal coherence even between story and moral. The lack of any overall structural principles is mirrored in the manuscripts, where the number and ordering of the tales varies widely, and where individual stories can be added or dropped at will; there are some hundred additional tales found in various versions. The editor of the *Gesta*, Hermann Oesterley, complained that there were almost as many texts as there were manuscripts. There was also a distinctively English grouping of a selection of the tales, known as the Anglo-Latin *Gesta*, and an English translation of this was made in the early fifteenth century.[3]

A number of other frameless story-collections were similarly designed as quarries for sermon *exempla*. The forty-seven *Moralitates* of Robert Holcot, a Dominican friar associated with both Cambridge and Oxford, were written in about 1334–42,[4] and enjoyed wide popularity; they were also drawn on in an early revision of the *Gesta Romanorum*. Holcot was a notable and respected scholar, but the stories of the *Moralitates* are often unashamed fantasy, not totally outweighed by the length of the *expositio moralis* that follows each. They were printed in the sixteenth century at the end of his impressive and substantial commentary on the Wisdom of Solomon: clearly nobody saw any contradiction between weighty theology and story-telling. There are indeed plenty of exemplary stories in the course of the Wisdom commentary itself. Holcot cites his sources for the stories of the *Moralitates*, and they include Ovid, Pliny, the *Epistola Valerii*, and Jerome

---

[3] Ed. Herrtage p. xix.

[4] *In Librum Sapientiae Regis Salomonis Praelectiones CCXIII* (Bâle, 1586) pp. 703–50. The date is given by Beryl Smalley, *English Friars and Antiquity in the Early Fourteenth Century* (Oxford, 1960) p. 146.

against Jovinian – the last two occurring in close proximity again in Chaucer, as sources for his own *exempla* and in the 'book of wikked wyves' that was the favourite reading of the Wife of Bath's fifth husband, Jankin.[5] The lack of logical ordering in a collection of this kind inevitably reduced its value as a preaching aid since stories were hard to find; one expedient to get round the problem was to arrange the stories in alphabetical order of moral catchword, with cross-references. This is the method of the *Alphabetum Narrationum*, of which there is a fifteenth-century English translation, the *Alphabet of Tales*.[6] 'A' covers abbots and their duties, absolution, abstinence, *accidia*, flattery (*adulacio*), adultery, ambition, St. Andrew, angels, apostasy and so on: it works well as an ordering mechanism at the most practical level, but it could hardly be seen as a creative solution to a major structural and artistic difficulty. At least the stories of the *Alphabet*, unlike the *De jactantia*, illustrate their morals in a predictable fashion; usually, indeed, there is no separate moralisation, for the tales are sufficient to display their own meanings.

There is another group of story-collections that appear sometimes without any kind of frame and sometimes with an introduction: collections of saints' lives and miracles. If the assorted contents of the *Moralitates* and such works are associated by function, as preaching aids, the stories of legendaries are brought together by common content. A number of these collections have prologues informing the reader what he is looking at, sometimes quite aggressively: Osbern Bokenham, writing in the mid-fifteenth century, opens his *Legendys of Hooly Wummen* with the lines

> Two thyngys owyth euery clerk
> To aduertysyn, begynnyng a werk,
> If he procedyn wyl ordeneelly:
> The fyrste is 'what', the secunde is 'why'.[7]

The compiler of the *South English Legendary* (late thirteenth century) is quite clear as to why he is writing:

> Men wilneþ muche to hure telle. of bataille of kynge
> And of kniȝtes þat hardy were. þat muchedel is lesynge,[8]

and so he will tell true tales of God's knights, the apostles and the martyrs. He solves the problem of the order of the stories by working

---

[5] In the Wife of Bath's Prologue; he also uses Jerome's *Epistola Adversus Jovinianum* for Dorigen's long complaint in the Franklin's Tale.

[6] Ed. Mary Macleod Banks (EETS O.S. 126–7, 1904–5).

[7] Ed. M. S. Serjeantson (EETS O.S. 206, 1938) lines 1–4.

[8] Ed. Charlotte d'Evelyn and Anna J. Mill, Vol. I (EETS O.S. 235, 1956), Prologue 59–60.

through the church calendar, a common arrangement in legendaries. He may have taken it over from the *Golden Legend* of Jacobus a Voragine, which appeared earlier in the century.[9] Collections of secular biographies, such as those by Petrarch, Boccaccio and Chaucer,[10] use the same structural basis of prologue and separate lives, but generally give a chronological ordering, Petrarch starting with Romulus, Boccaccio with Adam and, in *De Claris Mulieribus*, Eve, Chaucer with Lucifer. The *Legend of Good Women* is the exception here; its lack of order probably reflects one of its chief sources, Ovid's *Heroides*, a story-collection *manqué* in which letters from grieving women are substituted for formal narratives.

Forms as familiar as legendaries and collections of miracles of the Virgin can rely on the nature of their contents to make the 'what' and the 'why' evident to the reader even without a prologue like Bokenham's; but there are many single-genre collections of other kinds of stories that have a greater need of a prologue to tell the reader what is going on. Collections of animal-fables are especially widespread. These 'Aesopets' – whose contents derive from various classical or other sources in which Aesop himself figures only slightly – often have a prologue stressing the need for the listener or reader to get below the surface of the fable to reach the truth beneath, and lest anyone should still miss the point they generally spell out the moral in a short exposition appended to each story. Aesopets were a favourite form throughout Europe.[11] Three collections were composed in England in the late twelfth and early thirteenth centuries: in Latin, the *Novus Aesopus* of Alexander Nequam,[12] and the *Fabulae* of Odo of Cheriton;[13] and in Anglo-Norman, the *Fables* of Marie de France.[14] Marie provides not only a prologue but an epilogue too, in the course of which she summarises the history of the animal fable and its roots in Greek and Latin, also mentioning a translation into Anglo-Saxon which she ascribes to King Alfred. Her work survives in twenty-three manuscripts, which bear witness to the lack of logical internal order-

[9] *Jacobi a Voragine Legenda Aurea* ed. Th. Graesse (2nd ed., Leipzig, 1850).

[10] Petrarch's *De Viris Illustribus Vitae* is edited by Luigi Razzolini (2 vols, Bologna, 1874); on Boccaccio's *De Casibus Virorum Illustrium* and *De Claris Mulieribus* and Chaucer's Monk's Tale and *Legend of Good Women*, see below pp. 26, 30–32.

[11] For a detailed survey see Klaus Grubmüller, *Meister Esopus: Untersuchungen zu Geschichte und Funktion der Fabel im Mittelalter* (Münchener Texte und Untersuchungen zur Deutschen Literatur des Mittelalters 56, Munich, 1977).

[12] Ed. Julia Bastin, in *Recueil général des Isopets* Vol. I (SATF, Paris, 1929); Nequam also wrote another fable collection, the *Novus Avianus*, of which only six fables now survive (p. xii).

[13] Ed. Léopold Hervieux in *Les Fabulistes Latins depuis le Siècle d'Auguste jusqu'à la fin du Moyen Age* (5 vols, Paris, 1884–99) Vol. IV.

[14] *Die Fabeln der Marie de France* ed. Karl Warnke (Bibliotheca Normannica VI, Halle, 1898).

ing in collections of this kind: there are big variations in the order of the stories between the various manuscript groups, and, as with the *Gesta Romanorum*, the variations make no difference to the end product. An interesting attempt to impose a greater coherence on story sequence was made by Vincent of Beauvais, who includes a collection of fables in the *Speculum Doctrinale*, the educational section of his universal encyclopaedia: he arranges them in ten groups linked by similarity of moral import.[15] The separate chapter headings announce the topic for each group ('On fictional fables against backbiters and deceivers', 'De fabulis fictis, contra calumniosos et insidiosos' and so on), so the individual fables would be easily locatable for use as sermon *exempla*. Their placing in the whole work suggests, however, that their primary function is as a simple introduction to literature.

Marie de France's other story-collection, the *Lais*, is again a single-genre collection of unlinked stories with a prologue, but of a rather less usual kind. It is hard to find parallels for so explicitly secular a collection. It is genre alone that holds the stories together, and she devotes most of her prologue to describing just what a Breton lai is. She is at some pains to stress that the stories do have meanings, but these are not of the extractable sort that can be appended to the end. Its lack of overt orthodox didacticism makes the work decisively different from most other story-collections before Boccaccio's, though it may also be true that the very association of story-collection with morals led to her audience's placing a greater emphasis on her *sens*, the inner meaning of her stories, rather than on their subject-matter, their *matière*.

The next group of story-collections, those which have an introduction and explicit linking of tale to tale though with no overriding frame story, have little to do with each other intrinsically and are discussed together purely for the convenience of this chapter. They include such things as histories, Ovid's *Metamorphoses* and various didactic works – a very mixed bag indeed.

It may seem odd to include histories, as they would seem to be a generically different kind of writing from story-collection; and some histories are indeed very different. In the Middle Ages, however, a good many were not. Geoffrey of Monmouth's *Historia Regum Britanniae*[16] is nothing if not a work of the imagination, and it is packed with good stories that were taken over separately or as part of a historical sequence by later writers. The kind of universal history that was written by Godfrey of Viterbo in the late twelfth century, the

---

[15] *Bibliotheca Mundi* (*Speculum Maius*), Vol. II, *Speculum Doctrinale* (Douai, 1624) III.cxiii–cxxiii (pp. 290–5).

[16] Ed. Jacob Hammer (Cambridge, Mass., 1951); translation by Lewis Thorpe, *Geoffrey of Monmouth: The History of the Kings of Britain* (Harmondsworth, 1966).

Pantheon,[17] outlining the great events of the world from Noah onwards, was a collection of myths, legends and pseudo-history from all kinds of different sources, including Geoffrey, and Gower found it an invaluable mine of stories for the *Confessio Amantis*. Its literary pretensions are indicated by the fact that it is written in alternating sections of prose and verse. It is true that mediaeval historians could not make the modern distinctions between history and legend: no one would have seen anything odd in Sir Thomas Gray of Heaton's description, in his *Scalacronica*, of the ladder of history resting on the Bible and the story of Troy.[18] The Trojan foundation of Britain, like the historicity of Arthur, was accepted without question. Historians of this kind were still very different from sober chroniclers, however; Robert Mannyng of Bourne tells the story of the Judgment of Paris in his history of England,[19] and Nicholas Trivet the folktale of Constance in his Anglo-Norman Chronicle – from where Gower and Chaucer borrowed it for their own story-collections.[20] History, as Mannyng points out, is inherently instructive so needs no defence:

> It is wisdom for to wytten
> þe state of þe land, & haf it wryten,   11–12

though he notes its entertainment value as well.

The forefather of all histories is the Bible itself. It is perverse to describe it as a story-collection, since clearly its prime purpose and function – especially in the Middle Ages – was very different; but any account of collections would none the less be incomplete without it. It was quarried by compilers in much the same way as other histories were, and Boccaccio in the *De Casibus*, Gower in the *Confessio*, and Chaucer in the Monk's Tale all set Biblical stories alongside others from pagan history or legend. Boccaccio does refuse to mix the kinds (Eve only excepted) in the *De Claris Mulieribus*. A re-telling of the Bible such as the fourteenth-century *Cursor Mundi* emphasises its value as a collection of profitable stories to counter worldly romances,[21] very much as the *South English Legendary* does. The stress here falls on story; readings of the Bible itself stressed allegorisation – a process that is reflected in collections such as the *Gesta*.

---

[17] In *Gotifredi Viterbiensis Opera* ed. G. Waitz (Monumenta Germaniae Historica: Scriptorum Vol. XXII, Hanover, 1872) pp. 107–307; unfortunately this omits the section on British history and Arthur.

[18] See Smalley pp. 13–17.

[19] *The Story of England* ed. F. J. Furnivall (Rolls Series, 2 vols, 1887) I ll.503–678; he rationalises the goddesses into 'wicches' (l.503).

[20] *Sources and Analogues of Chaucer's Canterbury Tales* ed. W. F. Bryan and Germaine Dempster (1941/New York, 1958) pp. 155–81.

[21] Ed. Rev. Richard Morris (EETS O.S. 57, 59, 62, 66, 68, 99, 101; 1874–93), Vol. 57, Prologue.

Ovid's *Metamorphoses*[22] is also, in a sense, a universal history, in that it is structured chronologically, from the emergence of the earth from Chaos down to the death of Julius Caesar and his own times. Its historical aspect is of course the least important thing about it. The principle of coherence within the work is the single repeated plot motif, of metamorphosis – a motif that guarantees its distance from historical fact. The tales grow out of each other as Ovid works down the generations, and the transitions are managed with quite remarkable skill; but the stories are easily separable, and were an endlessly renewable resource for the energy of later story-tellers. Chaucer draws on the *Metamorphoses* for many *exempla*, and for complete stories in the *Book of the Duchess*, the Manciple's Tale and the *Legend of Good Women* – though there Ovid's *Heroides* is more important as a source. The *Metamorphoses* has also been proposed as the structural model for the *Canterbury Tales*, either in its entirety – where it has been suggested as a thematic model as well[23] – or else in the episode of the daughters of Minyas, who tell a sequence of stories on the theme of love as they spin.[24] There are even fewer parallels between the works to prove either hypothesis than there are between the *Decameron* and the *Canterbury Tales*; but Chaucer did at least have Ovid's story-collection in mind when he wrote, for he makes an explicit comparison between the works in the Man of Law's Prologue. This section of the *Tales* may once have been intended for a more prominent place, as introducing the whole sequence of story-telling.[25] The Man of Law is reviewing Chaucer's poetic career, and he describes him as having told of lovers 'mo than Ovide' (II 54) – though the list that follows consists entirely of the stories that Chaucer had taken from Ovid. He goes on to contrast Chaucer's work with Gower's, and then refers back to Ovid:

> But of my tale how shal I doon this day?
> Me were looth be likned, doutelees,
> To Muses that men clepe Pierides –
> *Methamorphosios* woot what I mene;
> But nathelees, I recche noght a bene
> Though I come after hym with hawebake.   II 90–5

The term 'Pierides' is ambiguous. The Man of Law may simply be denying any great poetic inspiration; or there may be a reference to

---

[22] Ed. and trans. Frank Justus Miller (Loeb Classical Library, 2 vols, London, 1958–60).

[23] Judson Boyce Allen and Theresa Anne Moritz, *A Distinction of Stories: The Medieval Unity of Chaucer's Fair Chain of Narratives for Canterbury* (Columbus, Ohio, 1981).

[24] *Metamorphoses* IV 1–415; Bryan and Dempster pp. 9–10.

[25] See note 76 below and pp. 63–4.

the daughters of King Pierus, of *Metamorphoses* Book V, who contended with the Muses and were changed into magpies. In either case, the implication is that his words will be mere chatter compared with the true Muse of Chaucer; so Chaucer neatly manages to deprecate and compliment himself in the same set of words, since of course the Man of Law's Tale is equally his own. The strong Ovidian reference of the whole passage does none the less invite the listener to compare Ovid's story-telling and Chaucer's.

It is interesting that Chaucer should stress the quality of *artistic* comparison here – the Muses *versus* 'hawebake', starvation rations. Most of the mediaeval justification for reading the *Metamorphoses* had been sought in different directions. In the early Christian era the work had been regarded as both frivolous and dangerously pagan; the notion that these drawbacks could be avoided by allegorical interpretation began to emerge in the Carolingian era, and from the twelfth century onwards Ovid became the centre of a great amount of attention, both scholarly and poetic.[26] He was perhaps the most widely known of all classical authors – he was Chaucer's favourite – and in the fourteenth century the *Metamorphoses* were not only extensively read but also glossed, adapted and translated. The trickle of commentaries giving allegorical explanations of the work turns into a pan-European flood at this period. Many of them are anonymous or wrongly attributed;[27] Giovanni del Virgilio, Dante's commentator, probably did write the one ascribed to him;[28] Robert Holcot did not write his; the one universally attributed in the Renaissance to Thomas Waleys is by Pierre Bersuire; and the author of the vernacular French *Ovide moralisé* is unknown. The one thing that remains clear is that glossing Ovid was an inordinately popular activity. In view of this plethora of moralisation it is interesting that Chaucer and Gower should ignore it all so completely and concentrate instead on the stories. With short tales as with larger romances, the subject-matter, the 'matter' or *matière*, is traditional and preserved though all treatments, the inner meaning, 'sentence' or *sens* or moralisation, depends on the particular author.

'Taketh the fruyt, and lat the chaf be stille.'[29] It was a commonplace

[26] See L. P. Wilkinson, *Ovid Recalled* (Cambridge, 1955) ch. XI, and Fausto Ghisalberti, 'Mediaeval biographies of Ovid', *Journal of the Warburg and Courtauld Institutes* IX (1946) 10–59.

[27] Many of the wrong attributions are unfortunately perpetuated in Lester K. Born's 'Ovid and allegory', *Speculum* IX (1934) 362–79, which has generally been taken as the authoritative account of the subject. I am most grateful to Miss Beryl Smalley for confirming my suspicions of its accuracy.

[28] Philip H. Wicksteed and Edmund G. Gardner, *Dante and Giovanni del Virgilio* (Westminster, 1902) pp. 314–21, doubted his authorship, but it is accepted by Ghisalberti.

[29] *Canterbury Tales* VII 3443.

of mediaeval literary theory that the fable existed only as a cover for the inner truth, but just as in that line the Nun's Priest gives advice that can hardly be squared with the tale just told, practice and theory do not always fit. The Nun's Priest also quotes the Epistle to the Romans on the subject, 'Quaecumque enim scripta sunt, ad nostram doctrinam scripta sunt' (XV.4):

> For seint Paul seith that al that writen is,
> To oure doctrine it is ywrite, ywis.   VII 3441–2

The author of the *Ovide moralisé*, writing *c.* 1316–28, had made exactly the same point in the opening couplet of his work:

> *Se l'escripture ne me ment,*
> *Tout est pour nostre enseignement.*[30]

He insists that his 'fables' are 'profitables' – a favourite, and instructive, rhyme in both French and English.[31] The Nun's Priest makes the same point in different words. Chaucer and the author of the *Ovide moralisé* are however worlds apart in their application of the idea – probably even in the nature of their belief in it. Chaucer probably knew the French poem as well as the *Metamorphoses* proper,[32] but a comparison of Chaucer and the *Ovide* will indicate how different was their sense of the relationship of tale and meaning.

The interpretations given in the *Ovide moralisé* are often not merely didactic but allegorical too, in the manner of Biblical exegesis or the *Gesta*: Actaeon torn to pieces by his hounds is Christ destroyed by the Jews, while Diana, whom Actaeon saw naked, is the Trinity, seen by Christ 'purement' without the veil of human flesh assumed by God in the Incarnation.[33] The logic of the narrative, that Actaeon is destroyed in retribution for seeing Diana's naked beauty, gets entirely

---

[30] Ed. C. de Boer in Verhandelingen der Koninklijke Akademie van Wetenschappen te Amsterdam: Adfeeling Letterkunde, Nieuwe Reeks, Vols XV, XXI, XXX, XXXVII, XLIII (1915–38); Vol. I (XV of the series), Bk. I. 1–2. The date and authorship are discussed on pp. 9–20 of the same volume; de Boer concludes that the author was a Franco-Burgundian writing probably for Jeanne of Burgundy, wife of Philippe V.

[31] Ibid. 11. 53–4. The rhyme, and the notion underlying it, are found as late as Bunyan's Author's Apology for his Book in the *Pilgrim's Progress* (ed. Roger Sharrock, London, 1966):

> Art thou for something rare, and profitable?
> Wouldest thou see a Truth within a Fable?

[32] It seems to have contributed some details to his treatment of the Legends of Ariadne and Philomela in the *Legend of Good Women*: see Robinson's summaries of sources for each legend.

[33] Ed.cit. Vol. I (Vol. XV of the series), Bk. III 635–58.

lost in the allegorical transposition. It is instructive to contrast such arbitrary interpretations with a sympathetic handling of similar narrative content; and Chaucer's treatment of Ovidian stories stands out by the contrast as doing justice to the inner tones and motives of his material, just as his treatment of the story of the hanging-tree stands out by contrast with the *Gesta*. Ovid's account of Ceyx and Alcyone, from Book XI of the *Metamorphoses*, will serve as an example. Ceyx leaves his beloved wife Alcyone and embarks on a sea-voyage; the ship is wrecked in a storm, Ceyx is drowned, and Alcyone is granted a vision in which his drowned body seems to appear to her to tell her of his fate. His corpse is washed up on the shore, she dies of grief, and both are metamorphosed into birds. The author of the *Ovide moralisé* follows this up with his allegorical reading:[34] Ceyx is the soul undertaking the pilgrimage to heaven; then there follows a choice of interpretations, either at the level of the individual, in which the ship is the mortal body with the senses as sailors, conscience the sail and so on; or alternatively there is a more general meaning in which the ship is the Church, the sailors are apostles and priests, the mast the Cross and the sail Christ's flesh stretched upon it. The birds, in a separate interpretation, are those who loved the world too much, a reading curiously at odds with the author's insistence, which comes immediately afterwards and concludes the whole section, on how admirable was the strength of love between the pair. When Chaucer describes his reading of the same story in the *Book of the Duchess*[35] he follows the original narrative to the moment of Alcyone's death, and he treats it literally: any further meaning it takes on in the course of the poem is derived from its relationship to the narrator's dream that follows it, in which the Ovidian tale of the wife grieving for her lost husband is balanced by the Man in Black's account of his loss of his lady. As in almost all his borrowings from Ovid, however, Chaucer omits the final metamorphosis: he seems to have resisted any notion that even in myth noble human beings could be reduced to the level of beasts. There is a further reason for the omission in the *Book of the Duchess* in that in neither half of the poem, tale or dream, does Chaucer pursue his subjects beyond death. That in itself is a further indication of the strong human emphasis in his works, an emphasis that is equally inimical to allegory of the *Ovide moralisé* kind. Human values, of the kind that emerge in story and not in abstract moralisation, remain paramount.

Chaucer's lack of overt didactic content becomes increasingly marked the more one compares his treatment of his tales with those

---

[34] Ed.cit. Vol. IV (Vol. XXXVII of the series), Bk. XI; the story runs from 3003–3787, the interpretation from 3788–4147, with a final return to the story at 4148–55.
[35] *Book of the Duchess* 62–214.

of other authors. The *Ovide moralisé* is contemporary with the *Gesta Romanorum*, and both works show an unusual readiness to sacrifice narrative import to allegory; but story-collections that do not go this far still tend to have a strongly moral intention. The last group of story-collections of the kind where the tales are linked though there is no formal frame story are all works of explicit moral instruction: the *Disciplina Clericalis*, the *Book of the Knight of La Tour-Landry*, and William of Wadington's Anglo-Norman *Manuel des Pechiez* and its English adaptation, Robert Mannyng of Bourne's *Handlyng Synne*.

The *Disciplina Clericalis* of Petrus Alfonsi[36] is one of the surprisingly small number of story-collections traditionally discussed in relation to the *Canterbury Tales*, and it is almost always described as a framed series of tales, the frame being that of an Arab father giving advice to his son. There is in fact no coherent frame, nor any consistency of speaker throughout the work: the formulae linking the stories run on the pattern of 'A father said to his son . . .,' 'A teacher said to his pupil . . .,' 'A philosopher said . . .,' 'Another philosopher said . . . .' Its author was a Spanish Jew who was converted to Christianity in 1106, and who was able to draw on oriental sources for many of his tales. In his Prologue he stresses the moral and religious purpose of his work, though when it comes to the point worldly wisdom is as important as divine. The work is a mixture of precepts, proverbs and exemplary tales, thirty-four in all. There is some linking of the stories by theme: the first two are on friendship; there is a long series from story nine to story fifteen on the wiles of women, interrupted by the twelfth story, about two thousand sheep which have to be individually ferried across a river, which the master tells to dampen his listener's enthusiasm for such tales. Adjacent stories can be antithetical: the fifteenth is on a woman's help to a man, the next on the help given by a philosopher. The final stories urge the transience of earthly things and the need to prepare for death. Most often the stories are told to illustrate a precept that has just been given; occasionally the moral is made explicit within the story itself. The work was known throughout Europe, and its tales were widely borrowed for other story-collections. The first substantial English version of it is in the form of 'The Fables of Alfonce' appended to the end of Caxton's 1484 *Fables of Esope* – an interesting instance of how story-collections of very different kinds could be associated as examples of the same basic genre.

For all Petrus Alfonsi's declarations of Christian intent, the *Disci-*

---

[36] Ed. Alfons Hilka and Werner Söderhjelm in two editions in 1911; the Helsingfors edition (Acta Societatis Scientiarum Fennicae XXXVIII.4) gives more information on MSS, the Heidelberg edition (Sammlung Mittellateinischer Texte 1) gives more information on its influence. There is a translation by P. R. Quarrie from the edition and translation by Eberhard Hermes, *The 'Disciplina Clericalis' of Petrus Alfonsi* (London, 1977).

plina is a work of secular instruction in a Christian context. The same is true of a later widely known compilation, the *Book of the Knight of La Tour-Landry*, written in 1371–2 by a French knight for the instruction of his three daughters. The work was twice translated into English in the fifteenth century.[37] It is particularly interesting for the detail Geoffroy de la Tour-Landry gives of how he came to compile the work. Walking in a garden grieving for his lost youth and his dead wife, he saw his daughters coming towards him; he remembered the cavalier attitude to women displayed by his former companions, and decided 'to make a litelle boke' to illustrate the deeds of good and evil women, 'wherupon thei might rede and studie, to that intent that thei might lerne and see both good and euelle of the tyme passed, and forto kepe hem in good clennesse, and from alle euelle in tyme comyng'. He goes on to describe how he set about the work:

> Y parted and yede oute of the gardein, and fonde in my way ij prestes and ij clerkes that y had. And y said to hem that y wolde make a boke of ensaumples, for to teche my doughtres, that thei might vnderstond how thei shulde gouerne hem, and knowe good from euelle. And so y made hem extraie me ensaumples of the bible and other bokes that y had, as the gestis of kingges, the cronicleȝ of Fraunce, Grece, of Inglond, and of mani other straunge londes. And y made hem rede me eueri boke; and ther that y fonde a good ensaumple, y made extraie it oute. And thanne y made this boke.[38]

It is a description of the practice that can only be deduced from other story-collections, of raiding the Bible and histories for stories of didactic import. Part of the delight of the book, and a feature that distinguishes it from other story-collections, is that the Knight includes stories drawn from his own experience as well. There are also some fabliaux, some saints' lives, and a number of stories drawn from an earlier collection of moral female *exempla*, the *Miroir des bonnes femmes*.[39] The stories are grouped in a series of thematically related sequences – on conduct and clothing (a favourite topic), on examples of 'euelle women' and 'good ladyes', and so on. These biographies, like saints' lives, are often entirely separate from each other; the moral fables generally conclude with a discursive exposition of the lesson they teach which in turn leads on to the next example, so that the work has a closer structural and thematic coherence than might at first appear.

[37] *The Book of the Knight of La Tour-Landry* ed. Thomas Wright (EETS O.S. 33, 1868), from a mid-fifteenth century MS; and Caxton's translation, *The Book of the Knight of the Tower* ed. M. Y. Offord (EETS S.S. 2, 1971). I quote from the earlier translation in Wright's edition.
[38] Ed. Wright p. 3.
[39] See Offord's introduction to Caxton's translation, pp. xxxix–xliii.

The use of exemplary stories for the purposes of moral instruction was of course a widespread practice in sermons and manuals of all kinds, but few of these show the emphasis on story that would define them as story-collections. One work where the emphasis on the tales is so great as to bring it within a generous classification of story-collections is *Handlyng Synne*, a penitential manual and treatise on the lay Christian life. It was translated into English and adapted in the process by Robert Mannyng of Bourne, author of one of the more fanciful chronicles mentioned above, from William of Wadington's *Manuel des Pechiez* ('handlyng' being his felicitously eccentric rendering of 'manuel').[40] The *Manuel* dates from the late thirteenth century; Mannyng began his own version in 1303. As early vernacular texts, both works are remarkable for the degree to which they put exemplary tales to use; and Mannyng places an even greater emphasis on stories than the original, adapting many and adding new ones of his own.[41] The result is to tip the balance of the *Manuel* from instruction towards entertainment. Mannyng indicates the importance of the stories as stories when he insists that they are meant to compete with secular tales, but these will be profitable, not sinful. He is writing for 'lewde men' who enjoy listening to such things:

> For many ben of swyche manere
> þat talys and rymys wyl bleþly here.   45–6

He gives sixty-seven tales in all, a number approaching that of the big story-collections. Many recur in other collections such as the *Gesta Romanorum* and the *Alphabet of Tales*; they are drawn from such sources as St. Gregory's *Dialogues*, Bede, the Bible, and, most intriguingly, the oral traditions of eastern England, stories that Mannyng himself 'herd telle'. *Handlyng Synne* is divided up according to major topics of Christian instruction: the Ten Commandments, the seven deadly sins, the seven sacraments, the twelve points of shrift and the twelve graces. Most of the stories occur under the first three headings, where each instructional point is driven home by one or more exemplary tales. Despite this ordered analytical structure, Mannyng stresses that the book can be opened at any point: it does not have to be read sequentially, 'for euery-whare ys bygynnyng of synne' (l. 120). As with so many of these story-collections, logical thematic progression is of little concern.

Handlyng Synne has a moral organisation, not a frame story; but it is only a short step away from the penitential structuring of Gower's

---

[40] *Robert of Brunne's 'Handlyng Synne'* ed. Frederick J. Furnivall (EETS O.S. 119, 123; 1901, 1903); the *Manuel* text is given in parallel.

[41] They are discussed by S. A. Sullivan, *Handlyng Synne in its Tradition* (unpublished Ph.D. thesis, Cambridge, 1979).

Confessio Amantis, where the ordering by the sequence of deadly sins is set in the story of the lover's confession. The existence of a frame story does not in itself entail resemblance between collections. When one turns to the traditional story-collections that have the most fully developed frame stories, the *Directorium Vitae Humanae* and the *Seven Sages of Rome,* one finds a much greater difference from the great framed story-collections of the fourteenth century than many of the less closely cohering compilations show.

Both these works are of oriental origin, and they were already centuries old by the time they were transmitted to the mediaeval west. The *Directorium* is a thirteenth-century Latin translation by John of Capua of an Arabic translation of the work known as the *Book of Kalilâh and Dimnâh* or the *Fables of Bidpai.*[42] John's own Prologue to the work, and the Prologue he translates from the Arabic translation, both stress the instruction and delight that the book will bring: 'Iste liber est ad scientiam et ludum.' It has two layers of meaning, one manifest, the other hidden; and the reader, like a man eating a nut, must break open the shell to find the goodness hidden beneath.[43] The stories themselves are told by the philosopher Sendebar to 'Disles rex Indie', to teach him the nature of true wisdom and good kingship. The bulk of the work is devoted to an extended beast-fable – beast-epic would describe its size more accurately – in the course of which the animals themselves tell other inset fables, often about other beasts, sometimes about human beings. It employs the *mise-en-abîme* method of receding mirrors: it is a story about Sendebar telling stories about animals telling stories. The moral concern, however, remains consistently in the foreground whatever level the particular tale in hand belongs to.

The *Seven Sages of Rome* was perhaps nearly two millennia old by the time the story reached the West in the mid-twelfth century.[44] It was rapidly translated into most European languages, and survives in some forty different versions in over two hundred manuscripts. The Middle English translation, from a French version, was probably made

[42] Ed. Joseph Derenbourg, *Johannis de Capua Directorium Vitae Humanae* (Bibliothèque de l'École des Hautes Études 72, Paris, 1887–9). The earliest English translation was by Sir Thomas North (the translator of Plutarch), as *The Morall Philosophie of Doni* (1570), edited as *The Fables of Bidpai* by Joseph Jacobs (London, 1888). This version, which extends only about half-way through the original, is in fact the great-grandson of the *Directorium,* by way of Spanish and Italian translations; the 'Doni' of North's title was responsible for the Italian. There is a delightful short modern version, *Kalila and Dimna: Selected Fables of Bidpai* retold by Ramsay Wood (London, 1982).

[43] Ed. Derenbourg p. 6.

[44] Killis Campbell tentatively dates the parent version to the fifth century B.C. (*The Seven Sages of Rome* (Boston, 1907) p. xi). A summary of the history of the work is also given by Laura A. Hibbard in *Mediaeval Romance in England* (2nd ed., New York, 1960) pp. 174–83.

in the late thirteenth century;[45] and among the manuscripts to preserve it is the Auchinleck Manuscript, the great miscellany, compiled
in London *c.* 1340, which it has been suggested Chaucer may have
known.[46] Most of the Western versions, including the Middle English,
contain fifteen stories, many of them belonging to the common pool of
tales that supplies the *Directorium* and the *Disciplina Clericalis* and
later feeds into the *Gesta Romanorum*, the *Alphabet of Tales*, the
Decameron and the *Confessio Amantis*.

The *Seven Sages* is unique in having a powerful frame story that
could exist in its own right as a romance even without the inset tales.
After the death of his wife, Diocletian, Emperor of Rome, entrusts his
son Florentine to seven wise men for his education. The Emperor
remarries; and after seven years his wife, jealous of Florentine's existence, asks for him to be recalled to court. Through their wisdom,
Florentine and his masters perceive that he will be killed unless he
keeps silence for seven days. At court his stepmother attempts to
seduce him; when she fails, she accuses him of trying to rape her.
After this exciting opening comes the section of the work containing
the stories. Each night the Empress tells her husband a story urging
the dangers he is in, and Diocletian resolves to put his son to death
the next day; in the morning one of the sages tells a story urging
circumspection, or setting out the wiles of women, and the Emperor
relents. On the eighth morning Florentine himself tells a story of a
child who is cast away at sea by his father for fear of a prophecy but
eventually meets and forgives him. He also tells of the Empress's
wickedness, she is burnt, and in due course Florentine succeeds his
father and rules with honour and wisdom ever after. The themes of
the tales of the *Seven Sages* arise out of the frame story and their
morals are closely directed towards its progress, but the tales are still
of explicitly instructional import – that is why the Empress and the
wise men tell them – and their instruction can be extended beyond
the limits of the work. None the less the entertainment value of the
Seven Sages is much higher proportionally to its didactic value than
in most other story-collections: the inset tales, like the frame romance,
appeal primarily to the audience's sheer love of story.

It is perhaps worth pausing at this point to see what emerges from

[45] Campbell pp. xxxv-lix. The various Middle English versions apparently derive from
the same original translation; there is an edition by Karl Brunner, *The Seven Sages of
Rome* (EETS O.S. 191, 1933). There is also a different Scottish translation.

[46] There is a facsimile with introduction by Derek Pearsall and I. C. Cunningham,
The Auchinleck Manuscript (Ilkley and London, 1979). See also Laura Hibbard Loomis,
Adventures in the Middle Ages (New York, 1962) pp. 111–30, 'Chaucer and the Breton
lays of the Auchinleck manuscript' (reprinted from *Studies in Philology* XXXVIII (1941)
14–33), and pp. 131–49, 'Chaucer and the Auchinleck MS: *Thopas* and *Guy of Warwick*'
(reprinted from *Essays and Studies in Honor of Carleton Brown* (New York, 1940) pp.
111–28).

such a survey of the range of story-collections familiar in the early fourteenth century before moving on to the great names – to Boccaccio, Gower and Chaucer himself. Whatever the nature of an author's material, sacred or secular, primarily moral or primarily entertaining, the problems he faced remain the same: first, how to relate his stories to one another – what sort of framing device to use; and second, what the relationship should be between story and moral. These two questions become increasingly prominent in the fourteenth century, and are crucial for the three great authors.

The most striking thing about the relationship of overall structure to individual story in the earlier collections is the diversity of solutions to the problem. The *Seven Sages* makes the telling of the stories subordinate to the principal narrative of the young prince and his wicked stepmother, so that the framework is the most important feature; the *Gesta*, by contrast, has no framework whatsoever, not even an introduction. The *Gesta* has no ordering principle either: there is no reason why any particular story should follow another, nor any principle of coherence to hold them together except their implicit function as a quarry for preachers. Histories have a chronological framework to order the stories sequentially but little internal coherence between episodes; legendaries have a consistent didactic theme but derive their order from the external system of the church calendar, which contributes nothing to the collection itself. The dominant principles of coherence are usually either consistency of genre, as in the collections of beast-fables, or the *Lais* of Marie de France; or consistency of theme, whether that theme is a narrative motif such as metamorphosis or martyrdom, or a moral idea such as the wickedness of women or the way to salvation. Saints' legendaries and miracle collections combine all these, providing single-genre compilations with consistent narrative patterns and moral messages. Coherence deriving from a frame story, as in the *Seven Sages* and for long sections of the *Directorium*, is unusual and is found in no story-collection originating in the Middle Ages before the fourteenth century, though other frames are common, whether chronological, as in the histories, or moral, as in *Handlyng Synne*.

I started this chapter by distinguishing between story-collections and manuscript miscellanies; at this point it becomes necessary to bring the miscellanies back into the picture, since there is a certain kind that throws light on the story-collections. These are the miscellanies that have no consistency of authorship or genre but are assembled for their thematic coherence. Jankin's 'book of wikked wyves' is a fine fictional example – perhaps even not fictional, since Chaucer knew most or all of its contents and might have seen them together in just such a collection. The Wife of Bath lists its contents: they include the *Epistola Valerii*, treatises by Theophrastus, St Jerome and

Tertullian, Ovid's *Ars Amatoria*, and various lesser works, not all of them certainly identifiable. It is not a story-collection, but it does bear a clear relationship, by contrast, to Chaucer's book of good wives, the *Legend of Good Women*.

Most miscellanies contain a wide variety of generically different items – a characteristic that is paralleled in story-collections only by the *Canterbury Tales*. Occasionally, however, a single-genre miscellany will be compiled, and there is one kind of particular interest for concluding this chapter: the miscellany of story-collections. In this way stories from the *Disciplina Clericalis* will appear alongside collections of beast-fables, legends and miracles in a miscellany such as Harley 463; and, perhaps most interesting of all, the contents of Harley 7333 include the *Gesta Romanorum*, extracts from the *Confessio Amantis*, and the *Canterbury Tales*. Chaucer's work was not read in isolation: it was read as a story-collection, and understood in terms of the generic conventions associated with that form.

Boccaccio

The seed of all Boccaccio's story-collections, in both Italian and Latin, is probably to be found in his vernacular *Filocolo* (*c.* 1336). Four fully-fledged story-collections followed. The *Ameto* or the *Comedia delle Ninfe*, written five or six years later, is the first of his works to make the story-telling the main substance: it consists mostly of stories told by a group of nymphs, at least some of whom probably represent actual ladies in literary-mythological disguise, who talk about their past experiences in love. The *Decameron* followed at the end of the 1340s; and finally came two in Latin, the *De Claris Mulieribus*, a collection of lives of famous women, and the *De Casibus Virorum Illustrium*, on the downfalls of tyrants, both works being more didactic than historical in emphasis.[47] The problem of organising a story-collection into a work with some semblance of cohesion was tackled in various ways by Boccaccio in these works. The *Filocolo*, *Ameto* and *Decameron* show increasing elaboration; the Latin works have no full narrative framework, and the *De Claris Mulieribus* only a minimal prologue and epilogue.

[47] For the vernacular story-collections I have used the edition by Enrico Bianchi, Carlo Salinari and Natalino Sapegno, *Giovanni Boccaccio: Decameron, Filocolo, Ameto, Fiammetta* (La Letteratura Italiana 8, Milan, 1952). English quotations from the *Decameron* are from the translation by G. H. McWilliam (Harmondsworth, 1972). For the *De Claris Mulieribus* I have used the edition of Berne 1539, which was also used by Guido A. Guarini for his translation *Concerning Famous Women* (New Brunswick, N.J., 1963). The *De Casibus Illustrium Virorum* is available in a facsimile of the *c.* 1520 Paris edition with an introduction by Louis Brewer Hall (Scholars' Facsimiles and Reprints, Gainesville, Florida, 1962).

The episode in the *Filocolo* in which stories are told is a digression in the work as a whole, which is a long and elaborate version of the romance of Floris and Blauncheflour. In the course of his travels Florio and his companions come ashore at Naples and are entertained in a garden by a group of aristocratic ladies and gentleman led by a lady named Fiammetta. The company take it in turns to put to her problems concerning the nature of love, some consisting of bare questions, others illustrated with or arising out of stories. Two of these stories were used again in the *Decameron*, including the one that Chaucer drew on for the Franklin's Tale. In this section of the *Filocolo*, the fictional framework, with its assembly of characters in a specific location, and the nature of the stories as part of a game on a particular subject, both give the episode a marked degree of coherence that sets it off from the rest of the work; it was indeed separately translated into English in 1566.[48]

The *Ameto*, described by Tatlock as an 'extraordinary and rather sickish combination of pastoral, romance, frame-story, scandal, mythological history and devout allegory',[49] again uses a company of people to tell its stories. A rough Florentine youth Ameto falls in love with the nymph Lia. In the spring, on the day of a festival to Venus, he meets her and six of her companions as they are all making their way to Venus' shrine. After a singing-match between two shepherds, which turns into a quarrel, the nymphs each tell of their unsatisfactory husbands and rather more satisfactory lovers, with Ameto presiding. Lia speaks last; most of her speech is devoted to a eulogy of Florence, but in addition she acknowledges that she is happily married to her second husband, her first having died. As in the *Filocolo*, the coherence of the work derives from the elaboration of the fictional frame and the common theme of the stories; though whereas in the *Filocolo* the stories were to some degree incidental even within the digression, here they assume a much greater importance. In both works the setting for the story-telling is overtly exotic, belonging to the world of romance and looking towards the conditions of the real world only obliquely in some of the questions or the nymphs' confessional tales – though most of the questions are impossibly artificial, and the nymphs' crude accounts of their inadequate or elderly husbands are closer to caricature than realism. The thematic coherence of the *Ameto* takes a battering at the end, however, when the whole work rather startlingly turns into a vision of Christian love, the nymphs become agents of virtue, and Venus, whose earlier rôle in the stories had

[48] *Thirteene most pleasaunt and delectable questions . . . englished anno 1566 by H.G.*, with an introduction by Edward Hutton (London, 1927).

[49] John S. P. Tatlock, 'Boccaccio and the plan of Chaucer's *Canterbury Tales*', *Anglia* XXXVII (1913) 69–117, quotation from p. 81; the comment is followed by a summary of the work (pp. 81–5), especially useful as there is no English translation.

been as a kind of supernatural bawd, is re-defined as the Trinity. It is certainly a powerful *moralitas* with which to end the story sequence, but one as incongruously out of key as the interpretation given to the tale of the hanging-tree in the *Gesta*.

The *Decameron*, with its hundred stories, presents a bigger problem of organisation. The tales are the object of the work; but the fictional frame is none the less one of the triumphs of the book, and not least because romance is abandoned for a circumstantially detailed and persuasive, if not quite entirely credible, account of how the story-telling comes about. Ten young people, seven ladies and three men, retreat from the plague-stricken city of Florence to a succession of idyllic country houses, where they agree to pass their time by telling stories. The settings for each day's tales, in gardens or ideal retreats in the landscape, are described in detail – in more detail, indeed, than are the speakers. A queen or king is elected to rule the company for each day, and each ruler after the first day specifies a general theme for the next day's story-telling – except for the ninth day, when the tellers are given freedom to choose any story. In addition Dioneo, the wit and to some degree the cynic of the company, is allowed the privilege of always speaking last and on a subject of his own choice. After a fortnight (ten days of story-telling interrupted by breaks on Fridays and Saturdays, when the company fast and the ladies wash their hair), they return to the city and go their own ways.

For all the idyllicism of the outdoor settings, the framework conveys a brilliant quality of authenticity. It provides a mould in which the telling of a hundred stories becomes plausible. This effect probably depends less on the unusual naturalism with which Boccaccio intro-duces the work – his account of the Black Death is the most graphic we possess – than on the appropriateness of telling stories as a game. There is a perfect congruity between the light-heartedness of the tellers devising an entertainment for themselves once they have left Florence behind and the sheer delight of author and reader in writing and reading stories. Although Boccaccio in his own voice and his narrators in theirs will at times refer to the usefulness of their stories, their principal function is simply to give pleasure. Didactic moral earnestness is laid aside with the gloom of the dying city. Boccaccio's own lack of concern with possible inner meanings in his narratives is indicated in the preface, when he declares,

Intendo di raccontare cento novelle, o favole o parabole o istorie che dire le vogliamo.

I shall narrate a hundred stories or fables or parables or histories or whatever you choose to call them.[50]

[50] *Ed.cit., Proemio* p. v; trans. McWilliam p. 47.

It is entirely up to the reader if he wishes to turn *novella* into *favola*, story into a fictional cover for truth;[51] inner meaning is not going to be the point of these stories.

The lack of an overriding moral purpose[52] makes the centrifugal forces involved in telling a hundred stories all the more considerable, however convincing the framework, and Boccaccio uses a number of devices to stop them flying apart from each other. The main one is the specification of a theme for eight of the ten days. The second day, for instance, is to be on those who after suffering a series of misfortunes are brought to a state of unexpected happiness; the third on 'people who by dint of their own efforts have achieved an object they greatly desired or recovered a thing previously lost'; the final day's subject is 'those who have performed liberal or munificent deeds, whether in the course of love or otherwise'. Even the subjects laid down are sometimes directly related to each other: the fourth day's topic is love that ends unhappily, the fifth day's is love that ends happily. Within each day and at times across days the stories are held together by common themes. In addition, one story will often pick up directly some point of the previous tale: Panfilo tells a story about prophetic dreams to follow on a similar one from Filomena, and Emilia notes that both her tale and Panfilo's are set in gardens (IV.5, 6, 7). One story is described as celebrating pity, the next as punishing cruelty (V.7, 8). Consecutive stories are sometimes located in the same city; or there is a series about the same character (VIII.3, 6, 9, IX.3). Links between stories are especially necessary on the first and ninth days, when no subject is prescribed, and Boccaccio has Lauretta note how the ninth day's narrators have taken their cue from each other (IX.8). Links of this kind are sometimes perfunctory in the extreme, but they do at the least give more than just an illusion of unity, and that is quite sufficient for Boccaccio's purposes.

He does run the opposite risk as well: that the prescription of a set theme might make each day's stories too repetitive, despite the diversion of Dioneo's contrasting and usually irreverent tenth tale. In practice, however, there is never any risk of this happening. In marked

[51] See above pp. 17–18 and note 31; for Boccaccio's own discussion of *fabula* in his *De Genealogia Deorum* XIV.ix, see *Boccaccio on Poetry* translated by Charles G. Osgood (Princeton, 1930/Indianapolis, 1956) pp. 47–51.

[52] Various critics have attempted to find one, but without a great deal of success. The last day's stories are more morally uplifting than most, but there is no consistent rise in level of vision throughout the work. Vittore Branca sees recurring patterns of tales on Fortune, Love and Ingenuity, with the occasional interlude, and the final tale (of Griselda) as the summation of virtue (*Boccaccio: The Man and his Works* trans. Richard Monges (New York, 1976) pp. 206–7), but the terms are too generalised to be altogether convincing. Charles S. Singleton has argued forcefully that the art of the *Decameron* is designed precisely to contain no *sovrasenso* ('On meaning in the *Decameron*', *Italica* XXI (1944) 117–24).

contrast to the didactic story-collections, the tales of the *Decameron* never take their morals too seriously. The very first tale of the second day, the first story, that is, that needs to conform to a set subject, illustrates the rise from misfortune to happiness by way of a scoundrel who narrowly escapes hanging. The morals derived from individual stories may show an equally witty disregard of higher morality. The fabliaux, the comic verse tales which are the closest relatives of many of the stories of the *Decameron*, have something of a tradition of spoof morals of this kind, where the advice is much less likely to be to behave well than not to get caught. The most outrageous tales of the *Decameron* will finish by piously urging their hearers to follow the example just set. The last tale of the third day – a tale about a novel method of putting the Devil in Hell, of a kind that for centuries made translators and editors retreat to asterisks or total silence – concludes:

> And so, young ladies, if you stand in need of God's grace, see that you learn to put the devil back in Hell, for it is greatly to His liking and pleasurable to the parties concerned, and a great deal of good can arise and flow in the process.[53]

On the surface Dioneo is conforming to the principle that 'all that is written, is written for our doctrine', but his application of it could hardly be more delightedly wicked.

If the prescription of themes is one of the main devices for holding the stories of the *Decameron* together, the play of wit in setting off story against moral helps to raise it far above the repetitive didacticism of so many compilations. Boccaccio's two Latin story-collections, written a decade or so later, tend to sink back to that level of dreary moralism, enlivened only by occasional flashes of his narrative skill.

Such moralism was immensely popular in the Middle Ages and Renaissance. The *De Casibus* was then his best known work; there are over eighty manuscripts surviving, and over a hundred of Laurent de Premierfait's French translation,[54] which was in turn the basis of Lydgate's *Falls of Princes*. It recounts the undeserved rise to fame and usually well-deserved falls of great men, and a few women, from the Creation (it starts, indeed, with Adam, who does not quite fit the specifications), to the present, interspersed with laments, warnings against vice, incitements to virtue, and more laments. He sees virtue, and especially poverty, as the one sure bulwark against Fortune. The stories are held together by their conformity to the same narrative outline of rise and fall, and by their expression of more or less the

---

[53] Trans. McWilliam p. 319; 'E per ciò voi, giovani donne, alle quali la grazia di Dio bisogna, apparate a rimettere il diavolo in inferno, per ciò che egli è forte a grado a Dio e piacer delle parti, e molto bene ne può nascere e seguire' (ed.cit. p. 270).

[54] See Hall's introduction to the facsimile p. v.

same kernel of inner meaning: the turning of Fortune's wheel, nemesis for pride, and the supreme power of God over the most apparently mighty of the earth. Their coherence is reinforced by a minimal connecting framework in that Boccaccio imagines many of the figures, including Fortuna herself at one point, passing before his eyes; and the discourse – 'narrative' is too strong a word – is more or less continuous within each of the nine books that constitute the work. It is sometimes described as a dream vision, but it is not: the figures enter his waking thoughts, and his laments and warnings are written literally open-eyed. We are never allowed to forget the *utilitas* of the work – his favourite word in the preface.

The *De Claris Mulieribus* lacks even a minimal framework of this kind. It was written partly as a companion piece to Petrarch's all-male *De Viris Illustribus*, and contains a hundred and four lives of women who deserved fame for whatever reason, good or bad:

> It is not my intention to give the word 'famous' so strict a meaning that it will always seem to signify 'virtuous', but rather to give it a wider sense, if the reader will forgive me, and to consider as famous those women whom I know to have become renowned to the world through any sort of deed.[55]

The biographies follow in individual chapters. There is no consistent narrative structure or moral shaping to the stories, and they are drawn from a wide array of mythological, Classical and occasionally historical sources, with the mythological figures (Ceres, Circe and so on) being rationalised into historical women. Hebrew and Christian women are excluded on the grounds that their stories and virtues have been plentifully celebrated by others; the only exceptions he allows are Eve, and a small closing handful of more recent women whose Christianity is secondary to their political fame or personal notoriety (Pope Joan, for instance). His final subject is Joanna, Queen of Sicily and Jerusalem, to whom the whole work is dedicated. The euhemerism is so marked, and the resistance to all kinds of superstition so explicit, that Guido Guarino, the modern translator of the work, has suggested that it may be itself an attack on the credulity of the average *Vitae Sanctorum*.[56] Whether this is so, or whether Boccaccio, with all the zeal of an early humanist, was trying to give Classical pagan literature

---

[55] Trans. Guarino pp. xxxvii–viii; 'Non enim est animus mihi hoc claritatis nomen, adeo strictim sumere, ut semper in uirtutem videatur exire, quinimo in ampliorem sensu (bona cum pace legentium) trahere, et illas intelligere claras, quas quocumque ex facinore, orbi vulgato sermone, notissimas nouero' (ed.cit.sig. a v^r (contractions expanded)).

[56] Guarino p. xxv. A more likely explanation, however, would be that the rationalism was necessitated by the change of genre from legendary to history.

a non-fictional status, he certainly saw the work as being morally useful. He describes it at the end of the preface as a 'pious work', and the exemplary function of each life is carefully pointed out, as he deplores vice and celebrates virtue. Beyond this rather perfunctory *ad hoc* moralisation, the only common criterion for the stories is that the subjects are all women, and all more or less famous.

Boccaccio's Latin works were disseminated across Europe with a speed not matched by the vernacular writings. The *De Casibus* and *De Claris Mulieribus* were known and indeed translated in England in the fifteenth century, by Lydgate at second hand in the *Falls of Princes* and by an anonymous poet who seems never to have found the patronage he needed to get beyond the first twenty lives of famous women.[57] Chaucer also knew them, though he drew on them surprisingly little considering how close his own Monk's Tale and *Legend of Good Women* are in theme and subject. In a number of manuscripts the Monk's Tale is given the sub-title 'De Casibus Virorum Illustrium', but there is no way of knowing whether that heading is Chaucer's own or whether it was added by a scribe. Very little of the content of the Monk's Tale can be traced to the *De Casibus* with any certainty, and the case is similar with the *De Claris Mulieribus*. The one story he certainly drew from it, the history of Xenobia, he uses not in the *Legend* but as one of the Monk's tragedies; in the *Legend* itself the only story derived from Boccaccio is that of Cleopatra, who appears in both the Latin works.

The bigger question is whether, or how much, Chaucer knew of Boccaccio's vernacular story-collections with their fuller fictional frameworks. There is some evidence that he may have drawn on the *Ameto* for his descriptions of an old husband and a young wife in the Merchant's Tale.[58] Karl Young demonstrated many years ago that the *Filocolo* may well have influenced some episodes and passages in

---

[57] *Die Mittelenglische Umdichtung von Boccaccios De Claris Mulieribus* ed. Gustav Schleich (Palaestra 144, Leipzig, 1924); on the question of patronage, see stanzas IV and CCLVI (the last):

> Without grete ayde of sum noble pryncess
> All in veyne shuld be my besyness;
> For poetys ben of litell reputacion
> That of estatys have no sustentacion.
>
> . . . . .
>
> If it fortune to be acceptable
> And please the herers, forth I wyll procede
> To the residue of ladyes notable;
> But fyrste of all, to se howe this shall spede,
> I will take counsell, er it go on brede,
> Leste that I eyre the baren se-banke
> And gete me more of laboure than of thanke.

[58] See Tatlock pp. 80–108, Bryan and Dempster pp. 339–40.

Troilus and Criseyde.[59] The *Filocolo* also contains a fuller version of the story found again in the *Decameron* of the wife who promises her love in return for the impossible – the story that became the Franklin's Tale.

Did Chaucer know the *Decameron*? The magisterial *Sources and Analogues of Chaucer's Canterbury Tales* decrees that he did not.[60] Early this century, R. K. Root and others argued strongly that he did,[61] though he may not have possessed a copy of his own. J. S. P. Tatlock picked up the argument by demonstrating that most of the points used to prove Chaucer's knowledge of the work applied equally well to the *Filocolo* and the *Ameto*.[62] More recent research has failed to resolve the matter; the parallels remain just as striking, and firm proof remains just as elusive.[63] The theory that Chaucer may have come across the *Decameron* in Italy but had only a memory of it, not a text, has received intermittent support; recently Donald McGrady has argued for an even closer relationship, of Chaucer's 'deliberate comparison of variant texts during the creative process' – texts that included the *Decameron*.[64]

The essence of the problem is this: five of the *Canterbury Tales*, the Reeve's, Clerk's, Merchant's, Franklin's and Shipman's, all have close analogues in the *Decameron*; there is a more distant analogue to the Man of Law's Tale, and there are strong similarities of motifs between the Miller's Tale and the Pardoner's Prologue and other of Boccaccio's tales.[65] Even if these last two are discounted and only complete tales are compared, then six of Chaucer's twenty-four stories – a full quarter of the total – are paralleled in the *Decameron*. The proportion seems

---

[59] *The Origin and Development of the Story of Criseyde* (Chaucer Society 1908/New York, 1968) pp. 139–81.

[60] In this they follow Hubertis S. Cummings' *The Indebtedness of Chaucer's Works to the Italian Works of Boccaccio* (University of Cincinnati Studies X, 1916/New York 1967) and Willard Farnham, 'England's discovery of the *Decameron*', *PMLA* XXXIX (1924) 123–39. Both works, especially Cummings, are seriously inadequate: see the long overdue critique by Donald McGrady, 'Chaucer and the *Decameron* reconsidered,' *Chaucer Review* XII (1977–8) 1–26.

[61] R. K. Root, 'Chaucer and the Decameron', *Englische Studien* XLIV (1911) 1–7, in which he elaborates on an article by Lorenz Morsbach, 'Chaucers Plan der *Canterbury Tales* und Boccaccios *Decamerone*,' *Englische Studien* XLII (1910) 43–52.

[62] See n. 49 above.

[63] The fullest and most judicious study known to me is an unpublished Oxford B.Litt. thesis by Moira F. Bovill, *The Decameron and the Canterbury Tales: A Comparative Study* (1966).

[64] McGrady p. 13 (see n. 60 above).

[65] For the Reeve's Tale cf. *Decameron* IX, 6; Clerk's Tale cf. X, 10; Merchant's cf. VII, 9 (a less close analogue than the others, but which uses the motifs of old husband, young wife, amorous servant and pear-tree; II, x provides further parallels to other motifs in the tale); Franklin's cf. X, 5; Shipman's cf. VII, 1; Man of Law's cf. V, 2; Miller's Tale cf. III, 4 (and possibly VIII, 7 and VII, 4: see McGrady pp. 13–14); Pardoner's Prologue cf. VI, 10.

too high to be coincidence: none of the other story-collections in circulation can provide anything approaching the same proportion of analogues. And yet, with the possible exception of the Franklin's Tale, none of the analogues in the *Decameron* apparently served as a source. The Clerk's Tale of patient Griselda does go back to Boccaccio's version, but only at second or third hand: Chaucer was working from Petrarch's Latin version of the story and an anonymous French translation of that.[66] It has been argued that he was also using the *Decameron* version,[67] but the point is less decisively demonstrable. As with the Clerk's Tale, so with the rest: for every story common to both collections, there are one or more other versions that are closer to Chaucer's telling than Boccaccio's.

It is still not altogether certain, however, that the *Decameron* provides no direct sources. Boccaccio based the fifth story of the tenth day on his own *Filocolo*, and there is singularly little clear evidence as to which was Chaucer's source for the Franklin's Tale. In conciseness of telling and in some details (such as that the question as to which character was the most generous is debated but never answered), the *Decameron* version is distinctly closer to Chaucer's, but he changes the story so much that it is impossible to know which he was using, or indeed whether he used both. Only the assumption that he knew the *Filocolo* has led to that being preferred as the source, but Chaucer's knowledge of the *Filocolo* in fact rests on no surer evidence than his knowledge of the *Decameron*. The other story which might have the *Decameron* as its immediate source is the Shipman's Tale; the alternatives suggested are from a conjectural lost old French fabliau, or from a tale in the *Novelle* of Giovanni Sercambi, who based his own version of the story on Boccaccio's.[68] Sercambi's work is discussed in more detail below; it is enough to say here that the version of his work that Chaucer might conceivably have known was the *Novelliero*, written probably in 1374, and this is lost; the revised version, dating from 1385 or later, almost certainly too late for Chaucer to have used it, is still extant, and is likely to be closely similar to the original collection. Given the largely trivial differences of detail that are held to demonstrate Chaucer's greater closeness to Sercambi than Boccaccio, however, it seems rash to base too strong a case on a work whose precise content can only be conjectural. In some significant respects, notably the distaste shown by both Boccaccio and Chaucer over the wife's sale of her sexual favours for cash, Chaucer is closer to the *Decameron*.[69]

[66] See the account by J. Burke Severs in Bryan and Dempster pp. 288–91.
[67] McGrady p. 9.
[68] See John Webster Spargo's section on the Shipman's Tale in Bryan and Dempster pp. 439–46.
[69] See Bovill ch. 7.

As with the Franklin's Tale, however, Chaucer changes the story substantially – so far as to make it impossible to tell whether one is looking at a source at all, or just at an analogue. Even apparent verbal similarities between the *Decameron* and the *Canterbury Tales* are not decisive: the comparison of an old lecher to a leek with a white head and a green tail may, or may not, have been proverbial; and although both authors apologise for the bawdy element of their work and blame their own fictional characters for it, this need not prove imitation.[70]

That, then, is the problem in outline; to go into more detail would take up this entire book, and still not produce any final answer. One other point is perhaps worth making: all the closest analogues to the *Tales* occur in the last third of the *Decameron*, in the last three days' story-telling and the Epilogue. This again proves nothing, but it does perhaps strengthen the case for Chaucer's having read or heard part of the work in Italy and brought back a memory of it with him, enough to give him ideas for the framework and to put him on the look-out for certain tales in other versions wherever they were accessible. What one can say with complete certainty is this: that if Chaucer did not know the *Decameron*, he did at least recognise the same problems in compiling a story-collection as Boccaccio did, and often tackled them in similar ways. The authors of the two greatest story-collections of the Middle Ages were both aware of the particular challenges and difficulties of the form, and they alone got to grips with the problem of coherence both through the framework and through the narrative and thematic properties of the stories themselves.

Whether or not the *Decameron* inspired the *Canterbury Tales*, it certainly inspired a new outburst of Italian story-collections in the later fourteenth century, more or less contemporary with Chaucer's career. The most notable of these were Sercambi's *Novelle*, the *Pecorone* of Giovanni Fiorentino, and the *Paradiso degli Alberti* of Franco Sacchetti. Sercambi's work is the only one that may possibly have been known to Chaucer, though the dating of even the early version makes it unlikely. It is much the most interesting in its solution to the problem of how to organise a story-collection; it has indeed been suggested as the model, not only for the Shipman's Tale and one or two other episodes in the *Canterbury Tales*, but for the framework of the whole piece.[71] Its attraction as the model for Chaucer's work lies

[70] Chaucer, Reeve's Prologue I 3878–9 and Decameron IV, Introduction; Miller's Prologue I 3167–86 and Boccaccio's Epilogue (Conclusione dell'Autore). See also McGrady pp. 3, 12, 17 note 10, and Bovill pp. 18–21, 28–31.

[71] On the framework, see the discussion by Robert A. Pratt and Karl Young in Bryan and Dempster pp. 20–33 and the extracts on pp. 33–81 (most printed here for the first time); for analogous passages on the activities of a religious trickster comparable to the Pardoner see pp. 413–14, and of an alchemist like the one in the Canon's Yeoman's Tale see pp. 694–5. Sercambi also gives a version of the story of Griselda (p. 288).

in the fact that the tales are told on a journey in which Sercambi himself claims to take part – it is indeed he who tells all the stories. The travellers are a group of men and women of assorted ranks and occupations from Lucca, who agree to travel through Italy until the plague in their home town has subsided. They appoint a leader from their number, one of whose functions is to be master of ceremonies; and Sercambi tells his stories along the way and at various stopping-places such as gardens and inn yards. Indoor entertainment is provided in the evenings by singing – the work includes a number of songs, on the model of the *Decameron* – dancing, and moral addresses from those members of the company who are in religious orders.

The similarities to Chaucer's plan are obvious: the mixed company, the journey setting, the first-person narrator, the 'Host' figure. None the less, Sercambi's work shows fewer similarities over all to the *Canterbury Tales* than does the *Decameron*. It is true that the stories are told while travelling, but if Sercambi was capable of thinking up that development, then so was Chaucer. Sercambi's carefully established (if sometimes slightly fanciful) geographical framework is certainly not reflected in Chaucer's haphazard itinerary: we are always told where Sercambi's travellers stop, never where Chaucer's pilgrims do. Sercambi's method of ordering his stories is distinctly perfunctory – the tales are often set in the particular town the travellers are approaching or passing. Chaucer's attempts to order his own stories are much subtler and more profound, and much closer to Boccaccio's methods, though he develops them differently. The difference in quality must also be taken into account. The *Decameron* is found in numerous manuscripts, printed editions and translations, and it spawned many imitations. Sercambi has not stirred even a modern scholar to print him complete.[72] It strains credibility less to believe that Chaucer knew the *Decameron*, than to believe that the circumstantial evidence for his knowledge of it is all mere coincidence, or that he found the inspiration for the *Canterbury Tales* in Boccaccio's uninspired imitators.

Gower

Sheer delight in telling or listening to stories characterised late fourteenth-century England as it did Italy. The interest in narrative shown by the great poets of the age of Richard II has been picked out

---

[72] The fullest edition is by R. Renier, *Novelle Inedite di Giovanni Sercambi* (Turin, 1889).

as their leading common characteristic.[73] And the more stories the better: the scheme outlined by the Host for the *Canterbury Tales* would produce a hundred and twenty stories, four for each of thirty or so pilgrims, so decisively overgoing Boccaccio's hundred; and the framework devised by Gower for the *Confessio Amantis* threatens to be infinitely expandable, though he too settles for something over a hundred – an exact count is impossible as there is no way to draw a precise line between the shortest of his stories and a name mentioned for exemplary purposes with a brief explanation of its appropriateness attached. Rhetoric used for wrong ends, for instance, is illustrated by this example:

> Of Uluxes thus I rede,
> As in the bok of Troie is founde,
> His eloquence and his facounde
> Of goodly wordes whiche he tolde,
> Hath mad that Anthenor him solde
> The toun, which he with tresoun wan.[74]

This is hardly a 'story'; but some of the stories proper are little longer. The variety in length of Gower's stories makes the work very different from most collections. The *Decameron*, the *Gesta* or the *Canterbury Tales* will have the longest stories ten times or so as long as the shortest; Gower's will commonly run from a dozen lines or even less to several hundred, his longest being almost two thousand.

Gower organises the *Confessio*, as its title indicates, on the model of a penitential manual. A work such as Robert Mannyng's *Handlyng Synne* has close similarities to Gower's poem, with the sins being listed and analysed in turn and each variety and sub-division illustrated by an example of the sin in action. Gower gives a secular version of the same thing. For the direct speech of the preacher he substitutes a fictional framework in which he presents himself as an unrequited and, it finally transpires, elderly lover, who meets the god and goddess of Love in the course of a May walk and is bidden by Venus to make his confession to her priest Genius. The rest of the work is taken up with Genius' interrogation of the lover as to whether he has committed any sin against love, the lover's replies, and Genius' exposition of the nature of these sins, well illustrated with stories. One book is devoted to each sin – Pride, Envy, Wrath, Sloth, Avarice

---

[73] J. A. Burrow, *Ricardian Poetry* (London, 1971) ch. 2. See also Piero Boitani, *English Medieval Narrative in the Thirteenth and Fourteenth Centuries* trans. Joan Krakover Hall (Cambridge, 1982) for a recent study of the place of Gower and Chaucer in the development of narrative and story-collections.

[74] *Confessio Amantis* VII 1558–63, in *The English Works of John Gower* ed. G. C. Macaulay (2 vols, EETS E.S. 81–2, 1900–01).

and Gluttony; the seventh, which one might expect to be on Lust, is instead on the education of princes (though Gower does note that Chastity is especially important for kings); and the eighth is on lawful, or more particularly unlawful, love, especially incest. At the end the lover is brought to recognise his age, Reason returns to him and he is freed from his passion. In addition to the narrative of the framework and the inset stories, there is a persistent thematic emphasis on the condition of the world in general and the body politic in particular. There is a long prologue on this subject, Book VII is concerned with it, and Gower closes the poem with a survey of the ills attending the clergy, 'chevalerie' and the middle classes, and of the duties of a king.

It might seem that with the exception of this curious double emphasis on the public alongside the personal, the political alongside the emotional, Gower had succeeded in finding a balance between frame and stories that can provide coherence without also imposing the monotony of a single theme. This is largely, but not entirely, true. In a story-collection the emphasis falls on the tales; and for long stretches of Gower's stories, especially the lengthiest, one forgets the frame completely, and with it the moral point the tale is supposed to be illustrating. There are times indeed when the sin under consideration seems as incidental an excuse for telling a particular tale as is the mention of a place-name in the *Decameron* or the *Novelle*. Even for Gower's most famous stories – the tale of Florent, for instance (which is the same story as that told by the Wife of Bath, about the young knight who promises to marry an old hag in return for her telling him what women most desire), or the tale of Constance – I would guess that few people who have read them could remember or even deduce which sin or concomitant virtue they are supposed to illustrate. In the *Decameron* the oblique relationship between tale and theme or moral is often deliberately witty; in the *Confessio*, once Genius is armed with an excuse for telling a story, the narrative tends to take over from the moral. There are of course many exceptions to this, especially with the most functionally exemplary stories – Book VII, for instance, is packed with instances of good and bad rulers; but generally, the closer the connection between story and application, the less interesting the story. The tales need to have a life independent of the framework if they are to succeed fully as stories. The progression through all the sub-divisions of the sins avoids the monotony imposed by the choice of a single topic; but it does not stimulate enough variety in the tales themselves to make the reader or listener eager for the next with the same degree of curiosity that one experiences in the *Decameron* or the *Canterbury Tales*.

All the stories of the *Confessio* are told in a single voice, that of Genius. There is one other principal speaker in the poem, the Lover making his confession; and while many of his interjections are very brief indeed, no more than a denial that he has committed a particular sin or a request to Genius to tell another story, there are passages where he describes the progress – or lack of progress – of his love-affair and his feelings for his lady. There is a germ of dramatic inter-play here, between confessor and penitent or, indirectly, between lover and lady, that is missing in the stories themselves and that gives a welcome sharpness to the movement of the whole poem. The tales, however, maintain a common tone, Gower's regular octosyllabics maintain an unvarying level of poetic competence, and the work lacks the dazzle that Boccaccio and Chaucer can give. In genre, too, Gower brings all his narratives towards a common centre, in which the con-sistency of style smoothes over the generic distinctions that the nature of the individual stories might suggest. The *Confessio* is unquestion-ably a remarkable achievement. It was widely copied and read in the Middle Ages: some forty complete manuscripts survive and there are extracts in many others, a number that suggests that it did not fall too far short of the *Canterbury Tales* in popularity and far outstripped Chaucer's other works. It was translated into Spanish, and printed by Caxton in 1483 and by Berthelette in 1532 and 1554. There were no Elizabethan editions, however: the Renaissance poetic revival was the movement that finally distinguished Chaucer as the supreme English poet of the Middle Ages. The opening chorus of the part-Shakespear-ean *Pericles* stresses the antiquity of both Gower himself and the story of Apollonius taken from him, and for some centuries after that date the *Confessio* was little read and never reprinted.

Gower's emphasis on story in the *Confessio* can easily conceal the place that the work holds in his wider ambitions for his whole *oeuvre*. He wrote three major works, in French, Latin and English: the *Speculum Meditantis* (a title he substituted for the original *Miroir de l'Omme*) in the late 1370s, the *Vox Clamantis* early in the next decade, and the *Confessio Amantis* itself. The deliberate patterning of the titles is an indication of the close relationship he came to see between the works, as three books of moral instruction bearing on different aspects of experience. He made some alterations to the *Confessio* to bring it closer into line with the others.[75] The poems are written in the three languages of Anglo-French culture spoken in England; and they are concerned with the public sphere of the common weal, the spiritual path to salvation, and the nature of individual emotion, love. Gower's long poems together present a kind of *summa* of human

[75] See John H. Fisher, *John Gower: Moral Philosopher and Friend of Chaucer* (London, 1965) pp. 88–90, 121–2, 135–7. Gower set out the relationship between the works in a colophon originally composed in about 1390: its various forms are given by Fisher, pp. 88–90, 311–12. Gower's works in all languages are edited by G. C. Macaulay, *The Complete Works of John Gower* (4 vols, Oxford, 1899–1902).

experience. The serious poet in the Middle Ages was thought of as a teacher; Gower sets out to teach across the whole range of human affairs. Although the *Miroir* contains some stories – some, indeed, that are used again with a similar application in the *Confessio* – it is an avowedly serious and didactic work. The *Confessio* threatens to be the lightweight member of the group, and this may be one reason for the intrusive emphasis there on the state of the world. It does indeed to some degree draw the subjects of the earlier poems into its purview: the indictment of social abuse and the sense of cosmic disorder work together with the notion of confession, of spiritual cleansing, towards an ideal of self-knowledge such as the Lover himself reaches in the course of his own inner analysis at the end of the poem.

The *Confessio*, then, is an ambitious poem by reason of more than mere length. Implicitly, and as the last of three works that form a series of sorts, it makes large claims for itself as a poem, for the nature of poetry and for the skill and understanding of the man who wrote it. Chaucer, however, was not going to let Gower have everything his own way. In a passage that he may possibly once have intended to introduce the story-telling[76] he has the Man of Law take objection to the immorality of some of Gower's stories by contrast with Chaucer's own:

> But certeinly no word writeth he
> Of thilke wikke example of Canacee,
> That loved hir owene brother sinfully;
> (Of swiche cursed stories I sey fy!)
> Or ellis of Tyro Appollonius,
> How that the cursed kyng Antiochus
> Birafte his doghter of hir maydenhede,
> That is so horrible a tale for to rede,
> Whan he hir threw upon the pavement.
> And therfore he, of ful avysement,
> Nolde nevere write in none of his sermons
> Of swiche unkynde abhomynacions.   II 77–88

The Man of Law's tone is moralistic and serious, Chaucer's tone is at least partly playful. If the lines advertise this story-collection at the expense of its rival, they do also point out a genuine distinction between the content of the works of the two poets. Chaucer tends to avoid 'unnatural' love, except in *exempla*, just as he avoids the metamorphosis of man into beast, and perhaps for similar reasons. More

---

[76] The evidence is internal, in the content of the section; all the manuscripts follow the General Prologue with the Knight's Tale. On the possibility that the Introduction to the Man of Law's Tale was intended to open the story-telling see Carleton Brown, 'The Man of Law's head-link and the Prologue of the Canterbury Tales', *Studies in Philology* XXXIV (1937) 8–35, esp. 23–6.

important, however playfully expressed, is the idea that the *Canter-bury Tales* will in some sense 'overgo' the *Confessio*. The *Tales* is also an ambitious work, and it makes claims for itself that go beyond Gower's.

Chaucer

From the time of his earliest work Chaucer evinced a keen interest not only in stories but in what could be done with them. He delighted in them for their own sakes; and he explored new ways of making them significant, not by deducing morals from them, nor even by exploring the *sentence* within the subject-matter – though this is cer-tainly important – but above all by letting meaning emerge from setting one story alongside another, or placing a story in a context that re-defines its meaning.

This kind of juxtaposition underlies Chaucer's use of inset stories in both the *Book of the Duchess* and the *House of Fame*, and it is most easily illustrated by those before one moves on to the greater com-plexities of his story-collections themselves. The story of Ceyx and Alcyone in the *Book of the Duchess* works in much the same way as a sub-plot in Elizabethan drama, to reflect or contrast with the prin-cipal theme of the play; though in Chaucer's poem the tale precedes the main action, rather than being interwoven with it as a sub-plot would be. The narrator describes himself as sleepless from a cause that appears to be love-sickness. To 'drive the night away' he starts reading, and the tale he picks on is the story of the king who is drowned and his wife who prays to Juno for a dream in which she will learn of her husband's welfare. Through the agency of Morpheus the dream is sent, and Alcyone dies of grief 'within the thridde morwe'. Then follows the one explicit connection between the story and the main action of the poem: the narrator decides that he too will pray to Morpheus in the hope that he will fall asleep as speedily as Alcyone did. He tries it, and it works.

The story obviously is much more than a mere sleep-inducing device. It introduces the whole idea of dreams and their significance, so that when the dreamer speaks of the 'sweven' that came to him we already endow it with the resonance that Alcyone's vision has brought. The content of the dreams is overtly contrasted: not the gruesomeness of Ceyx's drowned corpse, but a remarkable release from grief in the brightness of a May morning full of birdsong. The central figure of the dream is a man in black – at once a projection of the narrator's waking melancholy, for the melancholy man dreams of black just as the hen Pertelote assumes her mate to be choleric when he dreams of red; and also a counterpart to the Ovidian characters, for where Alcyone had lost her husband, the man in black has lost his lady. Chaucer the narrator appears to be split in two within the dream: the intense emotion of his waking life and his melancholy are projected on to the knight, while the 'I' continues as the recording eyes and ears of his dreaming consciousness. Only at the very end does the dreamer, like Alcyone at the end of her dream, realise the fact of death, but he can wake and continue his life, where her waking can lead only to her own death. The parallelism of meaning between story and dream is emphasised by the way Chaucer avoids any reference to anything beyond death. It is not Ceyx's spirit but a god animating his drowned corpse that speaks to Alcyone, and their metamorphosis into seabirds that concludes the story in Ovid is completely omitted by Chaucer. He also refrains from putting forward any idea that the Lady White may be in Heaven – a quite extraordinarily unconventional omission for a Christian elegy. As a result, all the emphasis falls on the worthwhile-ness of the love of knight and lady in earthly, human terms. For all his misery of loss, the man in black will not repent of loving. To do so would make him the worst traitor the world has ever known:

> 'Shulde y now repente me
> To love? Nay, certes, than were I wel
> Wers than was Achitofel,
> Or Anthenor, so have I joye,
> The traytor that betraysed Troye,
> Or the false Genelloun,
> He that purchased the tresoun
> Of Rowland and of Olyver.
> Nay, while I am alyve her,
> I nyl foryete hir never moo.'   1116–25

It is the knight's most impassioned outburst, and he defines his position by contrast with the villains of the story traditions of the Bible, Troy and the 'matter of France'. For all its dream setting, Chaucer is giving a deeply sympathetic account of human loving, explored not through action, as the Ovidian story is, but through the knight's expressed emotions and his memories of the Lady White that make her live to the hearer.

A footnote is necessary to this account of the *Book of the Duchess*, for readers will have noticed that I have not mentioned John of Gaunt. That the man in black is in some sense a representation of him, and the Lady White of his dead wife Blanche, has long been recognised. The curious thing is that he can be so entirely left out of an account of the poem, especially when Chaucer goes to some pains to confirm the identification at the end with his reference to Gaunt's name and his titles of Lancaster and Richmond.[77] In the transposition from his-

---

[77] A long castel with walles white,/ Be seynt Johan! on a ryche hil (1318–19).

tory to dream, however, the particularity of actual event is transcended. The black of the knight's clothing stands for death, grief, loss, mourning; the Lady White is associated with life, joy, beauty, love. Like all dream-poems, the *Book of the Duchess* makes a universal statement, not just a topical one. Even the nature of the consolation Chaucer is offering is subtler than has sometimes been suggested. Gaunt, like Chaucer the narrator, seems to have a double persona within the dream: publicly he is the emperor Octavian, the noble lord who rides hunting; privately he is the grieving widower. The two come together at the end, when the 'hert-huntyng' is completed and 'this kyng' rides home to his castle. The knight has never been described as a king, but the two figures seem to converge here – the private man resuming public action. If the man in black is within the movement of the poem also a projection of the narrator's own melancholy, then Chaucer is offering his patron sympathy through identification in grief. This is much more profound then the traditional notion of a deliberately obtuse dreamer drawing out his aristocratic patron in a tactless display of tact. Chaucer never allows the precise historical reference of his poem to dominate over its more general exposition of love and death, however: at the end he wakes, the book of Ceyx and Alcyone still in his hand. Immediately after giving the iconic signature of his patron, Chaucer reminds us of the unending relevance of that central theme, from the legendary past to his own present.

The story that occupies most of Book I of the *House of Fame* is equally significant for the poem as a whole, though Chaucer gives fewer overt clues as to just what that significance is. There is even less narrative connection here between the story and the rest of the poem than there is in the *Book of the Duchess*. Chaucer describes himself as falling asleep and dreaming that he finds himself in the temple of Venus, made of glass. On the walls is a summary of the *Aeneid*; this is mostly in pictorial form, but it starts with an inscription of the opening lines on a brass tablet, Virgil's famous 'Arma virumque cano':

> I wol now singen, yif I kan,
> The armes, and also the man . . .   143–4

The whole epic is described in brief, but the episode that most engages Chaucer's attention – and which he recounts in a degree of detail quite at odds with the claim that the story is told in wall-paintings – is the love-affair of Dido and Aeneas. His account of what he *sees*, 'Ther sawgh I grave . . .', does indeed give way to a different perceptual frame, 'But let us speke of . . .'. The story is told from Dido's point of view, and at the end Aeneas' treachery is compared to that of a good many other villains of classical legend (several of whom reappear in the *Legend of Good Women*) before Chaucer returns to his summary of the later books of the epic. When that is complete he steps outside the temple and finds himself in a desert; and an eagle appears and carries him off to the Palace of Fame.

Both structurally, by its isolation in a single book, and in narrative organisation, where the dreamer's sojourn in the temple of Venus has no introduction and no explicit relationship to anything that follows, the story of Dido is unrelated to the rest of the poem. The structure of dreams, however, operates on latent levels of understanding, as Chaucer and Langland well knew, and the very lack of overt connection forces the reader to complete the text, to make the thematic links between what Chaucer offers as unrelated phenomena within the dream. The most obvious of these occurs in the description of the pillars lining each side of Fame's hall. The pillars, of various non-precious metals associated with the most relevant gods, each support one or more famous writers, who in their turn bear up the fame of their subject on their shoulders. Among them,

> Tho saugh I stonde on a piler,
> That was of tynned yren cler,
> The Latyn poete, Virgile,
> That bore hath up a longe while
> The fame of Pius Eneas.   1481–5

Iron and tin are the metals of Mars and Jupiter; one suspects that they may also make an alloy of less than perfect strength. The whole message of the episode in Fame's house is that fame is distributed entirely capriciously, with no regard to merit. Virgil may support Aeneas' fame; Chaucer, in his own retelling of the *Aeneid*, has drawn a rather different conclusion. For him, Aeneas is 'pius' only on the surface:

> Ther may be under godlyhed
> Kevered many a shrewed vice.   274–5

On this interpretation Aeneas is a 'traytour' (267) and a model of 'untrouthe' (384) – a very strong word indeed. On either reading Aeneas is renowned – as in *De Claris Mulieribus* or the Sunday papers, one does not have to be good to be famous; but Virgil, Chaucer suggests, is according him renown for virtues he never possessed.

The *House of Fame*, it seems, is about poetry, and the function of the poet. As such, the *Aeneid* serves as the supreme example of poetry: Virgil was the accepted master-poet, and the epic was his greatest work. By his interpretation of the Dido episode, however (an interpretation derived in part from another Classical source, Ovid's *Heroides*, which is in effect a story-collection told by the various heroine-protagonists) Chaucer calls into question the *sentence* of the epic. He will accept its subject-matter as true, but not the implied moral. It is always story rather than inner meaning that is adopted by successive writers – Chaucer takes the matter of *Troilus* from *Il Filostrato*, the *sentence* is all his own; but often in the process of borrowing the meaning will become all the more profound. Chaucer's interpretation of the story of Dido and Aeneas is not a development from Virgil's, it is at odds with it; and the implication is that any poet who will offer such a hero as a model of *pietas* is perverting the central truth that a story should be designed to express. Such a meaning remains at the level of implication, none the less. The temple of Venus and the house of Fame belong to different sections of both dream and poem; and the dreamer finally abandons both for the revolving multi-coloured wickerwork gazebo of Rumour, 'tydynges', where any attempt to reach the truth is overwhelmed by the noise of gossiping, chattering, 'jangles', whispering, lies, and travellers' – and pilgrims' – tales.

At this point, according to one very tempting – and quite possibly true, though unprovable – line of argument, Chaucer broke off the poem and wrote the *Canterbury Tales* instead. The gazebo is sixty miles long, approximately the distance from London to Canterbury.[78] If it is impossible for the poet to discover the truth, he can at least offer the multiplicity of different voices of the pilgrimage.

We have little certain knowledge of the dating of Chaucer's works, not least of how close the *House of Fame* may have been to his idea for the story-collection. They may have followed on from each other, and certainly the ending of the *House of Fame* makes good sense in those terms, even if it was only gradually that Chaucer evolved the idea of how he could put the notion of 'tydynges' to poetic use. There is some evidence, however, that the Knight's Tale and Second Nun's Tale were still individual works, not yet absorbed into any story-collection, in 1394, the year in which he is thought to have revised the prologue to the *Legend of Good Women*.[79] His reference there to his work on 'al the love of Palamon and Arcite / of Thebes' (G 407–8) and his life of St. Cecilia make no mention of any frame for the poems. He may have started work on both the *Legend* with its original prologue and on some of the *Canterbury Tales* in about 1386.[80] The *Legend* certainly reached its final (though still unfinished) form before the *Tales* had progressed very far.

The *Legend* is probably Chaucer's first story-collection, but it shows

---

[78] See J. A. W. Bennett, *Chaucer's Book of Fame* (Oxford, 1968) pp. 178–87, esp. p. 183.

[79] The dating rests on the assumption that the couplet on the Queen (F 496–7) was excised in the revision because of her death.

[80] See R. W. Frank, jr, *Chaucer and The Legend of Good Women* (Cambridge, Mass., 1972) p. 1.

none of the subtlety in the use of story that the *Book of the Duchess* or the *House of Fame* had done. Both in the title and in the outline of the form of the work set out in the Prologue, Chaucer relates the poem to the saints' legendary with its series of exemplary biographies – though here they will be secular, and the heroines will be martyrs to the God of Love. The theme is prescribed by Alceste, the perfect pattern of a faithful wife, who appears to the poet in the company of the God of Love and orders him to spend his time

> In makyng of a glorious legende
> Of goode wymmen, maydenes and wyves,
> That weren trewe in lovyng al hire lyves;
> And telle of false men that hem bytraien.   F483–6 (G 473–6)

The task is imposed on him as a penance for writing such supposedly anti-feminist works as *Troilus and Criseyde* and the translation of the *Romaunt of the Rose*. Several models existed for this kind of story-collection apart from saints' legendaries. The generic homogeneity of the tales relates it to single-genre collections with a prologue such as those of Marie de France; or, rather more closely, the introduction and series of biographies of women recalls Boccaccio's *De Claris Mulieribus*, which Chaucer may have drawn on in his first legend, of Cleopatra. The criterion for selection laid down by Alceste, that the women should be 'trewe in lovyng', should give a sharper definition to the stories than the mere fact of fame gives to Boccaccio's; but in practice Chaucer's women conform peculiarly badly to Alceste's condition. Cleopatra is made to fit by the simple device of omitting all her various love-life before Antony appeared on the scene; the nature of Philomel's gruesome revenge on Tereus is also left out. The falseness of the men is indeed often more notable than the goodness of the women: Hypsipyle and Medea are coupled together in Legend IV as two victims of the treachery of Jason. There seems indeed little distinction between being a martyr and a victim; as R. W. Frank commented, 'Rape, suicide, abandonment, despair, callous abuse, and cynical seduction are the matter of his legends.'[81] The Prologue had seemed to promise something much more positive.

The curious relationship of story to prescribed theme, and the sparseness of the narrative in most of the tales, have caused some bewilderment. The boredom felt by many readers has resulted in the widespread theory that Chaucer abandoned the work because he was bored with it too. There is no falling off in the course of the work itself, however, and Frank has suggested that Chaucer may have wished to concentrate instead on the 'more rewarding scheme' offered

---

[81] Ibid. p. 26.

by the *Canterbury Tales*.[82] What is clear, is that in the *Legend* Chaucer did not succeed in overcoming the problems inherent in the story-collection form: the problems of coherence, repetitiveness and order. If Chaucer is to do justice to the stories in themselves he cannot also abide by the specified theme. His attempts to vary bald narrative with intense pathos – a tone he can be particularly good at conveying, as in the Clerk's or Prioress's Tales – themselves become monotonous. There is no order whatsoever, not even Boccaccio's chronological arrangement: the legends could be re-arranged with little or no effect on the poem as a whole.

The Monk's Tale resembles the *Legend* in many ways. It consists of an introduction and a series of unlinked biographies, some of only a single stanza, related only by their common nature as tragedies, as defined by the Monk in his prologue:

> Tragedie is to seyn a certeyn storie,
> As olde bookes maken us memorie,
> Of hym that stood in greet prosperitee,
> And is yfallen out of heigh degree
> Into myserie, and endeth wrecchedly.   VII 1973–7

This definition imposes both a common moral and a common narrative structure on the stories, and they all follow it faithfully. Too faithfully, indeed. It provides a basic principle of coherence for all the tragedies, and Chaucer also gives them a chronological arrangement to provide some system of order (despite the editorial debate, probably reflecting his own uncertainty, about the placing of the series of 'modern instances'); but the moral is shatteringly over-simple, to a point that denies everything else the stories may contain. Boccaccio's great men fall because of some kind of providential retribution. Chaucer jumbles the wicked, the great and the innocent together with no apparent recognition of the distinction. Lucifer and Nero, Alexander and Julius Caesar, and Ugolino and his little children all illustrate an identical moral, the turning of Fortune's wheel to bring sorrow after joy. If this is the universal truth exemplified by the surface narrative, then it is a very partial truth indeed.

Chaucer can hardly have been unaware of this central inadequacy: indeed, he has the Knight call attention to it, to drive the point home to any listener who might have missed it – a rare instance of Chaucer's taking pains to avoid misinterpretation. The very fact that he chooses to change the moral theme of the *De Casibus* from just retribution to capricious fortune also underlines the deliberateness of the move. Why did he do it? The traditional answer has been that the Monk's Tale

---

[82] See 'The legend of Chaucer's boredom', ibid. pp. 189–210.

was an early work, brought out of storage when the *Canterbury Tales* were conceived, and that its weaknesses are due to Chaucer's comparative inexperience at the time he wrote it. There is no external evidence for this, however, as there is for the Knight's or Second Nun's Tale; and it would seem odd that a writer as self-aware as Chaucer was from the time he wrote the *Book of the Duchess* should ever have produced a work whose flaws were so obvious as to require recantation. It would seem more likely that he devised it specifically for the *Canterbury Tales*, where it can function in ways that justify its existence as the organisation of the piece in itself does not. Its thematic concerns, with the nature of Fortune and the connection (or lack of it) between suffering and desert, will be discussed later. What is of interest here is its nature as story-collection; for the Monk's Tale is, quite specifically, everything that the *Canterbury Tales* is not.

The stories of the Monk's Tale have a single narrator – the Monk himself, that is. They are generically identical, all being tragedies. They are written in a single verse form, and they show little or no variation of style or tone. There is no suggestion of linking the biographies: they follow in series without there being any attempt to lead one on from another, historically or morally. The stories are never allowed to generate their own meaning. The prescribed moral drives a heavy lorry over all human experience, squashing it as flat as a hedgehog.

Chaucer preferred his animals live. He liked them of every species, too: the generic variety of the *Canterbury Tales* is enormous. In analyses of this variety the Monk's Tale has usually been classed according to the Monk's own definition, as tragedy; but it is also a story-collection in miniature, and so, for all its comparative insignificance in the complete work, stands in a special relationship to the greater story-collection that frames it. One of its major functions is to help to define by contrast just what Chaucer is doing in the *Canterbury Tales* as a whole.

The differences are immediately obvious. The *Canterbury Tales* are told primarily for entertainment, the Monk's for edification, even if he speaks within the game of the story-telling. The tales have a series of narrators with very different voices. In genre they are just about as mixed as they could be. The commonest prosodic medium is riding rhyme, the free-flowing narrative ancestor of the heroic couplet, but prose and various stanzaic forms are used too. Explicit morals of any kind are few and far between; no single theme is laid down for the whole series, and attempts to deduce one have not met with much success. The framework of the story-telling extends throughout the series, linking the stories in a general narrative progression, and giving them a sense of depth that more purely functional frames never achieve.

Few of these characteristics are found in other story-collections; the Monk's Tale would be much more typical of the genre in general. Where the *Canterbury Tales* has any parallels at all, they are generally with Boccaccio: most particularly with the *Decameron*, though the *Ameto* and *Filocolo* work in some similar ways. The series of narrators is one example, though the similarity here can be over-stressed, for the matching of tale to teller is unique to Chaucer – only Dioneo offers any parallel in the *Decameron*, and even he does not have a fully individualised voice. The fact has also been stressed that in both works a master of ceremonies controls the story-telling – the Host in the *Tales*, the day's king or queen in the *Decameron*, and Fiammetta has a similar rôle in the *Filocolo*. Once the action gets under way, however, they function in very different ways. In the *Decameron* they prescribe the subject and order the day's household arrangements; Fiammetta gives judgment on the questions put to her. Only Harry Bailey acts as instant literary critic, and has the problem of keeping his rather unruly company under some sort of control. The authenticity of the frame story in both the *Tales* and the *Decameron* is a more striking similarity, however different Tuscan palace gardens may be from the Canterbury road: both authors create a setting in which the telling of stories is plausible, where the frame imitates non-fiction. In both works, too, the story-telling is set up as a *game*, with all that this implies; and, as Huizinga notes, it implies a very great deal.

> Play lies outside the antitheses of wisdom and folly, and equally outside those of truth and falsehood, good and evil. Although it is a non-material activity, it has no moral function. The valuations of vice and virtue do not apply here.[83]

This formulation goes a long way towards explaining the remarkable freedom from didacticism of both the *Decameron* and the *Canterbury Tales*; any morals are undercut by the circumstances of their presentation. Huizinga goes on to specify the conditions of play. It must be voluntary; the ten aristocrats and the thirty pilgrims explicitly agree to join in, Chaucer giving some emphasis to the Host's request and the company's acceptance of it.

> 'If ye vouche sauf that it be so,
> Tel me anon, withouten wordes mo,
> And I wol erly shape me therfore.'
> This thyng was graunted, and oure othes swore
> With ful glad herte, and preyden hym also
> That he wolde vouche sauf for to do so,

[83] Johan Huizinga, *Homo Ludens* (1949 / London, 1970) p. 25.

And that he wolde been our governour,
And of oure tales juge and reportour,
And sette a soper at a certeyn pris,
And we wol reuled been at his devys
In heigh and lough; and thus by oon assent
We been acorded to his juggement.   I 807–18

Play must also be disinterested – the promised supper at the Tabard
is not going to affect anybody spiritually and barely materially; and
it must be limited in time and space – the ten days of holiday in the
countryside, the journey along the road to Canterbury. Play, moreover,

> creates order, *is* order. Into an imperfect world and into the confusion of
> life it brings a temporary, a limited perfection . . . The profound affinity
> between play and order is perhaps the reason why play . . . seems to lie
> to such a large extent in the field of aesthetics. Play has a tendency to be
> beautiful.[84]

The perfection of the story-telling game in the *Decameron* stands out
all the more for the horror of the plague. Chaucer's concern with order
is clear in many of the *Canterbury Tales*, though he is quite ready to
allow the squabbling disorder of the framework to spill over into some
of the tales. The movement between the overt artistic control of the
stories and the apparent free-for-all of the pilgrimage is none the less
carefully and precisely contrived. As soon as the game resumes after
each interlude, he carries us into a different world – not only the
particular world of the story, but the world of play. This does not mean
that the stories are less serious than the pilgrimage: the game, by its
very potential for order and perfection, may indeed be much more
significant.

There remain two characteristics of the *Canterbury Tales* that have
no parallels anywhere, and this very uniqueness suggests that they
should be looked at particularly closely. One is the generic variety of
the stories. Other story-collections, such as legendaries or Aesopets or
the Monk's Tale, concentrate on a single genre; potentially more var-
ied collections, such as the *Gesta* or the *Decameron* or the *Confessio*,
tend to reduce all their stories to the level of 'tale'. Only the stories of
the *Canterbury Tales* keep their individual structure and content as
romance or fabliau or saint's life or tract, with different verse or prose
forms to contain them. The second unique characteristic is that the
story-telling is set up, not as a series of *exempla* on a given theme nor
even merely as entertainment, but as a competition.

The element of competition in the *Canterbury Tales* has tended to

---

[84] Ibid. p. 29.

be ignored, and with some reason. The Host introduces it as part of his scheme for each pilgrim to tell four tales:

> Ech of yow, to shorte with oure weye,
> In this viage shal telle tales tweye
> To Canterbury-ward, I mene it so,
> And homward he shal tellen othere two,
> Of aventures that whilom han bifalle.
> And which of yow that bereth hym best of alle,
> That is to seyn, that telleth in this caas
> Tales of best sentence and moost solaas,
> Shal have a soper at oure aller cost
> Heere in this place, sittynge by this post,
> Whan that we come agayn fro Caunterbury.　　　I 791–801

The scheme is of course never completed, whether simply because the work is not finished or because in addition Chaucer changed his mind and reduced the planned number of stories to one per pilgrim. By the time of the link between the Squire's and Franklin's tales the Host himself has revised his scheme to 'a tale or two' from each pilgrim (V 698). One cannot ascribe the idea for a contest to the Host alone and not Chaucer, however: it would be a very perverse move for Chaucer to mislead his audience deliberately at this point. It is here that the plan for the work is set out, and it is these lines that inform the listener or reader what to expect – not a series of moral tales on a fixed theme, nor even a single-genre collection, but whatever story the tellers may choose. The stipulation that the tales should both entertain and instruct, contain *sentence* and *solaas*, is a commonplace of literary theory that the individual stories tend to interpret distinctly freely; if most of them fulfil both requirements, the Miller's has little that is didactic, and the Parson's, quite deliberately, has nothing that could be described as fun.

That the Host's rules for the game set it up as a contest is more than an empty phrase. It is true that it is not often referred to later,[85] and that when one tale is described as 'quiting' another the implied competition between them is usually on non-aesthetic grounds. A good many personal battles of a kind not envisaged by Harry Bailey are fought out through the stories. It is also true that no judgment is ever given, but that does not make the competition meaningless. At one level the question as to who should win is unanswerable – as unanswerable as the question as to what the landscape looks like beyond

---

[85] The contest (as distinct from the pilgrims' obligation to tell stories) is mentioned by the Knight at I 891, a passage probably added to the start of his tale specifically to fit it into the *Canterbury Tales* framework; possibly at I 3119; and at II 34–6, in a passage that has been proposed as the original start of the story-telling. ~~_____~~ *No*

Sire Man of Lawe quod he so have ye blis
Telle us a tale anon go forward is
If been submytted though youre free assent
To stonden in this cas at my juggement.
Aquiteth you now of youre biheeste
Thanne have ye do youre devoir atte leeste

the edge of the picture-frame, or what the Madonna of the Rocks is going to have for lunch. At another level, given the terms of Chaucer's fiction, it is answerable all too easily: the Knight must win, because the Host's social obsequiousness and the pilgrims' personal animosities and jealousies would never allow any of them to accept any other outcome. The poetic qualities of the stories, and which might be 'of best sentence and moost solaas', do not come into consideration at all – though it is probably no coincidence that Chaucer gives the Knight a tale that could have a claim to the prize on those grounds. Such speculation is however irrelevant. What matters is that the one criterion called to the audience's attention is that of *quality*. It is the best tale that shall win, and Chaucer is deliberately asking his readers to look at the sheer literary merit of what he writes. Every story-collection that has a prologue lays down at that point what the audience is listening to: examples of tyranny (the *De Casibus*), or sins against love (the *Confessio*), or old stories to be kept in remembrance (the *Lais* of Marie de France or the *Legend of Good Women*, both coupled with further morals). Through the Host's injunction, Chaucer informs his readers that these are the best stories, and they are to judge them as such – and one advantage of leaving the work incomplete is that the audience must take on Harry Bailey's rôle and consider which is best.

'Of best sentence and moost solaas' could perhaps be translated as 'most profound and delightful'. It directs attention to their moral worth and entertainment value; but any evaluation of those, and of the best story in general, must rely on poetic quality. Chaucer is calling attention to the *Canterbury Tales* as a work of art, and inviting judgment on those grounds. It is, after all, he and not the individual pilgrims who is responsible for the whole collection, whatever disclaimers he (like Boccaccio) may concoct to pretend to pass the buck for the immorality of some of them.[86] His claim to be a mere faithful reporter is one of the most tongue-in-cheek passages of the whole work. His pose as Chaucer the Pilgrim, the naïve journalist and bad story-teller, is counterbalanced – far outweighed, indeed – by the extraordinary assurance with which he stakes his claim to poetic excellence.

He is to excel, too, in every genre. The mixture of kinds in the *Canterbury Tales* has often been noted. It is indeed impossible to miss, and would have struck contemporary readers all the more forcefully for its departure from the conventions of the story-collection. Moreover, it is less a miscellany than an encyclopaedia. There are romances, of five distinct kinds; there are fabliaux, again of several

---

[86] I 3171–5, 3185; cf. the Epilogue to the *Decameron*, especially his defence, 'I could only transcribe the stories as they were actually told' (trans. McWilliam p. 831), 'Io non poteva nè doveva scrivere se non le raccontate' (Conclusione dell'Autore). This is one of the most telling similarities between the works: see p. 35 above.

varieties; there are moral tales of the kind that lie on the border
between romance and saint's life; there is a saint's life proper, and a
miracle of the Virgin; there are beast-fables, a sermon, a moral prose
tract, a penitential tract, the Monk's story-collection of tragedies, and,
in the General Prologue, an estates satire.[87] It is quite difficult to
think of any literary kind available to him that Chaucer has omitted.

Such a departure from the norm requires an explanation; it cannot
be mere accident. There would seem to be several reasons, two of
which can be summarised briefly, and a third which requires a chapter
to itself – Chapter 3 below. The first reason has already been suggested: that Chaucer wishes to demonstrate his poetic mastery not
just of a single literary kind but of the whole lot. The *Canterbury
Tales* is to be a masterwork, not by doing a single thing well, but by
doing everything well. The homage paid to Chaucer by succeeding
generations as the father of English poetry would not have surprised
him. At the end of *Troilus and Criseyde* he had made a specific claim,
disguised as modest reticence, to be regarded as continuing the highest
Classical tradition of poetry:

> But litel book, no makyng thow n'envie,
> But subgit be to alle poesye;
> And kis the steppes, where as thow seest pace
> Virgile, Ovide, Omer, Lucan and Stace.   V 1789–92

The same claim was implicit in the very first stanza of the poem, with
its Classical complexity of syntax – a complexity easily overlooked
now, as we read *Troilus* with a familiarity with such syntax derived
from centuries of later poetry, but which at the time was unparalleled
in English verse. In the *Canterbury Tales* he makes an even greater
claim, something approaching the notion that he will write the best
example of every genre, and so set himself up as the authoritative
master.

The second reason for the generic variety is inseparable from that,
and solves the practical problem raised by the setting up of the story
competition. If this is to mean anything at all, the stories must be
compared for quality; and if their quality is to be distinguished, there
must be some perceptible difference between them. If Chaucer were to
follow the usual pattern of a single-genre collection, he might have to
write weak stories just to make the possible winners stand out – an
obvious nonsense. By making the stories generically different from
each other, Chaucer can make each one excellent of its kind.

It also means that the tales are not, when it comes to the point,
directly comparable poetically. One cannot judge between them solely

---

[87] See Jill Mann's *Chaucer and Medieval Estates Satire* (Cambridge, 1973).

on aesthetic grounds. Different genres arise from, and imply, very different ways of looking at the world or interpreting human experience. 'Sentence and solaas' itself becomes a very equivocal formula in view of the stories that follow, for some literary kinds give greater stress to the moral and didactic, others to the entertaining. It is the age-old distinction between work and play, Carnival and Lent, joy in this world or joy in the next;[88] the distinction explored in *The Owl and the Nightingale*, or *L'Allegro* and *Il Penseroso*, or Eeyore and Tigger. *The Owl and the Nightingale* is set up as a debate between the proponents of two points of view, and if the Nightingale wins by sleight of argument it is strongly suggested that the Owl has truth on her side. *Il Penseroso* can be seen not only as a companion piece but as an answer to *L'Allegro*. In both these examples, however, the common ground between the different viewpoints is given more emphasis than might appear at first glance. The birds are both concerned with the same issues, Milton's poems are generic and prosodic twins. In the *Canterbury Tales* the contrasts are perpetually underlined.

In judging the tales one is also being compelled to judge the attitudes they embody; and again Chaucer's lack of, or avoidance of, a final verdict becomes significant. Critics who have given the answer that Chaucer omits in the narrative framework have derived it from his last words in the *Tales*, the Parson's Tale and the Retractions. The pilgrimage is complete – or so this line of argument runs; the pilgrims have reached Canterbury, their spiritual goal, and Chaucer now abandons mirth for doctrine, *solaas* for *sentence*, Carnival for Lent. Tigger-oriented critics point out that at one stage at least Chaucer intended the work to end not with a penitential tract but with the supper at the Tabard: a festive climax, not a Puritan one. Given the close connection of game and festivity, it would be rash to affirm that Chaucer never had such an intention: there would be a congruence, a fittingness, in such an ending that suggests it may have been integral to his idea of the work in more than a merely narrative sense. The Parson's Prologue does indicate some kind of a conclusion, even though Chaucer does not in fact say that the pilgrimage has reached Canterbury; but the tale is also no more than another genre, another attitude to life to be set beside the others. If it is meant to be a definitive answer, it is a reply that does not answer the question. The contradictions of the rest of the work, contradictions deliberately created and sustained through the use of traditional generic contrasts, are just as incompatible after one has read the Parson and the Retractions as they were before.

The Parson's Tale comes too late to turn the whole work into a *De*

---

[88] For a stimulating and informative discussion of these issues see the early chapters of C. L. Barber's *Shakespeare's Festive Comedy* (Princeton, 1954/Cleveland, Ohio, 1963).

Casibus on a fixed theme; and the Monk's Tale itself had shown the impossibility of doing that. To use the analogy of the 'house of fiction' developed by Henry James in the Preface to *Portrait of a Lady*, the single-genre collection would have a single watcher from a single window of a fixed shape interpreting everything he saw by predetermined principles. The *Canterbury Tales*, however, is not reducible to a formula. There, Chaucer is the watcher at every window; and what he sees is not 'life' alone, for 'life' comes to him ready defined by the perspectives of different literary genres, which for him constitute the multifarious windows of the house. Life for Chaucer takes the form described by Northrop Frye as 'the seed-plot of literature, a vast mass of potential literary forms'.[89] He will explore those potential forms, look through those windows, to see all he can through them; but by his consciousness that each gives a different view, and by giving each of those views in turn, he insists on the fact that they are only perspectives, and that what can be glimpsed through any one of them can never be more than a partial truth. If 'all of human life is there' in the *Canterbury Tales*, so is all of literature, all artistic interpretation and formulation of human experience.

[89] Northrop Frye, *Anatomy of Criticism* (Princeton, 1957/1971) p. 122.

2

The Ordering of the Canterbury Tales

There is little or no logical order in many story-collections, and it matters singularly little. The many forms of the *Gesta Romanorum* might just have well been produced by writing three hundred-odd stories (with their moralities) on separate strips of paper, shaking them up in a bag and extracting two hundred at random. When an order is imposed, it is often an external one: an alphabetical arrangement, or a chronological one; the cycle of the church calendar, the Biblical order of the Ten Commandments or the traditional sequences of the Seven Deadly Sins.

In the *Decameron*, the topic set for one day will often pick up in some way from the topic of the day before, and one story will be cued by another; but the stories are not so closely bound to their set theme as not to be interchangeable, and the points of comparison between tales cited by the speakers as the reason for their telling a particular story are often superficial, or tangential to the main issues. In the *Confessio Amantis* too the relationship of a tale to its particular placing in the framework can be decidedly casual, and little alteration would be needed to make it serve at another point. It is clear, however, that both Boccaccio and Gower were concerned to give their works a deeper structure than the more perfunctory kinds of imposed ordering, and the same process can be seen in many other collections. The growth of the single-theme story-collection is an indication of a similar concern for coherence; the *Decameron* itself is a collection of related single-theme collections.

At first glance, the state of the sixty or so manuscripts of the *Canterbury Tales* might suggest that the work is little more than another *Gesta Romanorum* with a prologue and a kind of epilogue. The tales come in a variety of orders (though not as wide as is sometimes implied).[1] Not only does the sequence of the groups of tales change, but

---

[1] John M. Manly and Edith Rickert, *The Text of the Canterbury Tales* (8 vols, Chicago, 1940) Vol. II esp. pp. 479–89.

some stories that we are accustomed by printed editions to think of as having a fixed place in a fragment float around all over the work: the Squire's, Merchant's and Franklin's Tales are the main offenders. After their extensive study of all the manuscripts Manly and Rickert decreed that none of the surviving orders could be attributed to Chaucer: 'the evidence of the MSS seems to show clearly that Chaucer was not responsible for any of the extant arrangements'.[2] The matter is not, however, as clearly settled as their pronouncement would suggest.

One might assume from the wide manuscript variations that, as in so many story collections, the order does not matter, and that Chaucer did not give his tales a final definitive order because he was not aiming at anything of the kind. There is general manuscript agreement that the Knight's Tale, with the rest of the first fragment, comes first, and the Parson's Tale and the Retractions last. The middle could be mere rag-bag; but this is very clearly not the case. The odd thing about the *Canterbury Tales* – odd when seen in the context either of other story-collections or of the state of the manuscripts – is that the order should matter so much. There is plenty of evidence that Chaucer moved tales around and re-arranged them (a process unimaginable in the *Gesta*) just as he would sometimes re-assign a tale to a new teller. All the evidence within the work suggests that he did care about ordering; that when a story comes to rest within a group, it is there for a good reason, and that there is more than just a missing narrative link to separate the fragments.

Chaucer seems, then, to have been much more concerned about the structure of his work than were most authors of story-collections. The problem remains to discover just what the structure is.

There is some interesting evidence in the way some of the manuscripts are arranged as to how early editors or scribes sought for such principles.[3] The Ellesmere manuscript has an elaborate marginal apparatus calling attention to the *sententiae*, the maxims, and the *auctoritates*, references to established authors, given by Chaucer in the course of the work. It thus turns the *Tales* into something resembling a widespread medieval genre, the *compilatio*, an assemblage of such statements; and the manuscript ends with a colophon referring to Chaucer as having 'compiled' the work. The story-telling, on this basis, is a device for arranging such maxims. Other manuscripts, notably Corpus Christi 198, stress much more the nature of the work as a

[2] Ibid. p. 475.

[3] In this account of Ellesmere and Corpus Christi 198 I follow A. I. Doyle and M. B. Parkes, 'The production of the *Canterbury Tales* and the *Confessio Amantis* in the early fifteenth century' in *Medieval Scribes, Manuscripts and Libraries: Essays presented to N. R. Ker* ed. M. B. Parkes and Andrew G. Watson (London, 1978) pp. 163–210, esp. pp. 190–3.

sequence of stories, assigning chapter numbers and attempting to cover up any narrative discontinuity.

Such devices are essentially scriptorial – they depend on the existence of a written record. The *Canterbury Tales*, however, was meant to be not only read but heard. The principles by which it works must not depend on marginal notes or numbered chapters, and they must be sufficiently clear to be picked up by readers or audience.

Modern editors and scholars have generally been less concerned to discover the structure of the *Canterbury Tales* in this interpretative sense than to reconstruct the work – to rebuild the broken fragments into the edifice Chaucer intended. They have most commonly used two kinds of evidence: the evidence of the references in the links to the chronological and geographical progress of the pilgrimage; and the evidence of the various orders found in the manuscripts. A third kind of evidence, the argument from theme, has also occasionally been brought in. The results derived from all three kinds of testimony remain equivocal and inconclusive.

The first way of attempting to recover Chaucer's structural intentions, by reconstructing the itinerary of the pilgrimage, is, I think, not only inconclusive but misguided. It is inconclusive because there are fragments which contain no references to time or place, and because the other references are so imprecise that they do not even answer the question as to whether Chaucer intended all the tales we have to be told on the outward journey or whether some should belong to the return.[4] The most famous, and drastic, emendation to the text of the *Canterbury Tales* was made on the principal of geographical consistency: the 'Bradshaw Shift' involved lifting the longest fragment of the *Tales*, VII (B²), from the late place it universally occupies in the manuscripts and putting it near the beginning, after the Man of Law's Tale, largely in order to bring its mention of Rochester back to a place before the Summoner's threat to tell

> tales two or thre
> Of freres, er I come to Sidyngborne.[5]

---

[4] The most forceful recent proponent of the two-way story-telling is Charles A. Owen, jr, *Pilgrimage and Storytelling in the Canterbury Tales* (Norman, Oklahoma, 1977) esp. ch. III.

[5] VII 1926, III 847. I leave out of account here the vexed question as to who should be named as the next speaker in the endlink of the Man of Law's Tale. The editors or scribes of the early manuscripts may have adjusted tale order to fit the name, or perhaps adjusted the name to fit the order. Scholars and editors have frequently adopted the best *ad hoc* solution, justifying their reading by arguing backwards from whatever purposes their preferred reading would serve. The scholarly bibliography on the subject is vast; E. T. Donaldson gives a useful critical summary in 'The ordering of the Canterbury Tales' in *Medieval Literature and Folklore Studies: Essays in Honor of Francis Lee Utley* ed. Jerome Mandel and Bruce A. Rosenberg (New Jersey, 1970) pp. 193–204.

That Sittingbourne could still be a long way away, so far that the
pilgrims need not have passed Rochester at the time he makes the
threat, makes nonsense of this kind of literal interpretation even on
its own terms.

A more serious criticism of the method of reconstructing the *Tales*
from the itinerary is the demonstrable fact that Chaucer himself does
not seem to have used the framework as an ordering device. Boccaccio
divides his story-telling clearly and distinctively into separate days;
Sercambi not only specifies the days but gives a detailed journey plan
too. Chaucer does neither. The remarkable thing about the links,
given the idea about the pilgrimage from Southwark to Canterbury,
is how very few such references there are. When Lydgate came to
write a further Canterbury Tale of his own, the *Siege of Thebes*, he
gave it a prologue that is a Chaucerian pastiche, and which abundantly demonstrates how closely familiar he was with Chaucer's text.
He tells the reader all about how he met up with the pilgrims at their
inn in Canterbury, what the Host suggested he should have for supper,
how they went to bed, got up at sunrise and set off intending to stop
at Ospring for dinner.[6] That is how one would expect the *Canterbury
Tales* to be written; but in point of fact there is nothing remotely like
it in Chaucer. After the pilgrims leave the Tabard, we never know
where they spend the night or what they do when they are travelling;
they never even pass through a town. The Pardoner has a drink at a
tavern, but that is the only hint of a physical setting for the story-
telling. The only two references to the date are irreconcilably contradictory.[7] As a narrative account of a journey, the *Canterbury Tales* is
a non-starter.

The evidence of the manuscript orders might appear equally baffling. The disorder is not, however, as extreme as it might look. There
can be little doubt that Chaucer did finally place the tales that float
around many of the manuscripts, the Merchant's after the Clerk's and
the Franklin's after the Squire's. The links between them sound too
quintessentially Chaucerian, and their appropriateness to those tales
and no others is too marked, for any other placing to be likely; and
the metre, rhyme and sense are all strained when the links are

---

[6] *Lydgate's Siege of Thebes* ed. Axel Erdmann, Part I (EETS E.S. 108, 1911) Prologus.
[7] The astronomical calculations in the Man of Law's Prologue give a date of 18 April,
those of the Parson's Prologue 'April 17 or earlier' (Sigmund Eisner, 'Chaucer's use of
Nicholas of Lynn's calendar', *Essays and Studies* XXIX (1976) 1–22, esp. p. 21). Eisner
suggests that Chaucer's reference to date serve a symbolic rather than a structural
purpose – though he also points out that in 1394 April 17 was the date of Good Friday,
a particularly appropriate day for the Parson's Tale.

adapted for other pilgrims.[8] Moreover, the separate fragments of firmly linked tales do tend to come in orders that show a surprising amount of consistency. Larry Benson has indeed recently argued that all the manuscripts are in fact derived from only two orders, and that both these can be ascribed to Chaucer.[9] He believes that the '*a*' arrangement represented by the Ellesmere manuscript preserves Chaucer's final plan for the work – the sequence familiar now from the Robinson text:

I	(A)	General Prologue, Knight, Miller, Reeve, Cook
II	(B^1)	Man of Law
III	(D)	Wife, Friar, Summoner
IV	(E)	Clerk, Merchant
V	(F)	Squire, Franklin
VI	(C)	Physician, Pardoner
VII	(B^2)	Shipman, Prioress, Chaucer's two tales, Monk, Nun's Priest
VIII	(G)	Second Nun, Canon's Yeoman
IX	(H)	Manciple
X	(I)	Parson

The other arrangement, which he suggests represents an earlier plan for the work, varies only slightly, in that fragment VIII (G), of the Second Nun's and Canon's Yeoman's Tales, is placed earlier, between fragments V and VI (F and C; that is, between the Franklin's and the Physician's Tales). He suggests in addition that this original scheme may not have contained the Manciple's and Parson's Tales.

It is an attractive theory; and its emphasis on the comparative consistency of the manuscript ordering seems unlikely to be challenged to any great extent. Most manuscripts do show remarkably little variation in their arrangement of most of the groups, except for fragment VIII (G), which has two alternative locations. Benson points out that the Retractions indicate that Chaucer had finished with the work, incomplete as it is, and since he was no longer working towards new arrangements his final draft would surely have left the fragments in some kind of order. That the '*a*' arrangement may indeed go back

---

[8] E.g. compare the Squire-Franklin link in Ellesmere,

> That knowe I wel sire/quod the Frankeleyn

with Hengwrt's use of the same link for the Squire and Merchant with its crude rhyme

> That knowe I wel sire/quod the Marchant certeyn,

or the other examples of awkwardness cited by Larry Benson, 'The order of the Canterbury Tales', *Studies in the Age of Chaucer* III (1981) 77–120.

[9] See the article cited in note 8 above.

to Chaucer, and not to early editors' attempts to arrange a series of disordered fragments as best they could, is made more likely by the fact that MS Gg.IV.27 apparently provides confirmation of this order independently of the Ellesmere exemplars.[10] It must be added, however, that other scholars have come to very different conclusions as to the state in which Chaucer left the *Tales*, and the most authoritative recent study of what is probably the earliest manuscript, Hengwrt, describes it as reflecting the 'lack of an established order in the whole collection'.[11]

Whether the Ellesmere order is indeed Chaucer's own is a question that can probably never finally be solved. It certainly works well; Benson comments, 'It is difficult to believe that anyone other than Chaucer could have made so satisfactory an arrangement.'[12] Whoever was responsible for the order, however, whether Chaucer or a brilliant early editor, the fact remains that it is still a provisional one, reflecting the incomplete state of the *Tales*. The stories within the separate fragments are firmly bound together, in terms of dramatic narrative and internal congruence; the breaks between the fragments are marked not only by a lack of narrative connection but by greater thematic discontinuity. There are two exceptions to this, however. There is some reason to believe that fragments IV and V (of Clerk, Merchant, Squire and Franklin) are more likely than the other fragments to have been linked by Chaucer; and near certainty that IX and X (Manciple and Parson) were so linked. The evidence for the first lies in the fact that the Merchant's endlink and the Squire's headlink always occur together regardless of which tales they connect.[13] The Manciple's Tale is given a different grouping from the Parson's only because modern editors were worried by the chronological inconsis-

---

[10] *The Poetical Works of Geoffrey Chaucer: A Facsimile of Cambridge University Library MS Gg.4.27* with introductions by M. B. Parkes and Richard Beadle (3 vols, Cambridge 1979–80) III 43.

[11] A. I. Doyle and Malcolm B. Parkes, 'A paleographical introduction' in *The Canterbury Tales: A Facsimile and Transcription of the Hengwrt Manuscript* ed. Paul G. Ruggiers (Norman, Oklahoma, 1979) p. xix. A rival account of the Hengwrt manuscript is given by N. F. Blake, who argues that it represents most accurately the state of the poem as Chaucer left it. He believes that passages missing from this – including the Merchant's Prologue and the entire Canon's Yeoman's Tale – are spurious additions. He would see twelve unrelated fragments in the *Tales*. See his *The Canterbury Tales by Geoffrey Chaucer edited from the Hengwrt Manuscript* (London, 1980) Introduction, and 'On editing the Canterbury Tales' in *Medieval Studies for J. A. W. Bennett* ed. P. L. Heyworth (Oxford, 1981) pp. 101–20. Few supporters have been found for the extremes of this argument, however; and it is striking how far even Hengwrt supports the consistency of manuscript ordering, allowing for the fact that the scribe apparently received his copy in bits and pieces. Benson sees Hengwrt as deriving from the earlier of his two orders (p. 108).

[12] Benson p. 111.

[13] Manly and Rickert II 489, 284, 476.

circulority of argument –

No

tency of the links that made the first tale apparently last six hours; there is no manuscript authority for this division, and Chaucer's casual attitude towards such references and the unrevised state of the final text make this an inadequate reason for separating them.[14]

Whether or not Chaucer arranged the fragments in the Ellesmere order or any other, we can be sure that he arranged the tales within separate fragments. This raises a question about structure which goes much deeper than the superficial matter of which tale should follow what: the question of why he put certain tales together, of what makes some stories hold together in groups. Again, if the sequence did not matter, there would be no reason for some tales being fixed in sequence but the fragments remaining discontinuous: Chaucer clearly had in mind a principle of ordering that went beyond merely following one tale with another. This brings back into the picture the third kind of evidence for ordering the tales, the argument from theme. This is an essential critical tool for studying the tales within the separate groups; if it is applied more widely, to arranging the fragments in some particular order, the argument can risk becoming circular. E. T. Donaldson pinpointed the problem in an excellent article on the difficulties of ordering the *Canterbury Tales*:

> There is, of course, a wealth of literary criticism justifying one order or another, but most of this seems to me to consist of *ex post facto* demonstrations of the literary effects – 'resonances' – that occur after a given order has been adopted ... Unfortunately, resonances tend to work equally well in either direction.[15]

There are indications that Chaucer may have found the same trouble. It seems to be precision of resonance that finally locks a story into place in its group; but each fragment constitutes a unit to itself. It is certainly possible to argue for resonances connecting the fragments, but they are rarely so clear as those connecting the firmly linked tales. It must also be said, however, that the Ellesmere order does provide a good progression from fragment to fragment, and however untrustworthy the argument from resonance may be, its arrangement can certainly be justified in those terms.

[14] In addition, the word 'Manciple' in line 1 of the Parson's Prologue is written over an erasure in Hengwrt, and one late and chaotic MS has the Parson follow the Canon's Yeoman; but these inconsistencies are trivial compared with many firmly accepted readings. A more serious discrepancy, though one less often mentioned, between the Manciple's and the Parson's prologues is that Chaucer seems to envisage a number of tales still remaining to be told in the former, whereas in the latter the Host says that only one remains. Given the strong evidence for connecting the two tales, this seems more likely to be an unrevised inconsistency than an indication that they do not belong together.

[15] Donaldson, 'Ordering' in Mandel and Rosenberg; the quotation is from the notes, p. 366 n. 33.

Z

—

The underlying principle of Chaucer's poetry, as of Gothic art, was juxtaposition: like the introductory sections and the dreams in his dream poems, the separate stories of the *Canterbury Tales* bear a significant relation to the story next to them. Chaucer follows no single definition of what this relationship is, however: each story defines its own possibilities. It is therefore particularly interesting to look at the traces remaining in the *Tales* of how certain arrangements came into being, especially as some of the ideas for ordering that apparently came to him latest were also some of the best.

Two examples will illustrate this: the Knight's Tale and the Merchant's. The manuscript evidence alone would suggest that the Knight's Tale had always followed the General Prologue and headed the story-telling, but there are distinct indications that this is not so. The Knight's Tale may still have been a separate work in 1394, many years after the date generally proposed for when Chaucer began work on the *Tales*.[16] The story-telling seems once to have begun with the introduction to the Man of Law's Prologue and Tale, when the Host notes the date and time of the day. It is ten o'clock on the eighteenth of April, as calculated by the angle of the sun with reference to the length of shadows and the latitude. No similarly precise indication of the time occurs again until before the very last tale, the Parson's, begun at four in the afternoon, as calculated by the length of Chaucer's own shadow. The two passages look as if they could be intended as a complementary pair, opening and closing the story-telling. In the first passage the Host urges the pilgrims to waste no more time. The injunction is hardly necessary if this tale is to follow on from the first fragment; and although it could alternatively be taken as starting the second day's entertainment, the speech seems to imply that the story-telling has not yet begun.

> 'Lordynges,' quod he, 'I warne yow, al this route,
> The fourthe party of this day is gon.
> Now, for the love of God and of Seint John,
> Leseth no tyme, as ferforth ye may . . .
> Let us not mowlen thus in ydelnesse.
> Sire Man of Lawe,' quod he, 'so have ye blis,
> Telle us a tale anon, as forward is.'   II 16–9; 32–4

---

[16] The evidence rests on a line in the *Legend of Good Women* (F420) referring to 'al the love of Palamon and Arcite' as if it were an independent poem. The reference does not prove its independence, however, although it is often taken to do so. It is not impossible that Chaucer wrote the Knight's Tale for the Canterbury scheme but allowed its separate publication in some form, if only by reading it at court. No individual manuscripts survive of the Knight's Tale or any of the other sections of the *Tales* that may have been written independently at an early date; but this again is not final proof that none ever existed.

This mention occurs before the CT was begun; it is retained in a revision, the earliest date for which is 1394.

Certainly the speech would fit perfectly well at the head of all the tales. The Man of Law's words that follow confirm this impression: he discusses Chaucer's skill at poetry, lists his poems, and compares his work with other leading story-collections, the *Confessio* and the *Metamorphoses*. All this looks again very like introductory material. He then promises something in prose, which was probably once the *Tale of Melibee*,[17] to contrast with Chaucer's own 'rymes' (96) – a point of contrast that suggests that the eventual attribution of *Melibee* to Chaucer himself was not entirely serious.

Chaucer criticism has tended to take the form of constructing hypothesis upon hypothesis. One could speculate intriguingly on what a *Canterbury Tales* opening with *Melibee* might have been like. Whatever the possible results, Chaucer did not follow them up; the poem on 'al the love of Palamon and Arcite' that he mentions in the *Legend of Good Women* was brought in to become the *Knight's Tale*. If it was originally an independent work, as this mention of it suggests, it is possible that Chaucer added only a couple of short interpolations to fit it into the Canterbury scheme. The only overt reference to its place in the story-telling is confined to four lines near the beginning, after Chaucer has summarised the substantial sections of the *Teseida* he is not going to narrate in full. The reason for this abbreviation, which thematically is already entirely justified, can now be fathered on the story competition:

> I wol nat letten eek noon of this route;
> Lat every felawe telle his tale aboute,
> And lat se now who shal the soper wynne;
> And ther I lefte, I wol ayeyn bigynne.   I 889–92

There is also a final couplet in which the Knight exclaims, 'God save al this faire compaignye!' There could have been a general revision of the whole poem at this stage; but there is little hard evidence for it. There are plenty of references to *telling* the story, such as would fit recitation on the pilgrimage; but these are also found in works such as *Troilus* (though not so densely), and could have little implication beyond the practice of reading aloud. There are also several references to 'endyting' the tale,[18] a word associated more with written than oral composition; and once there is a mention, though a negative one, of 'writing':

---

[17] The most likely alternative would be the translation (now lost) of Pope Innocent III's *De Contemptu Mundi* which Chaucer speaks of having made in the *Legend* G 414–15. Most of the Man of Law's Prologue is taken from this work; but the relevant passage is also quoted in both the Latin and French versions of *Melibee* (see Manly and Rickert III 448), so it could easily have introduced either translation – and would indeed have fitted either better than it fits the present tale of Custance.

[18] I 1209, 1380, 2741.

Of that storie list me nat to write.   1201

There is no reason why the 'me' should refer to the Knight rather than Chaucer. The voice, as in all the tales, is suited to the particular genre, and it is that which serves to define the rhetorical level. A high courtly romance with epic pretensions, as this is, demands high style; this is how Chaucer will write this tale, and as such it is appropriate for the Knight. The man of highest social rank is given the most courtly tale and the highest level of rhetoric. Any further attempts to deduce the character of the Knight from his telling of the tale are likely to produce something more like an analysis of the story, or a characterisation of Chaucer's art. It is Chaucer, for instance, who manipulates the style so that it does not always preserve the height demanded by the decorum of genre and speaker, and so opens up possibilities beyond the Knight's immediate purposes of telling a story.

However much or little Chaucer needed to revise the Knight's Tale, it makes an ideal beginning to the story-telling. Its widespread stylistic formality marks it off immediately from the humdrum, inconsequential tone so brilliantly established in the General Prologue, and sets a poetic standard of a kind that may not be rhetorically appropriate for all the other tales but which in their own particular ways they will need to attempt to match. It also introduces many of the major themes of the *Canterbury Tales* as a whole. Human love, the nature of ideals, the metaphysical context for human action, are all explored – and explored as problems, not to give a ready-made *moralitas* of the ordinary story-collection kind. Many of the recurrent *topoi* and plot motifs are introduced: female beauty, the love-garden, the rivalry of two men for the same woman. The pilgrimage, for the first time, is glimpsed as having an allegorical as well as a literal meaning:

> This world nys but a thurghfare ful of wo,
> And we been pilgrymes, passynge to and fro.   2847–8

The tale of Palamon and Arcite has the potential for setting the *Canterbury Tales* on a much more exciting course than any other single tale, not least the *Melibee*, could suggest.

The Merchant's Tale is another example of a tale that apparently found its place only late in Chaucer's development of his scheme, though the evidence is more ambiguous. The tale of January and May seems to have been originally composed with a different teller in mind: the references to 'folk in secular estaat' (IV 1322) and, more particularly, 'thise fooles that been seculeer' (1251) suggest an ecclesiastical narrator. The tale appears in many manuscripts without its own headlink, or with one adapted from somewhere else, and often follows the Squire's Tale. A single explanation that would account for all these features could be that Chaucer decided to link the Merchant's Tale to the Clerk's late in the development of the *Tales*.[19] The juxtaposition of tales that now seems so necessarily right and obvious may have resulted from Chaucer's moving around the pieces of his jigsaw until they fell into place. Further evidence for this lies in the wide textual variations in different manuscripts for the ending of the Clerk's Tale. A number omit the final stanza and the Envoy, which make the tale explicitly refer back to the Wife of Bath. Other manuscripts arrange the stanzas of the Envoy in a different order, so that the last line,

And lat him care, and wepe, wringe, and waille!

which is picked up in the first line of the Merchant's Prologue, there comes in the middle.[20] These features again suggest that Chaucer decided at a late stage to emphasise the marriage theme in these tales; so he added the Clerk's reference to the Wife of Bath, brought in the tale of January and May to provide a strongly contrasting example of marital experience, and gave it to a narrator who could be redefined as an unhappily married man. The Merchant of the Prologue and Tale is not totally incompatible with the Merchant of the General Prologue, but there is certainly no necessary continuity between them.

If this sort of rearrangement of tales is an accurate reflection of the way the work was put together – and the manuscripts indicate something of the kind – then it suggests a very close concern indeed on Chaucer's part with getting the order *right*. There will be nothing haphazard in the arrangement: tales will be assigned or juxtaposed for a good reason, but if the good reason is superseded by a better one they can still be moved around.

Digging into the archaeology of the *Canterbury Tales* is a very uncertain business. There is no clear succession of strata identifiable by any literary version of carbon dating or dendrochronology. The following two paragraphs are therefore the most hypothetical in this entire book, and readers are accordingly given due warning. I include them because even if they do not give an accurate reconstruction of what actually happened in the course of the making of the *Canterbury Tales*, they do, I think, offer a possible, and plausible, model of the way Chaucer worked.

[19] This would still be before Chaucer reached the stage of the earlier of the fixed orders suggested by Benson, if that theory is accepted, when the arrangement was still flexible. Different explanations to account for the state of the manuscripts are given by Benson himself and by Blake, Blake's being that the Merchant's headlink is not late Chaucerian but post-Chaucerian. The suggestion of late composition and organisation is however not incompatible with the views of Benson, or of Doyle and Parkes in their introduction to Ruggiers' facsimile of Hengwrt.

[20] See Manly and Rickert II 243–4, 265.

If the tale of January and May was only assigned to the Merchant and given its place after the Clerk's at a late stage, what did Chaucer intend to do with it before? The narrator was apparently an ecclesiastic; and critical opinion has generally favoured the Friar as the original teller.[21] J. M. Manly, however, once suggested the Monk, on the intriguing grounds that the Monk might have been 'retaliating for the satire on monks in the Wife of Bath's Tale (now the Shipman's)'.[22] The Shipman's Tale, it will be remembered, is the tale about the wife who has an affair with a monk in return for payment, the money for which the monk borrows off her husband. Early in the tale there is a passage referring to wives as 'we', 'us', making an original attribution to the Wife of Bath as certain as such things can be. The Monk has generally been rejected as the teller of the story of January and May because the tale does not fit his character; but it only fails to fit his character as it is derived not only from the original portrait in the General Prologue but from the tragedies he tells as the Monk's Tale. There is nothing in the General Prologue picture of the worldly hunting Monk, with the possible word-play on 'venerie', that would prevent his telling the mixture of preaching and pornography that constitutes the story of January and May. Even the stylistic level, of fabliau content aspiring to the high style rhetoric of courtly romance, would fit his social pretensions.

The contrasting of Knight and Monk in the General Prologue reinforces this attribution. In the version of the *Canterbury Tales* that we have, the Knight, who has told of the reverses of Fortune counterpointed with its benefactions, puts a stop to the Monk's tragedies with their endless falls from Fortune's wheel. After the Knight's own tale, however, it is the Monk whom the Host invites to follow on:

> Now telleth ye, sir Monk, if that ye konne
> Somwhat to quite with the Knyghtes tale.   I 3118–19

In fact, of course, the Miller interrupts, and it is he who 'wol now quite the Knight's tale'. 'Quite' implies rebuttal rather than a mere following on; and the tale of January and May would have been even more devastating a parody of the Knight's Tale than the Miller's is. It may indeed have been the extent of the threat it posed that led Chaucer to substitute a less destructive parody. Emily, on her first appearance, is mentioned alternately with May, in a way that defines her by the qualities of the month. She appears 'in a morwe of May',

The Knight's Tale as late in its place.

---

[21] See A. C. Baugh, 'The original teller of the Merchant's Tale', *Modern Philology* XXXV (1937) 15–26.

[22] In his edition of *The Canterbury Tales* (New York, 1928) p. 624.

And fressher than the *May* with flowres newe . . .   I 1037

She was arisen and al redy dight;
For *May* wole have no slogardie a-nyght . . .   1041–2

This maked *Emelye* have remembraunce
To doon honour to *May*, and for to ryse.   1046–7

After all that, it is impossible to separate the two. The heroine of the other tale is actually named May, usually 'fresshe May', though the epithet becomes increasingly sarcastic as its bearer becomes more unsavoury. May is also sought by two men, and sought solely for their sexual interest in her: there is nothing resembling Palamon's belief that he has seen a goddess, a spiritual being. January wants to marry in order to give himself a lawful outlet for his lechery. The walled garden in which the knights first glimpse Emily from their prison symbolises her inaccessibility; the walled garden that January builds as a place in which to 'paye his wyf hir dette' (IV 2048) is all too accessible, and Chaucer notes in passing that it is Priapus who is god of gardens (2035). In both tales, the gods are introduced to cut the gordian knot of the plot, and they are precisely selected to match the protagonists: they are gods of love, war and virginity, and of winter and spring. In the Knight's Tale they may be cruel and capricious, but they are unquestionably powerful; in the Merchant's Tale, the gods are those of the underworld, Pluto and Proserpina, not of the heavens, and they are further reduced to bickering fairies engaged in their own marital squabble. Courtly ideals are shown to be mere delusions, and high style is no more than a veneer for ugly action. If Chaucer did once think of following Palamon and Arcite with January and May, he was wise to think again. There would have been very little of the Knight's Tale left after that, whereas the story of Alisoun and Nicholas sends up the Knight's Tale in a way which enhances them both.

It is time to return to the *Tales* as we have them, not to the work that Chaucer decided against writing. The tale of January and May is now told by the Merchant to follow his cynical prologue; the Wife of Bath now has the story of the old hag whose youth and beauty are restored, and not the tale of the adulterous wife and the monk. In the Wife's case a story that fitted her has been replaced by one that fits her even better; the tale of January and May was apparently taken from one suitable narrator and given to a more suitable one. The finer kind of psychological appropriateness of the kind we associate with the Wife of Bath seems to have been introduced only late in Chaucer's scheme. It is there in the Wife's and the Pardoner's lengthy Prologues, and in the Merchant's short one, but the assignment of the Wife of Bath's Tale to the Wife, or the Merchant's Prologue to the story of January and May, were apparently both second thoughts.

What we have in the *Canterbury Tales*, then, is a series of grouped stories. The groups are of uncertain order, the degree of uncertainty varying according to individual scholarly interpretation, but in any case reflecting the incomplete state of the work. There are in addition perceptible relics of some earlier arrangements beneath the existing fragments. Both the uncertainty and the alterations probably reflect Chaucer's method of composition. He clearly cared deeply about the relationship of one tale to another, or of tale to teller. The various stories are linked by his concern to bring out a number of interrelated themes in them, to set up a pattern of multiple perspectives. The result is a kind of cobweb effect, of lines of contact going off in a number of directions from any given point. But the hard fact that the stories have to be read sequentially, one after the other, just as they are told sequentially on the journey, means that they cannot be read as a cobweb: Chaucer has to start at some point on the thread and follow it in a certain direction. The possibilities of different orderings are clearly numerous. He arranged them; he re-arranged them; that he may never have fixed on a final order for them is perhaps not the result of disability, religious conversion or death – the explanations most often given – but an inevitable corollary of the way he wrote the *Tales*. It opens up too many possibilities. The problems in reaching a final arrangement are inherent in his conception of what a story-collection can do.

The debate over how to order the *Tales* may then be an artificial one. Chaucer himself, for all his care with the ordering of the stories we have, did not insist that they should be read in sequence:

> Whoso list it nat yheere,
> Turne over the leef and chese another tale.   I 3176–7

This might seem paradoxical, given his interest in juxtaposing tales appropriately (not least at this point, between the Knight's and Miller's; and whether or not the lines are a paradox, they are certainly a joke, as he knows no one will take up the suggestion). The lines still indicate that a sequential reading is not essential; but this need not jar with the cobweb analogy. Just as Mannyng points out that one can open *Handlyng Synne* anywhere, 'for every-whare ys bygynnyng of synne', so perhaps with the *Canterbury Tales*:

> Whedyr þou wylt opon þe boke,
> þou shalt fynde begynnyng oueral to loke.[23]

---

[23] *Handlyng Synne* 120, 121–2.

The relationship between the tales within each fragment may be most strongly developed, but the cobweb extends over the whole work, and the thread can be picked up and followed from any point.

Each tale, very obviously, has its own unique qualities and tone and creates its own world. It may seem that a stress on the interrelationship between the tales would deny this; in fact it works in the opposite way – as a glance at the first two tales will show. The Miller's Tale would be superb anywhere; in context, it is even better, and its distinctiveness is highlighted all the more sharply by the preceding stately and philosophical romance. A reading that stresses comparisons and contrasts between the tales heightens their individuality.

Such a reading may sound too complex, and appear too obscure, for Chaucer to have intended and for his audience to have followed. There are, however, certain kinds of mediaeval literature that show how well accustomed contemporary listeners and readers would have been to picking up meaning from juxtaposition and interrelationship. Chaucer's dream poems work in just this way, and he clearly felt no need to spell out the meaning. He lets them speak for themselves, just as Elizabethan dramatists allow their plots and sub-plots to define each other without discursive explanation. The *Book of the Duchess*, the *House of Fame* and the *Parliament of Fowls* all work in this way. The story of Ceyx and Alcyone, the summary of the *Aeneid* and the dream of Scipio function like sub-plots split off from the main action and treated as prologues; the main plots come later, with the appearance of the man in black, the palace of Fame, and the temple of Venus and the hill of Nature. The two parts of each poem present sequentially ideas that interrelate and contrast.

There is also one mediaeval genre that operates on a structural pattern closer to the interweaving of plot and sub-plot. This is the interlaced romance, where the simultaneous adventures of various heroes are followed by pursuing each for a section of narrative and returning to him later. There is more to it than this, however, as Rosemond Tuve points out in her excellent study of the form:

> One must distinguish entrelacement from the mere practice, ubiquitous in narrative, of taking one character through a series of actions, then deserting him temporarily – often with the object of introducing suspense – while another character is given primary attention, then returning to the first and so on ... But events connected by entrelacement are not juxtaposed; they are interlaced, and when we get back to our first character he is not where we left him as we finished his episode but in the psychological state or condition of meaningfulness to which he has been pulled by the events occurring in following episodes written about someone else ... We digress, or seem to, and then come back, not to precisely

what we left but to something we understand differently because of what we have since seen.[24]

The *Canterbury Tales* do not return to pick up the adventures of a character mentioned earlier; but they work in a rather similar way at the level of theme rather than narrative. An idea will be developed, dropped for a while, and picked up again, and when Chaucer returns to it our perception of it will be modified by what has intervened. The *Tales* work not merely sequentially, but cumulatively, like the interlaced romance. Like the *good* interlaced romance, that is: there are many romances that pursue different stories without also giving this subtle interrelationship between them, just as there are many story-collections that fail to add up to anything over all; and Chaucer does indeed write one such romance himself, in the Squire's Tale – a tale that, like the Monk's story-collection, is interrupted.

The *Canterbury Tales* provides more in the way of cues to aid audience understanding than do the dream poems or most romances. Particular points of comparison are often mentioned in the links, not least in the first fragment, so that a pattern of relationships is set up from the very beginning of the work. There are also occasional cross-references within tales, as when the Wife of Bath is mentioned in the course of the Merchant's Tale and in the Clerk's Envoy. These are mere hints, but they would be enough to set an audience in the right direction, especially an audience of the literary sophistication that Chaucer's listeners must have possessed. Moreover, their familiarity with the conventions of other story-collections, and Chaucer's striking departures from them, would also help to alert them to new levels of meaning. There are no separable *moralitates* here, no pattern of single plot outlines or genres: all the customary devices for cohesion are abandoned. Mediaeval readers would be used to such devices; and they would expect to find them not only in the framework but in the stories too, for that is where other story-collections locate their principles of coherence. They would look for such principles in the tales themselves; and by leaving out the more obvious kinds of consistency, Chaucer takes them beyond the superficial incoherence to where dream poems and interlaced romances and similar works had accustomed them to find meaning, in thematic patterns explored and developed through superficially discontinuous narrative.

Good point.

---

[24] Rosemond Tuve, *Allegorical Imagery: Some Mediaeval Books and their Posterity* (Princeton, 1966) pp. 362–3. Eugène Vinaver points out the feats of memory demanded by interlaced romance (*The Rise of Romance* (Oxford, 1971) p. 83).

3

An Encyclopaedia of Kinds

Chaucer's handling of his greatest story-collection gives it strong similarities to another kind of mediaeval writing: the *summa*. The word
implies less a genre than an attitude to life or learning. The *summa*
is, in effect, an encyclopaedia, a bringing together of all knowledge;
but the notion of *togetherness* is important. One uses a modern encyclopaedia to look up a single item, and some of the works of the great
mediaeval encyclopaedists, Vincent of Beauvais or Thomas Aquinas,
could be similarly used; but that was not their point. A *summa* was
intended to show the wholeness, the unity, of all creation and all
abstract or intellectual thought in all their diversity. The same ideal
was pursued by many scholars and, in a different way, by many poets.
Alan of Lille in Latin and Jean de Meung in French, both writers
whose works were known to Chaucer, were attempting something of
the kind. So was Dante, in his great survey of humanity *sub specie
aeternitatis*; and there the importance of the unity of the work is
especially apparent. One cannot pick out an episode from the *Divine
Comedy* and read it in isolation: an understanding of it depends on its
placing in the entire scheme. In Chaucer's own time, Gower presented
his three major works as a *summa*, and Langland's survey of good life
in the world and the revelations of faith is another. The *Canterbury
Tales* has the same all-encompassing intention, though the means for
achieving it are more overtly literary: for Dante's anagogical range of
Hell, Purgatory and Paradise, Chaucer gives a generic range. His
work barely touches on such ultimate religious experience as the
beatific vision (the Second Nun's Tale comes closest), but as an exploration of life through literature it is unsurpassed. His method is to
juxtapose the different perspectives offered by different genres and to
allow them to define or tell against each other. The effect is cumula-
tive, and selection or concentration on a single tale goes against the
tenor of the work. To read one story alone is a little like reading the
Murder of Gonzago without *Hamlet*.

Literature is in a poor way these days so far as form and content are concerned. The range and number of kinds of writing that can be recognised as 'literature' have been getting smaller and smaller ever since the Middle Ages. Chaucer was singularly fortunate in writing at the time when the generic variety was at its richest. A consideration of the genres he uses will indicate our present impoverishment. Many of them have now been assigned a place on the very fringes of 'serious' literature. The romance has become the stuff of women's magazines, or science fiction. The beast-fable has become the staple of children's literature, or if it is more adult (as *Watership Down* is, for instance), it is still regarded with suspicion by the critical establishment, and such suspicion is based primarily on genre, not on the degree of skill with which the genre is handled in a particular work. Few sermons have been accepted as significant literature since the seventeenth century. A modern epic, in poetic form, is all but unthinkable. The fabliau has descended to the rugger club or the pub; the saint's life, if it still exists at all, exists as a vehicle for ideological propaganda. Almost all we are left with now is the novel – and although there are a good many varieties of that, they do not come with the richness of convention and tradition that the various genres of the Middle Ages did. The links between the stories in the *Canterbury Tales* deserve a special mention here. All novels until some of the most recent experimental examples – and perhaps even they – do set out to 'imitate life' in some fairly direct and naturalistic sense, however great the debates about what naturalism is and how one imitates nature in a verbal and structural form. It is this naturalism that distinguishes novels, historically and even at the present, from romances or beast-fables. In the links, Chaucer is providing something of the same extension from art towards life. This does not mean that the *Canterbury Tales* is a novel *manqué* or a forerunner of the novel or anything else of the kind: rather, that Chaucer identified the one area not covered by the traditional generic range, and allowed the trivial amoral non-order of everyday living to play its part alongside the various orderings proposed by the stories. The pilgrimage imposes some kind of overriding structure on the frame narrative, but the deeper meanings of the idea of pilgrimage, to which Chaucer directs attention in the first and last of the tales, impinge singularly little on the pilgrims themselves, or on their stories.[1] They are blissfully unaware of any rôle they may have in a greater spiritual allegory, and Chaucer is not going to allow a single meaning to emerge from the progression of tales. To do that, as he does in the Monk's Tale, would be to deny too much.

---

[1] See Ralph Baldwin, *The Unity of the Canterbury Tales* (Anglistica 5, Copenhagen, 1955). Baldwin would deny that the tales are independent of the pilgrimage framework, but the one weakness of his work – and it is a crucial one – is that his account of the *Canterbury Tales* leaves out the stories almost entirely. The Parson's Tale is the only one that can be significantly linked to the pilgrimage.

To interpret the pilgrimage in too exclusively spiritual a sense is to overlook the strong claims of the world. The *Canterbury Tales*, most of the time, is much more a secular work than a religious one. The claims of the spirit are not entirely disregarded, however, even outside the overtly secular tales. The famous opening, with its description of the fertile April showers engendering the flowers, the birds wakeful with the pricking of their 'corages', and men and women setting out on pilgrimage, is more than ironic in its association of the sexual and the spiritual, though the irony is there. There is also beyond that an entirely serious level on which it is right and fitting that at the time of the springing of new life pilgrims should set out

> The hooly blisful martir for to seke,
> That hem hath holpen whan that they were seeke.   17–18

The pilgrimage has a potential for spiritual renewal to match the physical regeneration of the sick. The secular is given a generous weighting, but it is balanced by the sacred.

The same kind of all-inclusiveness of perspective is found throughout the General Prologue, and throughout the *Canterbury Tales* as a whole. Some examples of the way Chaucer works in the Prologue may help to demonstrate the kind of richness of approach that he uses later with greater complexity in the stories. Some of the pilgrims are ideal figures; some are villains; most are described in superlatives, with a surface naiveté coupled with a precise moral pointing that overtly leaves all judgment to the reader but in practice leaves little room for manoeuvre. Some of the pilgrims are to be judged in two ways at once: the Prioress, for instance, is delightful as a woman, but she is far from being the ideal embodiment of her office. None of the portraits is psychological or character-oriented after the fashion of characterisation in the classic novel. All the pilgrims are placed through reference to systems beyond themselves as individuals: to the offices they hold and the standards demanded by those, to their function in society, to their approximation to, or distance from, the ideals set out in those mediaeval anatomies of the social order, the estates satires. On a larger scale, the stories are handled in the same multiplicity of ways. Some of the tales give an idealised portrayal of the world, emphasising human nobility or the providential order; others give a kind of debased caricature. If the pilgrims are all the best of their kind, so are the tales, and if moral judgment is harder to reach in this inner fictional world it is not held in suspense. Some of the tales too must be evaluated in two ways at once, not least where aesthetic and didactic values part company; the Pardoner's Tale demands a particularly complex response since it demands two mutually exclusive moral readings, and the *Melibee* presents a complexity that is still to be untangled. None of the tales has the characteristics or concerns of the traditional novel; they are defined by their particular genre and must be read with all the literary sophistication suggested by that, with an alertness to where they are fulfilling conventional expectations and where and why they leave those behind.

It follows that the relationship between teller and tale is a good deal more complicated than the traditional notion of dramatic projection. Chaucer was certainly keenly aware of the relationship between speech and the man who speaks it: so much is not merely a matter of deduction from the *Tales*, but is given a distinctive formulation in the *House of Fame*:

> Whan any speche ycomen ys
> Up to the paleys, anon-ryght
> Hyt wexeth lyk the same wight
> Which that the word in erthe spak,
> Be hyt clothed red or blak;
> And hath so verray hys lyknesse
> That spak the word, that thou wilt gesse
> That it the same body be,
> Man or woman, he or she. 1074–82

The interesting thing about this is that the speech re-creates the speaker: the character is a projection of the thing said, not the other way round. In much the same way the stories of the *Canterbury Tales* can be seen as defining or creating their speakers. Mario Praz suggested many years ago that the pilgrims 'sprung up from the stories themselves' through 'an embodiment of the spirit of each work in a concrete person'.[2] This is obviously not the whole story, as the shifting around of tales from teller to teller indicates, and the final fit is still not always very good, dramatically or generically. It may none the less be much less misleading than a reading based on character alone.

The way in which both pilgrim and speech can be grounded in literary sources is demonstrated particularly clearly by the Wife of Bath. Estates satires analysed society into its constituent parts, from the pope or emperor downwards, and defined the shortcomings and abuses of each. In this scheme, women constituted a social order to themselves, and the Wife is nothing if not archetypal woman.[3] As Jill Mann has pointed out, some of the details of her portrayal become additionally delightful when she is set in this conventional context: where the satirists inveigh against the expense of women's clothes, and especially headdresses, the Wife's Sunday 'coverchiefs' for her

[2] 'Chaucer and the great Italian writers of the Italian Trecento', *Monthly Criterion* VI (1927) 50. Similar points are made by Allen and Moritz pp. 186–7, and Gabriel Josipovici, *The World and the Book* (2nd ed., London, 1979) pp. 82, 86.

[3] Mann p. 121; the following reference is to pp. 124–5.

head did not *cost* ten pounds but *weighed* ten pounds. All mediaeval anti-feminism was focused in the estates satires; and the Wife is every anti-feminist's dream (or nightmare) come true. She is sexually predatory, extravagantly dressed, ultra-sensitive to her social position, and, worst of all, irresistibly attractive. The 'confession' she gives in the Prologue to her tale is of a piece with this. It is only incidentally autobiographical: all the details of her life, and of her arguments with all her husbands, not least the Oxford clerk Jankin, are drawn from the traditions of anti-feminist literature. The result of all this is something infinitely more rich and delightful than any portrayal of a historical Wife of Bath, such as scholars still occasionally try to find, could ever be. Her Tale itself, of the young knight who marries an old hag, is all the more surprising for this background. Its theme of women's sovereignty is predictable enough; its motif of the old woman regaining her youth is entirely appropriate. What one might not have expected is the romance treatment of the fairy-tale, so that the story becomes an assertion, and a forceful one, of the good to be found in this world. That too is appropriate, but at a deeper level than the rest. After the Wife's exposition of matrimonial woe, the image of secular bliss of the end of the tale demands a re-orientation from the reader.

The richness of the *Canterbury Tales* does not spring only from the relationship of tale to teller, whether this is seen in psychological or literary terms. If the Wife, her Prologue and Tale all define and redefine each other, a similar process also goes on between different stories, or different pilgrims. A more detailed look at some of the portraits of the General Prologue may serve to illustrate in miniature these poetic and conceptual relationships.

The stories of the *Canterbury Tales* can be very roughly divided into three spheres of action and interest: the exotic world of chivalry and courtesy in the romances, the everyday world of the fabliaux, and the spiritual world of the pious tales. Social analysis divided men according to their three main functions, parallel to these worlds: those who fight, those who work, and those who pray. Both Langland and Chaucer recognise this primary grouping, though it was of course acknowledged that society is a good deal more complex than that – the genre of the estates satire existed to demonstrate the point. Chaucer, however, makes the representatives of those three estates the ideal characters of the pilgrimage: the Knight, the Ploughman and the Parson. A fourth character who comes close to setting a similar pattern for his profession is the Clerk: perhaps Chaucer felt the lack of a place for learning, the labour of the intellect as distinct from the body or soul, in the model of the three estates. Knight, Parson and Ploughman, however, are archetypal figures for the estates.

The Ploughman is described in terms very close to Langland's ideal ploughman:

A trewe swynkere and a good was he,
Lyvynge in pees and parfit charitee.
God loved he best with al his hoole herte . . .
He wolde thresshe, and therto dyke and delve,
For Cristes sake, for every povre wight.   I 531–7

Langland's Piers, who in his first and most human manifestation speaks of being Truth's pilgrim at plough for poor men's sake,[4] embodies exactly the same ideal. Some influence is possible, given the popularity of Langland's poem, and indeed the fact that he and Chaucer must have lived within a mile of each other for some years;[5] but it is not necessary to assume it. These are the accepted traditions of the labourer's virtues, though the close connection of duty to the church and duty to the poor is found in no other character in either work.[6] The presence of the Ploughman is a salutary reminder that human perfection should be the norm.

The Parson is the Ploughman's brother: their blood relationship is symptomatic of their equal moral standing in their separate worlds, symbolic of their social functions as labouring to support the body and the soul. Where Chaucer describes what the Ploughman *is*, however, he describes what the Parson is *not*. After the opening lines, the portrait of the Parson is the portrait of a bad priest, annulled throughout by negatives:

Ful looth were hym to cursen for his tithes . . .   486

He sette nat his benefice to hyre
And leet his sheep encombred in the myre
And ran to Londoun unto Seinte Poules
To seken hym a chaunterie for soules . . .   507–10

He was to synful men nat despitous,
Ne of his speche daungerous ne digne . . .   516–17

By the time Chaucer ends his portrayal of the ideal priest, we have a very good idea of the abuses practised by the beneficed clergy.

The Knight is more complex than either of these other estates ideals. Chaucer puts him first, at the head of the series of portraits, not only

[4] *The Vision of William concerning Piers the Plowman* ed. Walter W. Skeat (2 vols, 1886/London, 1965) B.VI.104.
[5] Chaucer lived in 'a dwelling above the gate of Aldgate' from 1374 to 1386 (*Chaucer Life-Records* ed. Martin M. Crow and Clair C. Olson (Oxford, 1966) pp. 144–7); Langland speaks of his cottage on Cornhill in a famous passage in the C-text (C.VI.1–4), written probably in the late 1370s. For a fascinating study of the links between Chaucer and Langland see J. A. W. Bennett, 'Chaucer's contemporary' in *Piers Plowman: Critical Approaches* ed. S. S. Hussey (London, 1969) pp. 310–24.
[6] Ibid. pp. 317–18. See also the discussion in Mann pp. 67–74.

for reasons of social precedence but also because the standards by which the Knight is described as living are to be relevant to many of the portraits that follow. Terry Jones, in a fascinating study of the Knight's campaigns, has recently argued that the portrait is a travesty and that the Knight is far from ideal.[7] This is not, I think, what Chaucer is doing. That war is always and inevitably a bloody business in every sense of the word was perfectly well known in the Middle Ages (and is emphasised in the Knight's Tale), but that did not affect the almost universal assumption that the proper function of knights was to fight: even Langland, with all his moral stringency, never questions that.[8] It was generally acknowledged that the killing of Christians was a bad thing (though that rarely stopped anyone from doing it), but only a small group in the late fourteenth century, the Lollard knights at the court of Richard II, some of them closely known to Chaucer, were opposed to the killing of pagans. Whatever his own views may have been, Chaucer in his portrait of his own Knight is recalling the solid tradition of Christian chivalry. The Knight does not fulfil the lower form of his rôle, of fighting for his feudal lord, but the highest form, of fighting for God. Jones would have him fighting for money – he subtitles his book 'The Portrait of a Medieval Mercenary' – but Chaucer, who can so unerringly identify the ecclesiastics who substitute Mammon for God, never hints at that.[9] There is a curious critical assumption that since Chaucer is often ironic in the *Canterbury Tales*, he must always be ironic. If that were so, there would be little bite left in the irony. It is precisely because the Knight is an ideal that the imperfection of some of the later characters tells so strongly; and most of the characteristics Chaucer gives him have an immediate, and a positive, function in the General Prologue itself.[10]

The Knight, whom one might expect to be portrayed as the well-to-do secular country gentleman, is in fact an ascetic who has devoted his life to the service of Christianity. The Monk, who follows shortly

[7] *Chaucer's Knight: The Portrait of a Medieval Mercenary* (London, 1980).

[8] See C.VI.72–5; he does also, of course, recognise other social functions, such as maintaining justice and hunting vermin (B.VI.28–46).

[9] Jones's arguments are largely based on the fact that there were a great many English mercenaries around in Europe in the fourteenth century, and that the word 'armee' was used for a mercenary army. But Chaucer could easily have dropped a word that the Knight had been in one of the mercenary groups if he had wished to; he does not – the Knight's campaigns are all on the fringes of Christendom. 'Armee' (a disputed reading, as Jones acknowledges) is, on Jones's own evidence, not used in the sense of 'mercenary army' in the derogatory sense he would have it: the examples he gives suggest that 'armee' means a host made up of fighters who are not the lord's own vassals – and since the King of England was not fighting in any Crusades, Chaucer's Knight necessarily has to serve under a different lord.

[10] The details of the Knight's clothing and horses appear highly suspicious to Jones; but that they should be interpreted positively becomes unquestionable when they are set against the description of the Monk (see below).

afterwards, and whom one might expect to be portrayed as an ascetic
who had devoted his life to the service of Christianity, is in fact
portrayed much more as a well-to-do country gentleman. R. E. Kaske
has set out the close verbal parallels that Chaucer uses in the two
portraits:[11] the Knight who

> fro the tyme that he first bigan
> To riden out, he loved chivalrie,   I 44–5

the Monk 'an outridere, that lovede venerie'; the Knight's 'good' but
not 'gay' horses, the Monk's 'ful many a deyntee hors', 'his hors in
greet estaat'; the ascetic plainness of the Knight's clothing, the Monk's
fur sleeves and gold pin. The contrast extends to internal qualities as
well as attributes: the Knight is 'of his port as meeke as is a mayde',
the Monk 'a manly man, to been an abbot able'. We are made aware
of how the world values the Knight: he has been 'evere honoured for
his worthynesse', 'everemoor he hadde a sovereyn prys', and the voice
is Chaucer's echoing a wider valuation, with no room for irony. In the
Monk's portrait, however, it is perpetually his own estimate of himself
that we keep hearing in the lines. That he is fit to be an abbot follows
too suddenly on the reference to his hunting for it to be acceptable at
face value, and his own voice is so distinct later in the description that
his qualification for promotion – 'to been an abbot able' – gets infected
by it. We never hear the Knight's voice: he is entirely reticent about
his exploits, and Chaucer does all the speaking for him. The Knight
is summed up in terms of the achievements of his career and his moral
qualities; the Monk is described in terms of his attributes, his clothing,
his fondness for good hunting, good horses and (above all) good food,
and his cheerful contempt of the old-fashioned monastic rule.

Apart from his horse, no animal is mentioned in the portrait of the
Knight. The Monk comes surrounded with them: not only the fine
horse he rides and the others back home in the stable, but greyhounds
'as swift as fowel in flight' (a simile that suggests hawking to add to
his fondness for hunting), the hare he chases; and when he is not
hunting he is eating, with the fat swan as his favourite roast, and at
the other extreme, as expressions of worthlessness, the plucked hen
and the oyster. All this gives the portrait a very different texture from
the abstract moral adjectives – 'worthy', 'wys', 'meeke' – used for the
Knight, or the Miltonic roll-call of the names of the places where he
had fought. Animal imagery is used in a number of other portraits to
make an effect different again from the Monk's. In a description such
as that of the Miller the animals are not ones he possesses or uses as

[11] 'The Knight's interruption of the Monk's Tale', *ELH* XXIV (1957) 249–68, esp. pp. 256–8.

speech idioms, but are used as similes to associate him with beasts: his beard 'as any sowe or fox was reed', the bristles on his nose are 'reed as the brustles of a sowes eeres'. In a selection of similes full of nastier implications,[12] the Pardoner's eyes are like a hare's, his voice like a goat's, he himself 'a geldyng or a mare'. His holy relics are mere pigs' bones, and he reduces the people he dupes to the sub-human level of 'apes'.

The General Prologue is a very complex piece of writing, and one could analyse these differences of poetic treatment indefinitely; how characters fulfil, or more commonly fail to fulfil, their estates ideals, how far their attributes are conventional (a surprising number of them are) and which are individual, how the different tones and textures of the various portraits are achieved. What emerges from even such a brief survey as I have given here, is how few psychologically individualising elements there are. The pilgrims are not characters of post-Freudian depth, but individualised types controlled by convention – whether they fulfil expectations or contradict them – and by the poetic manipulation of language and imagery.

As in the General Prologue, so in the tales: the aims and methods are not those of psychological exploration, but of poetry: of imagery, language, genre, manipulation of convention and so on. The 'confessions' of the Wife of Bath and the Pardoner in their respective prologues are clearly tailored to fit the characters, but even they are deeply rooted in convention, in well-known social and ecclesiastical abuses or in the familiar traditions of anti-feminism, and none of the tales shows as tight a connection with its narrator as do these first-person passages. The primary reason for assigning a tale to a particular teller is likely to be rhetorical, not psychological: the ascription derives from the story rather than the pilgrim. Rhetoric demands decorum, 'appropriateness'; and first and foremost it is a fit at that level that Chaucer offers. Even the 'cherles tales' are decorous in this sense:

> The Millere is a cherl, ye knowe wel this;
> So was the Reve eek and othere mo,
> And harlotrie they tolden bothe two.   I 3182–4

At one level this can imply a social ranking: high romance for the Knight, bawdy fabliaux for the low-class ruffians. Per Nykrog established some years ago that fabliau and romance do not in fact belong to different authors and audiences,[13] and the *Canterbury Tales* is the

---

[12] See Beryl Rowland, *Blind Beasts: Chaucer's Animal World* (Kent, Ohio, 1971), esp. pp. 100–2.

[13] Per Nykrog, *Les Fabliaux* (1957/Publications Romanes et Françaises 123, Geneva, 1973) ch. I.

perfect illustration of that; but Chaucer will pretend that the division is true, and divide his pilgrims into 'cherles' and 'gentils'. Decorum can also provide a contrast, sometimes a subtle one, between the religious and the lay members of the pilgrimage: pious romance for the Man of Law, Miracle of the Virgin for the Prioress. But just as easy divisions of this kind are blurred in the General Prologue, with the Monk's secularity, the Pardoner's greed and the social climbing of almost everyone except the ideal figures, so the assignment of genre to particular kinds of pilgrims gets confused. The tales are less significant for what they tell us about the characters of the individual pilgrims than for what the assignment to a particular narrator tells us about the kind of story it is. Just as in the General Prologue one has to be alive to expressions of the ideal and departures from it, to levels of imagery, to the play of conventions, to links and reflections and contrasts between portraits, so the tales work in the same way. Just as the portrait of the Monk is qualified by the portraits of the Knight and Parson, so every tale is qualified by the presence of the others.

The process is most clearly visible at the level of genre. Mediaeval literary genres are very sharply differentiated – in essence, at least: there are always grey areas – and Chaucer is keenly aware of the points of differentiation. Every other writer of a story-collection works to bring his tales towards a common generic centre, to give them a tonal and stylistic consistency and to reduce their differences of narrative outline or thematic import. Chaucer works in exactly the opposite way, to enhance the differences and point them up in every way he can.

The points of difference he exploits are explicit in the genres themselves. The leading genre of secular literature, the romance, idealises the world and those who live in it. Its heroes are young, strong, handsome and noble, its heroines young, beautiful, noble, and chaste before marriage. There are no romances of adultery in Chaucer,[14] and indeed very few in Middle English. (The main exception is the story of Lancelot and Guinevere, and that was invented by the French. It was in France, not England, that adultery was a common romance motif – though it was still less common in French romances than it is in French novels.) The bulk of any romance is likely to be devoted to the suffering and hardship endured by its characters, but a happy ending is guaranteed, and rewards are dealt out in this world to ensure a happy-ever-after ending. Romances are set far away or long ago, well apart from the triviality of everyday living, and their scope is

---

[14] *Troilus and Criseyde* is sometimes described as if it were, but that would be unimaginable if Criseyde had a living husband. The Merchant's Tale is not a romance, partly because the adultery reduces it far below any ideal: see below, pp. 142–3.

large both geographically and temporally. They are, above all, stories. Narrative is what counts in romance; but in the more courtly or self-aware romances there is also a deeper level of implied meaning, the *sens* or *sentence* underlying the *matière*. Courtly romance is also concerned with ideals of human behaviour; and the highest value is set on human love.

In the saint's life, the highest value is out of this world: its absolute is a divine imperative. The worldly end of its hero – or more often heroine, since the qualities of being young, beautiful and chaste are again essential, and these have more sensation value in women than in men – the worldly end of its heroine is likely to be a sticky one. The setting is again often exotic: more typical than St. Thomas à Becket with his historically and geographically identifiable context would be St. Margaret of Antioch, who was swallowed by a dragon which split when she made the sign of the cross (Jacobus a Voragine, to give him due credit, doubts whether it actually ate her), but duly martyred by beheading with a sword. What happens to the body is, luckily, unimportant: the soul is what matters. Rewards in the saint's life, by way of spiritual enlightenment in this life and salvation after death, are unmeasurable, or even invisible, to the worldly eye.

The romance stresses the highest earthly ideals, the saint's life the highest spiritual ones; in the fabliau, men and women leave all ideals far behind, and act with an eye to instant gratification that allows no postponement of the reward to a distant happy ending or to life after death. The ruling code in the fabliau is animal instinct. The physical functions of the body, especially sex (and as a close second in Chaucer, farting), provide the primary plot motifs. In fabliaux there is none of the nobility of blood or exoticism of setting associated with romance: the characters are at best middle-class, and the plots are worked out in a single house in a local town or village. Further meanings are minimal or non-existent. If mediaeval fictions are supposed to teach and delight, the authors of the fabliaux were not listening to the first half of the injunction. Entertainment value is all.

Beast-fables are also delightfully entertaining; but traditionally they come with their morals firmly attached. If the fabliau scarcely distinguishes human action from animal instinct, the beast-fable has its animals imitate rational human action. In contrast with the courtly ideals of the romance or the spiritual absolute of the saint's life, the beast-fable teaches worldly common sense.

And so one might continue through the various genres of mediaeval literature, and the *Canterbury Tales*. If romance emphasises the upward movement of Fortune's wheel, *tragedie*, in the mediaeval non-dramatic definition derived from Boethius, is concerned solely with its downward turning:

What other thyng bewaylen the cryinges of tragedyes but oonly the dedes of Fortune, that with unwar strook overturneth the realmes of greet nobleye?

Glose. Tragedye is to seyn a dite of a prosperite for a tyme, that endeth in wrecchidnesse.[15]

If romance concerns itself with marvels and the irruption of the super-natural into the world, miracles of the Virgin, even more than saints' lives, concern themselves with miracles and the irruption of the divine into the world. Between the saint's life and the romance lies an area of secular hagiography, the realm of Custance and Griselda, which examines standards of divine perfection operating within the world; and the Physician's Tale will give another such story a pagan setting. Didacticism can take the form of discursive prose, or, in the Pardoner's Tale, a lengthy sermon *exemplum* can become a gripping murder-story. Traditional wisdom can be embodied in the actions of irrational beasts, or in proverbs and the maxims and *sententiae* of the great teachers of the past.

If the fabliau is all entertaining story and no moral instruction, the penitential tract is all moral instruction and no entertaining story. Robert Mannyng may have enlivened his poem on the good Christian life with an abundance of exemplary tales, but Chaucer's Parson will allow no such compromises with the world:

> Thou getest fable noon ytoold for me;
> For Paul, that writeth unto Thymothee,
> Repreveth hem that weyven soothfastnesse,
> And tellen fables and swich wrecchednesse.
> Why sholde I sowen draf out of my fest,
> Whan I may sowen whete, if that me lest?
> For which I seye, if that yow list to here
> Moralitee and vertuous mateere. X 31–8

Verse, whether rhymed or alliterative, is excluded along with fiction; Chaucer's exploration of the limits of genre results finally in the rejection of poetry and fiction – in the rejection of creative literature.

Until the very end of the *Tales*, there is the constant alternation of the world of poetry and the imagination, in the stories, and the imitation of real life, with all its apparent disorder and triviality, in the framework. The frame is in fact of course as highly-wrought and fully imagined as any of the tales; but where the stories look away from everyday life towards their own worlds, or perhaps look at this world from the perspective imposed by their genre, the frame looks at ordinary life from a point of view within it.

[15] *Boece* Book II pr.2.67–72.

This matter of perspective, of point of view, becomes crucial for any understanding of the *Canterbury Tales*. To ascribe the attitudes expressed in the tales to the narrators is an over-simplification and denies much of the richness of what Chaucer is doing. It is precisely because so many of the differences in perspective are already inherent in the kinds of story told that they can work together for an effect much greater than the sum of its parts. The similarities and contrasts between the different genres that I have set out above are implicit or explicit in every leaf of the *Canterbury Tales*. Chaucer plays off these differences against each other, not just by using so many different genres, but by drawing on an extensive stock of ideas and motifs that recur throughout the work, each time treated from a different angle appropriate first of all to the tale and only secondarily, through the tale, to the teller. The pilgrims may be allowed their say in the links, but in very few of the stories does the voice of any of the ostensible narrators replace Chaucer's. The pilgrims are as much part of his fiction as are their stories.

The recurring themes of the *Canterbury Tales* are enormously various. They include such things as ideas about literary theory, the nature of fiction, and the relation of art and morality; they include metaphysical speculation about divine justice or the balance between Fortune and Providence. Modes of human behaviour, especially the perennially fascinating topic of sex *versus* chastity, are perpetually discussed. Marriage is one such issue, and the one that every reader of Chaucer knows all about; it is certainly important, but not as all-important as is sometimes implied, nor do the tales of the 'marriage group' stand out in isolation from the rest as the only ones to be thematically linked. There is a vast pattern of similarly related themes woven throughout the whole fabric of the tales. Narrative and rhetorical *topoi* come in for the same kind of treatment: female beauty, or gardens, or sworn brotherhood, or the concept of meeting one's fate by the wayside, and many others, are repeated many times throughout the *Tales*, each time from a different angle suggested by the nature of the story. The interplay of themes and ideas can cover everything from details of style to the discussion of what men – or women – most desire, whether it be love, money, sovereignty or salvation.

The objection may be raised that there is such variety here that all literature is going to cover such themes, and that their presence in the *Canterbury Tales* is both accidental and unavoidable. Chaucer often goes to some trouble to point out the similarities, however; and a comparison of his tales with their sources or closest analogues shows up very precisely how he stresses or develops or adds characteristics of this kind. A collection of the sources of the tales would show very few of these links. Neither Boccaccio's *Teseida* nor his *De Casibus*, for instance, reveals any of the hard metaphysical questioning of the nature of Providence and the relationship of worldly misery to guilt or innocence that Chaucer examines so persistently in the Knight's and Monk's Tales; and it is impossible to imagine any source for the portrait of Alisoun that would provide its detailed counter-pointing of the portrait of Emily. Even when tales do have traditional elements that are used by Chaucer in this way – the ruling passions of the Pardoner's and Wife of Bath's tales, for instance, *cupiditas* and women's love of sovereignty – the very selection of such tales can be seen as deliberate. The only proof possible must lie in the text, and this will be the concern of the later chapters of this book; I believe that the precision and detail with which the interrelationships between these various themes are worked out must be seen as conclusive. As Kolve comments on visual imagery, 'It is context that turns a sign into a communication, defining its exact and immediate intent.'[16] The context provided by the *Tales* is very rich indeed, and its communications all the more significant, and precise.

The next question must be, what is the point of writing the *Canterbury Tales* in this way? There are many possible answers to this, some practical and technical, others more profound and far-reaching. The most immediate practical point relates to the question of coherence that the compilers of so many story-collections had come up against: this process of interrelation locks the tales together, and with each additional story the edifice becomes not more diffuse and disordered, like a child's magazine collage, but tighter and firmer, like building an arch. The thematic implications are more significant. The *House of Fame* had suggested that multiplicity of tidings must take the place of the poet's attempt to find an undiscoverable single truth; the Monk's Tale suggests how inadequate a single moral must be. The *Canterbury Tales* is a presentation of the world, and of men's apprehension of the world, in all its richness and relativity. The very diversity of attitudes enforced by the division of literature into different genres means that there cannot be any authoritative 'answers'. There is one answer given by romance, another by fabliau, another by saint's life.

Even this way of proceeding is not without precedent, or indeed without generic classification. The anatomy, or Menippean satire, works on just such a basis.[17] Northrop Frye gives the classic account of the form:

---

[16] 'Chaucer and the visual arts' in *Writers and their Background: Geoffrey Chaucer* ed. Derek Brewer (London, 1974) p. 312.

[17] There is a valuable discussion of this aspect of the *Tales* in Derek Brewer's article 'Gothic Chaucer' in his *Writers and their Background*, esp. pp. 27–9. F. Anne Payne's *Chaucer and Menippean Satire* (Madison, Wis., 1981) concentrates on *Troilus and Criseyde*, the Knight's Tale and the Nun's Priest's Tale as individual examples of the form and does not develop any ideas about the *Canterbury Tales* as a whole.

The Menippean satire deals less with people as such than with mental attitudes. Pedants, bigots, cranks, parvenus, virtuosi, enthusiasts, rapacious and incompetent professional men of all kinds, are handled in terms of their occupational approach to life as distinct from their social behavior. The Menippean satire thus resembles the confession in its ability to handle abstract ideas and theories, and differs from the novel in its characterization, which is stylized rather than naturalistic, and presents people as mouthpieces of the ideas they represent.[18]

It 'deals with intellectual themes and attitudes', and in its simplest form will take the shape of a dialogue or colloquy. Boethius' *Consolation of Philosophy* is one such dialogue example well-known to Chaucer: its clash of ideas and its pattern of alternating prose and verse are both typical of the genre. If there are many speakers involved, 'the setting then is usually a *cena* or symposium' – a symposium in its Greek sense of a drinking-party as well as its modern meaning. Frye cites Apuleius, Rabelais, *Gulliver's Travels* and the Alice books as instances of the form; but his account is also a perfect description of the *Canterbury Tales*, which is a symposium in both senses – an intellectual debate between opposing attitudes, and with the promised supper at the Tabard Inn to look forward to. The 'anatomy' basis of the General Prologue has long been recognised; but the anatomy of literary attitudes and of ways of understanding the world extends throughout the work, and adds up to something much larger than the social anatomy of the Prologue.

Such a process might imply that all the tales should be seen on a level, as all equally valuable or 'meaningful'. This is not in practice what happens. The audience's moral judgment is kept perpetually on the alert throughout the *Tales*, just as it is in the General Prologue: that the Knight, Monk, Friar and Parson are there all described in superlatives does not mean that they are all to be taken at face value. There is a clear level of irony at work in the tales as in the Prologue; but very often it is an irony arising primarily from context, from the counterpointing of one tale with another. The *Melibee* was a favourite tract throughout Europe, and taken in isolation Chaucer's translation is entirely faithful; the Prioress's Tale, compared with other miracles of the Virgin, is atypical only by virtue of being so much better. The section on *Sir Thopas* in Bryan and Dempster's *Sources and Analogues* is one of the longest in the work, and demonstrates amply that similar doggerel was being perpetrated in abundance. Put the tales together, however, and rather different things start to happen. The Miller's Tale does not cancel out the Knight's, but the vigour and detail of its parody prevent us from taking the Knight's Tale as the only word to be said

---

[18] *Anatomy of Criticism* p. 309; the further quotations are from pp. 311 and 310.

on its subject. The difference in stylistic level between the poetics of *Sir Thopas* and the other Canterbury tales damns it instantly.

The notion that the stories are to be told in competition with each other enhances this series of contrasts and relationships. The idea of competition may direct the audience to appreciate the high poetic qualities of the tales; but within the fiction it affects the pilgrims rather differently. The word Chaucer uses – or has his characters use – to describe their understanding of the competition is *quite*, 'requite' or 'repay'. The narrators very often set out not to surpass the previous story but to *answer it back*. The stories parody, comically or seriously, each other's generic conventions and attitudes. The high idealism of the Knight's Tale is answered by the cheerful earthiness of the Miller's:

> 'By armes, and by blood and bones,
> I kan a noble tale for the nones,
> With which I wol now quite the Knyghtes tale.'   I 3125–7

The Miller's tale of the carpenter is taken by the Reeve as a personal insult, and he insists three times over[19] that his story will 'quite' the Miller's. It does so by more than just reversing the insult, however: there is a more literal overgoing of the Miller's Tale, too. There, one student slept with one woman; in the Reeve's, two students sleep with two women. Oxford is 'quited' by Cambridge, in a fourteenth-century equivalent of the Boat Race, and Cambridge wins by a length. The three tales of the first fragment, to summarise, respond to the 'competition' element, first, in the Knight's Tale, with sheer poetic quality; then by generic parody; then by an elaboration and multiplication of identical plot motifs. The generic contrasting of the tales, here and throughout the work, is backed up by its dramatic projection from the framework, from the pilgrims and their rivalries, but its implications go far beyond individual psychology or dramatic conflict.

Generic contrast can work at many levels, from pervasive themes of cosmic import down to single lines and phrases. It shows in the attitudes to Providence or to authority adopted in different tales; it shows in the various ideals, or lack of them, by which men can live; it highlights different attitudes towards women, marriage and sex. It also gives a sharper point to such a line as

> Allone, withouten any compaignye.   I 2779, 3204

Once it is used for Arcite contemplating the grave, at the end of the Knight's Tale; at the beginning of the next story, it describes the

---

[19] I 3864, 3916, 4324.

amorous Nicholas in his lodgings, preparing to get together with Alisoun. The repetition is too closely juxtaposed, and too brilliantly contrasted, for it not to be intentional.

Not every repetition is significant, however. There is a strong formulaic element in mediaeval literature: conventional plot motifs, rhetorical *topoi* and proverbial or oral formulae abound, in Chaucer as in every writer of his time. The existence of certain resemblances between different sections or lines of the *Canterbury Tales* therefore in itself proves nothing; some may be significant, others equally clearly are not. There is a genuine difficulty here which every reader will solve in a different way, drawing the line between an incidental relationship and a more profound one in a different place. Chaucer's intentions as to which mean something and which do not must remain speculative when the evidence of the text is inconclusive; and reflections or repetitions that he may not have inserted deliberately still throw a good deal of light on the way the *Tales* work. A few examples will illustrate the various processes and problems.

Some verbal formulae remain at that minimally formulaic level, and their repetition will be incidental and not incremental. That the Knight's Yeoman, the statue of Cupid in the Knight's Tale, and the yeoman-devil in the Friar's Tale, all bear 'arwes brighte and kene',[20] is an example of this kind, where the repeated phrase remains formulaic. Proverbial similes also need carry no significant weight: 'as fayn as fowel is of the brighte sonne' is used by the Knight, and, with only small variations, by the Shipman and the Canon's Yeoman.[21] On other occasions a simile of this kind can help to define the differences between tales even though it seems too much to ask that any audience, or Chaucer himself, should have the earlier usage in mind when the second occurs. 'As drunk as a mouse' is a simile used by both the Knight and the Wife of Bath (mice having had the habit of falling into beer vats). To the Knight, the phrase is a simile for the state of mankind:

> We witen nat what thing we preyen heere:
> We faren as he that dronke is as a mous.   I 1260–1

The Wife uses it to insult her husbands:

> Thou comest home as dronken as a mous!   III 246

The use of the same words in the two different contexts epitomises the differences between the sections: the Knight's Tale with its deep philosophical reach, ready to use the humblest similes in the service of the

---

[20] I 104, 1966, III 1381.
[21] I 2437, VII 38, 51, VIII 1342.

search for truth; the Wife's Prologue with its vivid colloquialism and concern for the everyday domestic world. When the Wife says 'drunk as a mouse', she means just that; when Arcite says it, it is a simile within a simile – '*as* he that drunk is *as* a mouse' – and ideas of inebriation and small furry animals are alike distanced by his agonized questioning of the nature of human life.

Single lines or aphorisms can present similar problems. Chaucer was not a man to avoid using a good line twice, or even four times.

Pitee renneth soone in gentil herte

occurs not only in the Knight's, Merchant's and Squire's Tales, and with a slight variation in the Man of Law's, but also in the Prologue to the *Legend of Good Women*.[22] If a poem outside the *Tales* can contain the same line, it would seem to weaken the case for the usages within the *Tales* being significant. This does not necessarily follow, however. The line in the *Legend* confirms that the idea was a lasting concern of Chaucer's – the theme, if not the actual wording, is found again in *Troilus and Criseyde* – and so enforces the likelihood that he was aware of the repetitions in the *Tales*. Given the detailed counterpointing of the Knight's and Merchant's Tales, the uses of the line in those strike particularly hard: it is used once for Theseus tempering anger and ruthless justice with compassion, the second time for May deciding to have an affair with her husband's squire. In the Squire's Tale the line again occurs in the context of a love affair, but here there is no irony: the heroine Canacee's true pity and *gentillesse* are contrasted with the unfaithful tercelet's hollow imitation. The repetition gains extra weight from the likelihood that Chaucer intended the Squire's Tale to follow the Merchant's; but its significance does not depend on the juxtaposition. The Knight's Tale uses the line straight, to mean what it says. The Merchant's turns it inside out, so that *pitee* and *gentil* are both ironically redefined, and even 'soone' has a cynical ring in view of how closely May's plans for adultery follow her marriage. In the Squire's Tale the line has a double meaning: it applies literally to Canacee, but given the context of a lover's unfaithfulness it carries a reminder that its opposite is also true.

Lines and phrases such as these illustrate on a small scale what Chaucer is doing with motifs of every size from a few words to ideas of cosmic import. In order to be perceptible to the listeners, even to ones so alert to literary meaning as late fourteenth-century audiences seem to have been, significant repetitions must be given in a way that will make them noticeable. Adjacent tales can rely on finer cues, or more detailed 'quiting', than more widely spaced stories. For all Chau-

[22] I 1761, IV 1986, V 479, II 660; *Legend* F 503.

cer's invitation to turn over the leaf to a different tale, there is a presumption that they will be read in sequence. The locking together of one tale to the next within the fragments by both thematic relationship and narrative connection suggests that a sequential reading of linked tales is preferable, from Chaucer's point of view, and likely, from the reader's. When a motif reappears in tales from different fragments it must be more prominent. The occasional cross-references (such as those to the Wife of Bath) help here, but there are few of them. Chaucer's use of literary conventions helps more: since they would already be familiar to the audience, his variations on them, or his refusal to fulfil the expectations they arouse, would be all the more noticeable. In addition, many of the themes and motifs found pervasively throughout the work are given their first clear statement in the opening tale, the Knight's. The rest can then build on the foundations laid there.

4

An Opening: The Knight's Tale

The Knight's Tale is a dynamic introduction to the story-telling: it leads in many directions and opens out on to many of the problems and perspectives explored later in the work. Many of the reflections of it that occur later are very precise indeed, as in the parodies given by the Miller's and Merchant's Tales; I shall discuss connections of this kind, of specific echoes of plot motif or rhetorical commonplaces, in later chapters, for they only affect the Knight's Tale by hindsight. My concern here is with the tale alone, as it stands – for there is as yet at this point in the work nothing apart from the General Prologue to relate it to. What emerges most clearly from the Knight's Tale by itself is the immensity of the issues it raises. These themes are not complete in themselves, as plot motifs are, but are often presented as questions. Later stories take up the questions in different forms, or occasionally even suggest answers; but all such concerns open out from the first of the tales. This open-ended exploration is contained in a brilliantly controlled narrative and rhetorical structure, and given form through a handling of genre that in itself suggests that there is no single or simple way of looking at the world. The tales in which Chaucer brings together different genres are indeed often the finest in the whole work, and the Knight's Tale acts as the model.

The Host had requested stories 'of aventures that whilom han bifalle': 'once upon a time' stories. The Knight takes up the injunction very precisely, but at once endows it with a force and breadth such as the original formula had not suggested:

> Whilom, as olde stories tellen us,
> Ther was a duc that highte Theseus;
> Of Atthenes he was lord and governour,
> And in his tyme swich a conquerour,
> That gretter was ther noon under the sonne.
> Ful many a riche contree hadde he wonne.   I 859–64

The lines immediately establish a sense of epic range and grandeur.

This impression is reinforced by the epigraph from Statius' *Thebaid* that heads the tale in some manuscripts,[1] lines which not only introduce the action of the tale but affirm its antecedents in heroic poetry. This aspect of the tale has sometimes been played down, since Chaucer reduces the epic qualities of his major source, Boccaccio's *Teseida* (a 'Theseid' to match the 'Aeneid'); but Dryden, who did not have the *Teseida* to contrast it with, still saw the work as an epic. For him it was 'the Noble Poem of Palamon and Arcite, which is of the Epique kind, and perhaps not much inferiour to the *Ilias* or the *Æneis*'.[2]

Chaucer does none the less concentrate on the romance elements in the story. His poem is only a fifth the length of Boccaccio's, and it is the heroic sections of legendary history and military campaigns that are most ruthlessly cut. Love, and the lovers' rivalry, come to dominate the tale; but the epic quality of the poem has still been affirmed strongly in the opening section. Chaucer differentiates the five romances of the *Canterbury Tales* very precisely. The Wife of Bath's Tale comes from the edge of the genre where romance touches folk-tale; the Squire's Tale is the opening of an interlaced romance; the Franklin's is a Breton lai; *Sir Thopas* is a parody of the popular romance. The Knight's Tale starts the sequence at the noblest level, where romance shares a border with epic.

Romance and epic are on a single narrative continuum; but Chaucer rapidly qualifies the nature of the Knight's Tale as a romance in a more startling way, by fusing it with its opposite, tragedy – tragedy in that Boethian sense of the 'unwar strookes' of Fortune. Romance has more than a conventional expectation of a happy ending: generically it is partially definable in terms of the upward movement of Fortune's wheel. At the very beginning of the story, before the introduction of Palamon and Arcite and the main action, Chaucer insists on this contrast, that oné man's victory is another's overthrow. As

---

[1]   Iamque domos patrias, Scithice post aspera gentis
        Prelia, laurigero, &c.

And now after his fierce battles with the Scythians, [Theseus approached] his native land in his laurel-decked [chariot]

(*Thebaid* XII 519–20). The epigraph may have been added by copyists, but the point remains the same whether it was Chaucer or a scribe who saw the epic appropriateness of the lines.

[2] *Preface* to *Fables Ancient and Modern*, in *The Poems and Fables of John Dryden* ed. James Kinsley (London, 1970) p. 536 11. 637–9. For interesting discussions of the genre of the Knight's Tale see Robert S. Haller, 'The *Knight's Tale* and the epic tradition', *Chaucer Review* I (1966–7) 67–84, and John Burrow, *Medieval Writers and their Work* (Oxford, 1982) pp. 57–8. Boccaccio's work insists much more than Chaucer's on its nature as epic, but the title he chose qualifies that conception: it is in full the *Teseida delle Nozze d'Emilia*. Virgil would not have called his own epic the *Aeneid of the Marriage of Lavinia*.

Theseus enters Athens in triumph he is met by 'a compaignye of
ladyes', dressed in black, who kneel before him to ask for his help. The
oldest of them, widow of King Capaneus, addresses him like this:

> 'Lord, to whom Fortune hath yiven
> Victorie, and as a conqueror to lyven . . .
> Certes, lord, ther is noon of us alle,
> That she ne hath been a duchesse or a queene.
> Now be we caytyves, as it is wel seene,
> Thanked be Fortune and hire false wheel,
> That noon estaat assureth to be weel.'   915–16, 922–6

Capaneus himself is a victim of Fortune in the manner of the subjects
of the Monk's tragedies. This is the first of many passages emphasising
the mingled web of good and ill, joy and grief, in the world. The
romance vision is one of suffering and hardship as a means to a blissful
ending; the vision of the Knight's Tale is more complex. The ladies
beg Theseus to attack Creon, lord of Thebes, who has not only killed
their husbands but refused them burial and 'maketh houndes ete hem
in despite'. Theseus responds to their plea for 'som drope of pitee'; and
he at once sets off to attack Creon 'as he that hadde his deeth ful wel
deserved', to act as the agent of justice and restore the decencies of
human order. But to get to the ceremony of the funeral pyre, Theseus
must first destroy the city; and his victory brings with it not only the
restoration of the proper ceremonial obsequies and a new triumphal
entry, but, for Palamon and Arcite, discovered among the heaps of the
dead, perpetual imprisonment. The contrast is again brought out by
sharp juxtaposition:

> Hoom he rit anon
> With laurer crowned as a conquerour;
> And ther he lyveth in joye and in honour
> Terme of his lyf; what nedeth wordes mo?
> And in a tour, in angwissh and in wo,
> This Palamon and his felaw Arcite
> For everemoore.   1026–32

Only at the very end of the Knight's Tale – and perhaps not even
there – are we allowed to think of joy without also thinking of its
opposite. The poem is Palamon's romance, in which his faithfulness
and endurance at last win him his lady; but it is at the same time the
tragedy of Arcite, whose equal mental suffering and greater physical
pain are rewarded only by death.

The architectonic form in which these generic contrasts are held is
one of Chaucer's most remarkable, and unsung, achievements. He
compressed Boccaccio's lengthy amplification of the story into a much

tighter structure of a kind only paralleled in contemporary literature by *Sir Gawain and the Green Knight* – to which indeed it bears a surprisingly close resemblance. Both works are structured symmetrically, with equivalent scenes or episodes occurring at each end and working inwards towards a crucial central core of three: the three bedroom scenes and hunts in *Gawain*, the three temples in the Knight's Tale. The triads are central in both senses: they occupy the mid-point of this symmetrical structure (though they occur in the third of each poem's four sections); and they are also in some way definitive for the rest of the work.

Such symmetry of structure is very unusual indeed in the Middle Ages.[3] Most mediaeval imaginative literature operates on a linear basis, often represented in the narrative by a journey. All romance quests do this; so does the *Divine Comedy*, with Dante's journey from Hell to Heaven; so do many saints' lives, such as the voyages of St. Brendan; so does *Piers Plowman*, though the dreamer's journeying is located only in the field full of folk; so does the *Canterbury Tales* itself, with its pilgrimage frame. That the hero returns to his society at the end of his quest, or that Chaucer may have intended to bring his pilgrims back to the Tabard, does not significantly affect this linearity. In *Gawain*, however, there is a careful mirroring of events and even lines: the references to Troy at the beginning and end; within those, the scenes at Camelot; the references to Arthur as Gawain's uncle and to Morgan as his aunt; the beheading and the return blow; the winter journeys to Bertilak's castle and the Green Chapel. The Knight's Tale works similarly. It opens and closes with a wedding: Theseus' to Hippolyta at the beginning, Palamon's to Emily at the end. Within those are the two funeral scenes, of the pyres for the widows' husbands at the start, for Arcite at the end. After the first of these comes the lovers' rivalry for Emily; before the last, Arcite yields her to Palamon. Arcite's metaphorical death at his exile from Emily, which results in an illness so severe that he is no longer recognisable for his old self and so can return under a new identity, is balanced by his actual death.[4] The fight in the wood gives way in the second half of the poem to the tournament. At the centre is the triad of the three temples, of Venus, Mars and Diana, described with iconographic detail that gives them a significance extending far beyond the confines of the poem.

---

[3] I mean specifically symmetry of the kind that works from the outside in. Repeated patterns are often found in romances (including the Knight's Tale: see p. 95 below); see Vinaver ch. VI.

[4] This is the one point where the strict symmetry of the mirror effect is broken, in that according to that arrangement his death should precede his entrusting of Emily to Palamon – an obvious narrative impossibility. The overall effect of the sequence is not disturbed. A similar thing happens in *Gawain*, where the episodes of his arming necessarily come before the two journeys.

The symmetrical structuring of the Knight's Tale accounts for less of the poem than it does for *Sir Gawain*, but in Chaucer's work it runs alongside other structural patterns. The initial episode, of the widows' appeal for help and the destruction of Thebes, acts rather like the prologues to the dream poems, to introduce and reflect on some of the main themes by juxtaposition. It serves to define the poem as something more than romance: grief, death, and the imposition of order on disorder are its dominant motifs. It is also the first of several repeated sequences in the tale. The opening series of the widows kneeling to ask for mercy, the battle at Thebes and the funeral is repeated on a larger scale later, when the ladies fall on their knees to beg mercy for the lovers, the tournament takes place and Arcite's body is burnt. The parallelism of phrasing is at times very striking:

> Ther kneled in the heighe weye
> A compaignye of ladyes   897–8

who cry,

> 'Have on us wrecched wommen som mercy!'   950

In the forest, 'all the ladyes in the compaignye' cry

> 'Have mercy, Lord, upon us wommen alle!'
> And on hir bare knees adoun they falle.   1757–8

On both occasions the 'gentil duc' reacts 'with herte pitous' (952–3),

> For pitee renneth soone in gentil herte.   1761

The funeral obsequies are not the only ceremony to be repeated: Emily's 'observaunce' of May when the cousins see her in the garden is repeated in Arcite's maying in the forest, and both episodes lead to rivalry between the knights, the first time a quarrel, the second a combat. In both cases the darkness of disorder replaces the brilliance of the celebrations of 'faire, fresshe May'.

There are a number of other striking oppositions of this kind. Before the cousins' quarrel, Emily's appearance in the garden, with all the densely clustered imagery of colour, lilies and roses, the daybreak and the spring, is brought up sharply against the fact of the knights' imprisonment: garden and prison are literally as well as thematically contiguous. The passage is worth quoting at length as it shows so well Chaucer's superb manipulation of conventional materials: by their means he defines Emily as the ideal romance heroine *par excellence*, unsurpassable in beauty and symbolic association, and so the inevitable object of the cousins' adoration.

> It fil ones, in a morwe of May,
> That Emelye, that fairer was to sene
> Than is the lylie upon his stalke grene,
> And fressher than the May with floures newe –
> For with the rose colour stroof hire hewe,
> I noot which was the fyner of hem two –
> Er it were day, as was hir wone to do,
> She was arisen and al redy dight . . .
> Yclothed was she fressh, for to devyse:
> Hir yelow heer was broyded in a tresse
> Bihynde hir bak, a yerde long, I gesse.
> And in the gardyn, at the sonne upriste,
> She walketh up and doun, and as hire liste
> She gadereth floures, party white and rede,
> To make a subtil gerland for hire hede;
> And as an aungel hevenysshly she soong.
> The grete tour, that was so thikke and stroong,
> Which of the castel was the chief dongeoun,
> (Ther as the knyghtes weren in prisoun
> Of which I tolde yow and tellen shal)
> Was evene joynant to the gardyn wal
> There as this Emelye hadde hir pleyynge.
> Bright was the sonne and cleer that morwenynge,
> And Palamoun, this woful prisoner,
> As was his wone, by leve of his gayler,
> Was risen and romed in a chambre an heigh.   1034–41, 1048–65

As in the opening scene of Theseus' triumph and the weeping widows, the light and dark sides of life are inextricable.

Chaucer also uses juxtaposition to contrast ideal action with its opposite. The cousins have a violent quarrel over who has the first claim on Emily, and Arcite brutally renounces the values of blood relationship and of sworn brotherhood in favour of love:

> ' "Who shall yeve a lovere any lawe?" . . .
> And therfore, at the kynges court, my brother,
> Ech man for hymself, ther is noon oother.'   1164, 1181–2

This is immediately followed by a reference to the love between Perotheus and Theseus, which was so great

> That whan that oon was deed, soothly to telle,
> His felawe wente and soughte hym doun in helle.   1199–1200

The Classical legend of Pirithous is different: it is Chaucer who specifically turns it into an example of friendship stronger than death. The same contrast of ideal brotherhood with actual enmity is expressed more concisely, almost with the force of oxymoron, in the preparations for the fight in the forest – a fight intended to be to the death:

> Ther nas no good day, ne no saluyng,
> But streight, withouten word or rehersyng,
> Everich of hem heelp for to armen oother
> As freendly as he were his owene brother.   1649–52

The irony lies in the fact that they are indeed 'brothers' by oath and kinship.

These structural and thematic oppositions reach a climax in the descriptions of the three temples. It is there, at the centre of the mirror patterning of the work, that the strongest statement of the disorder of the world is made. The lovers had complained against the state of the universe, and their complaints were more than the expression of mere personal opinion; but they were none the less in the first instance dramatic utterances appropriate to the speaker and his circumstances. The descriptions of the gods are presented as incontrovertible fact. These gods are not mythic fictions: as planetary influences they represent the literal truth of life in the world.

They shock in the first instance because they are not what one expects. In a courtly romance the principles of decorum would seem to prescribe idealised gods, an enchantingly beautiful Venus, a Mars in glittering armour, a Belphoebe-like Diana. Chaucer has established from the beginning, however, that such a mode of easy idealism is alien to this work, and he presents the gods as emblematic of all the cosmic capriciousness and disorder the human characters have sensed. Good and bad now appear not merely juxtaposed but inextricably jumbled. Lovers' oaths, hope, rashness, beauty, pimping, riches, rape and jealousy are tumbled out in a single heap as morally indistinguishable attributes of Venus: 'wroght on the wal' of her temple are

> The firy strokes of the desirynge
> That loves servantz in this lyf enduren;
> The othes that hir covenantz assuren;
> Plesaunce and Hope, Desir, Foolhardynesse,
> Beautee and Youthe, Bauderie, Richesse,
> Charmes and Force, Lesynges, Flaterye,
> Despense, Bisynesse, and Jalousye,
> That wered of yelewe gooldes a gerland,
> And a cokkow sittynge on hir hand.   1922–30

The *exempla* that follow, of famous lovers of legend, are equally suspect. Some died for love; passion led Solomon to 'folye'; the enchantments of Medea and Circe are ascribed to Venus. Arcite had denied that any law could be stronger than love, and the account of Venus' temple leads to a conclusion that gives his denial the force of divinely sanctioned truth.

> Thus may ye seen that wysdom ne richesse,
> Beautee ne sleighte, strengthe ne hardynesse,
> Ne May with Venus holde champartie,
> For as hir list the world than may she gye.   1947–50

This is a vision of the world very different from the 'faire cheyne of love' binding the cosmos that Theseus envisages. Venus overturns all human ideals of moral action.

The temple of Mars is even nastier. He is the god not only of battle – that is mentioned surprisingly little – but of all irrational violence: of theft and conspiracy, suicide and murder, human and animal blood-lust, fatal accidents:

> Ther saugh I first the derke ymaginyng
> Of Felonye, and al the compassyng;
> The crueel Ire, reed as any gleede;
> The pykepurs, and eek the pale Drede;
> The smylere with the knyf under the cloke;
> The shepne brennynge with the blake smoke;
> The tresoun of the mordrynge in the bedde;
> The open werre, with woundes al bibledde;
> Contek, with blody knyf and sharp manace . . .   1995–2003
>
> Amyddes of the temple sat Meschaunce . . .   2009
>
> The careyne in the busk, with throte ycorve;
> A thousand slayn, and nat of qualm ystorve;
> The tiraunt, with the pray by force yraft;
> The toun destroyed, ther was no thyng laft.
> Yet saugh I brent the shippes hoppesteres;
> The hunte strangled with the wilde beres;
> The sowe freeten the child right in the cradel;
> The cook yscalded, for al his longe ladel.
> Noght was foryeten by the infortune of Marte
> The cartere overryden with his carte:
> Under the wheel ful lowe he lay adoun.   2012–23

That final image gives a startlingly literal interpretation to an image associated with the wheel of Fortune. It is not only the great who fall (though they are there too, in the next section, with Conquest 'sittynge in greet honour' with a sword suspended above him by a thread); there is no condition of life that is safe from the power of these gods. Carters and tyrants are alike crushed. It is no surprise when Arcite, who commits himself to this god of casualties, dies a victim of 'meschaunce'.

Diana would seem to offer the fewest opportunities for such a bleak interpretation, but she provides no alleviation of this pessimistic vision. Her rôle as goddess of chastity is mentioned briefly at the start, but Chaucer swiftly moves on to less attractive aspects of her influence. As the lunar deity, she is the principle of change:

> Undernethe hir feet she hadde a moone, –
> Wexynge it was and sholde wanye soone.   2077–8

Such a theme is appropriate for the narrative since Emily must change her allegiance from maidenhood to marriage; but if that is a positive transformation, the 'change' depicted in the temple is not. The very ordering of waxing followed by waning implies a falling away, the downward turn of Fortune's wheel. The specific examples of transformation are of a more sinister violence. Chaucer's avoidance throughout the rest of his work of the metamorphosis of man into a lower order of life has already been mentioned; this passage is the great exception.

> Ther saugh I how woful Calistopee,
> Whan that Diane agreved was with here,
> Was turned from a womman til a bere . . .   2056–8

> Ther saugh I Dane, yturned til a tree . . .   2062

> Ther saugh I Attheon an hert ymaked,
> For vengeaunce that he saugh Diane al naked;
> I saugh how that his houndes have hym caught
> And freten hym, for that they knewe hym naught.   2065–8

The violence and the reduction of human being to passive victim are of a piece with the descriptions of the activities of Mars and Venus. As triple Hecate, Diana also has connections with the 'derke regioun' of Pluto. Her role as Lucina, goddess of childbirth, is depicted as non-ideally as all the rest: the woman in labour who cries out to her for help 'for hir child so longe was unborn' is given no assurance of survival.

The other gods who play some part in the Tale are similarly presented. Juno is invariably mentioned with horror by the Theban princes. Arcite dreams that Mercury appears to him and bids,

> 'To Atthenes shaltou wende,
> Ther is thee shapen of thy wo an ende.'   1391–2

He follows the advice; but the god's implied promise of hope is cruelly misleading, for the 'ende' prepared for his woe is not joy but death. Saturn is the most sinister of them all:

> Myn is the drenchyng in the see so wan;
> Myn is the prison in the derke cote;
> Myn is the stranglyng and hangyng by the throte . . .   2456–8

In the careful parallelism between the human and divine characters, Emily is paired with Diana, Palamon with Venus, Arcite with Mars. Since Saturn resolves the dispute between the other gods, it might be expected that Theseus would correspond to him; but Chaucer does not allow this to happen. Theseus' father Egeus indeed seems to be introduced partly to forestall such an equation. Theseus is associated with the other three gods – he bears Mars on his banner, he has been a 'servant' of love in his youth, and in going hunting, 'after Mars he serveth now Dyane'. In his closing speech on the metaphysical ordering of the universe he looks beyond these three, and beyond anything Saturn can represent, to a philosophical or divine principle, the 'First Moevere', whom he identifies with Jupiter. Jupiter has already made a brief appearance (2442) as a rather ineffective peacemaker in the quarrel between the gods; the contrast between his inadequacy at that point and the omnipotent rôle Theseus ascribes to him highlights the difference between pagan pantheon and Christian truth. Theseus has no other name to give his First Mover. His identification is wrong, but his understanding of a higher divine providential principle beyond the capriciousness and cruelty of the lesser forces of destiny is certainly more important than his limited interpretation. For over two thousand lines of the narrative, the supernatural order is seen as a principle of disorder, disrupting all human attempts to live by ideals. Only in the least-two hundred lines is there any indication that those ideals may have a 'parfit and stable' root beyond the mutability of the world.

It is an answer, of sorts; but it does not altogether resolve the problem. Arcite has died still questioning the nature of 'felicity' with ever greater urgency:

> What is this world? what asketh men to have?
> Now with his love, now in his colde grave
> Allone, withouten any compaignye.   2777–9

Theseus' final great speech gives an answer in terms of faith, and offers a pragmatic solution that enables life to continue; but the question remains central to human thought and experience.

Not even this much of an answer is given until the very end. In the body of the poem the characters feel themselves helpless before the forces of destiny or the gods. At its simplest, this helplessness means that when they are at the bottom of the wheel they know they must endure patiently. The widows deny that they are grieved by Theseus's 'glorie and honour'; Arcite urges patience on Palamon when he cries out in prison. Such reactions at least imply a kind of understanding, that the universe is predictable though unpleasant; but things are rarely so straightforward. The cousins' inability to measure their own state is more unsettling. The damned and the saved in Dante's great *summa* at least know where they are; not so Arcite, released from prison at Perotheus' intercession, only to be exiled out of sight of Emily.

> He sayde, 'Allas that day that I was born!
> Now is my prisoun worse than biforn;
> Now is me shape eternally to dwelle
> Noght in purgatorie, but in helle.
> Allas, that evere knew I Perotheus!
> For elles hadde I dwelled with Theseus,
> Yfetered in his prisoun everemo.
> Thanne hadde I been in blisse, and nat in wo.' 1223–30

Only the proof will distinguish hell from heaven – and perhaps not even that, for at this point each of the cousins bitterly envies the other. There is no way of knowing how to achieve one's desire. Providence and Fortune may appear in such strange forms as to be unrecognisable. Arcite continues with a lament broadened out from a consideration of his own state to the state of mankind:

> Allas, why pleynen folk so in commune
> Or purveiaunce of God, or of Fortune,
> That yeveth hem ful ofte in many a gyse
> Wel bettre than they kan hemself devyse? 1251–4

A man may be murdered when he achieves the riches or the release from prison that he has desired:

> We witen nat what thing we prayen heere:
> We faren as he that dronke is as a mous.
> A dronke man woot wel he hath an hous,
> But he noot which the righte wey is thider,
> And to a dronke man the wey is slider.
> And certes, in this world so faren we;
> We seken fast after felicitee,
> But we goon wrong ful often, trewely. 1260–7

Universal in implication as the lines are, they are also especially appropriate to Arcite, who throughout the story confuses ends and means. He

> wende and hadde a greet opinioun
> That if I myghte escapen from prisoun,
> Thanne hadde I been in joye and perfit heele,
> Ther now I am exiled fro my wele.   1269–72

Later, before the tournament, he prays for victory, only to find that
his triumph is hollow. His speeches on the state of the world are thus
a dramatic projection; but they work the other way too – Chaucer
wants this point of view to be expressed, and he puts Arcite into the
appropriate situations to express it.

Palamon knows what he wants – Emily – and never loses sight of
that; but his suffering is just as intense, and just as all-embracing in
its implications. Chaucer always stresses the parallelism of the two
knights, from the moment when they are found lying side by side on
the battlefield wearing identical coats of arms. Each has a great speech
in which he declares his love for Emily, and each denounces the
condition of human life. Where Arcite laments man's erring pursuit
of felicity, Palamon indicts the 'cruel goddes' and their capricious,
even vicious, control of human affairs. He too sees man as little better
than a beast:

> What is mankynde moore unto you holde
> Than is the sheep that rouketh in the folde?
> For slayn is man right as another beest.   1307–9

A beast, moreover, ends its suffering with death, whereas

> man after his deeth moot wepe and pleyne,
> Though in this world he have care and wo.   1320–1

It is Palamon who asks the question that echoes down through the
Canterbury Tales, and indeed through the whole history of metaphysical thought:

> What governance is in this prescience,
> That giltelees tormenteth innocence?   1313–14

Different answers are given in different tales according to the system
of values they adopt; for the moment Palamon does not attempt to
answer it.

> The answere of this lete I to dyvynys,   1323

but the theological answers have never been entirely satisfactory.

The gods who take the greatest part in the action of the Knight's

Tale, Saturn, Mars, Venus and Diana, are all seen as malevolent. As planetary deities they are agents of destiny or Fortune:

> Fortune hath yeven us this adversitee.
> Som wikke aspect or disposicioun
> Of Saturne, by som constellacioun,
> Hath yeven us this.   1086–9

Theseus' attempts to impose order on the chaos of fortune are more persistent than successful. His retribution on Creon leads to the downfall of Thebes; his replacing of the fight in the forest by a tournament ends in death for the victor. He is none the less an ideal figure, a man of 'pitee', 'gentilesse', justice and mercy; but he is acting in an imperfect universe. The speeches on the state of the world that Chaucer gives to the knights are drawn from Boethius, from the prisoner's bitter attacks on Providence. Theseus' great closing speech is again Boethian, but taken this time from Philosophia's answers to Boethius' complaints.[5]

> The Firste Moevere of the cause above,
> Whan he first made the faire cheyne of love,
> Greet was th'effect, and heigh was his entente.   2987–9

There is a strong implication, however, that this is a matter to be taken on trust: the events of the tale hardly justify it, least of all the presentation of the gods. Theseus is making a declaration of faith; a faith that also has implications for action.

> Thanne is it wysdom, as it thynketh me,
> To maken vertue of necessitee,
> And take it weel that we may nat eschue.   3041–3

This may sound like a doctrine of passive acceptance, but it is more than that. It is true that in contrast to almost every other romance the Knight's Tale stresses endurance rather than action,[6] but Theseus' own interpretation of his dictum is more positive. He will stress the making virtue more than the necessity; and he accordingly marries Palamon to Emily to produce a happy ending from the tragedy like a conjuror's rabbit. 'Making virtue of necessity' thus becomes closer to the conventional generic perspective of the romance than one might expect: it turns into something very similar to the idea of taking the adventure that shall fall to you, accepting the challenge of the quest,

---

[5] J. A. W. Bennett gives the appropriate excerpts from Chaucer's translation in his edition, *The Knight's Tale* (2nd ed., London, 1958).

[6] See the study by Georgia Ronan Crampton, *The Condition of Creatures: Suffering and Action in Chaucer and Spenser* (New Haven, 1974) chs II, III.

in a way that turns passive endurance into active heroic endeavour. Old Egeus insists on a more tragic view of life. He is given a speech stressing the universality of death, which is platitudinous only because it is self-evidently and incontrovertibly true; and he uses the familiar metaphor of life as a pilgrimage. Theseus redefines the idea of the 'thurghfare ful of wo' into something more like a quest, and even produces the reward at the end of it in the shape of Emily. In the marriage, the human story and its metaphysical implications come together. The 'faire cheyne of love' binds the cosmos and the elements; it is also the force that brings together nations into alliance and people to matrimony.[7] That Palamon finally achieves Emily is a way of transcending the capriciousness of fortune to enact one's faith in the stability of the First Mover.

It is a process that comes impressively close to the heart of romance. As Northrop Frye has expounded,[8] romance is the mode of the natural cycle through winter to spring, through death to rebirth – the same turning that Chaucer envisages as the fall and rise of Fortune's wheel, but projected on to a series of more mythic metaphors and truths. It is also the essence of Christian doctrine, where death is superseded by resurrection. Christianity is the religion of romance. The Knight's Tale is not a Christian allegory; it is, consciously, a Christian analogy, in which the affirmation of continuing life after Arcite's death is seen as a reflection of the ultimate providential ordering of the universe. The setting is pagan: Palamon and Arcite have none of the special insight into God's workings vouchsafed to the saint. All they can see are the operations of Fortune and the malevolent gods, and those are very disordered indeed. But there is a higher vision possible, and it is there that Chaucer ends.

The depth of meaning in the Knight's Tale is impressive. Courtly romances since the time of Chretien de Troyes had consciously included a level of meaning beyond mere narrative, a *sens* to inform their traditional subject-matter; but there is nothing to equal the metaphysical reach of the Knight's Tale. The only comparable work is Chaucer's own *Troilus and Criseyde*, and there the inner meaning is given such extensive treatment that the story could almost be seen as an extended *exemplum* of love *versus* mutability. In the *Troilus*, romance is subsumed into tragedy; and the explicit Christianity of the close can only exist beyond the confines of the fiction. In the Knight's Tale Chaucer can find a place for Theseus' affirmation of faith within

---

[7] See Boethius II m. 8: 'This love halt togidres peples joyned with an holy boond, and knytteth sacrement of mariages of chaste loves.' Chaucer had already used the passage extensively in *Troilus* III 1744–64.

[8] See *Anatomy of Criticism*, Third Essay, and *The Secular Scripture: A Study of the Structure of Romance* (Cambridge, Mass., 1976).

the structure of the poem. In both poems, however, it is hard to reconcile the ending fully with what has gone before.

The Knight's Tale raises questions; it does not finally answer them. It can ask them quite specifically, as over the rival demerits of imprisonment or exile:

> Yow loveres axe I now this questioun:
> Who hath the worse, Arcite or Palamoun?   1347–8

In a work such as the *Filocolo* such questions are raised precisely in order to be resolved; but Chaucer does not stay to give an answer, any more than he answers Palamon's question about the order underlying the suffering of the innocent, 'What governance is in this prescience?', or Arcite's 'What is this world?' This refusal to resolve is echoed in the perpetual juxtapositions of joy and grief, brilliant colour and darkness. At the level of style too the Knight's Tale reaches out towards both extremes. Most immediately striking is the high rhetorical formality: the great set pieces of the descriptions of the temples or of the combatants in the tournament, the philosophical declamations, the elaboration of style through figures of speech. Chaucer's use of *occupatio*, the device of describing something under the pretence of refusing to do so, is notorious, and has even been seen as satirical. This is not usually the case: he often uses the device to summarise a section of the *Teseida* that he does not wish to give in full, and the figure can be strikingly effective for conveying a sense of richness of background, as if the poet finds even describing the tip of the iceberg overwhelming. Running in counterpoint to this use of high style, however, is a rougher, more idiomatic use of language that one would expect to be rhetorically indecorous, inappropriate, in an aristocratic romance, but which possesses a deeper decorum appropriate to the greater reach of the Knight's Tale.

Style is keyed very carefully to tone throughout the poem. High style demands, for instance, imagery of a certain level, and up to a point Chaucer fulfils that requirement. It is the lark that announces the dawn, not the more familiar cock that acts as timekeeper to the fabliaux; Palamon and Arcite are compared to the noblest beasts, lion and tiger or boars; Lygurge and Emetreus are accompanied by similarly noble beasts, bulls, an eagle, lions and leopards. Chaucer also, however, draws on a range of more commonplace animals that elsewhere in the *Canterbury Tales* are mentioned only in fabliaux or similarly colloquial stories. These references are always belittling. The drunk mouse and the huddled sheep are intentionally reductive images for the condition of mankind. Arcite's comparison of the cousins' rivalry to dogs fighting for a bone that is snatched away by a kite (1177–80) is a miniature beast-fable whose drop in style matches their falling away from noble ideals of behaviour. The sheer folly of their fighting for the love of a woman who knows nothing whatsoever about it is brusquely expressed by Theseus in a similarly colloquial image:

> She woot namoore of al this hoote fare,
> By God, than woot a cokkow or an hare!   1809–10

Cuckoos and hares both have sexual associations: the comparison not only mocks the pretensions of the lovers, it points up how far the cousins' passion is from any practical fulfilment. Such unworldly absolutism demands a little gentle mockery.

Most of these shifts in stylistic and tonal level have a clearly definable function. There are others, however, that are more unsettling, which introduce a note of flippancy when the serious potential of the work would seem to be at its greatest. Emily 'caste a freendlich ye' on the triumphant Arcite,

> For wommen, as to speken in comune,
> Thei folwen alle the favour of Fortune.   2681–2

His injury and death are treated with no rhetorical cushioning of hard facts.

> As blak he lay as any cole or crowe,
> So was the blood yronne in his face,   2692–3

as if the physical damage lessened his humanity. The description of the corruption of his wound is clinically analytic, and ends with a dismissive shrug:

> Ther Nature wol nat wirche,
> Fare wel phisik! go ber the man to chirche!   2759–60

The detachment from Arcite as a moral and emotional being is at least useful at this point, for the moment of death is usually the cue for a summing up of a man's life; and that would be an embarrassment here,[9] where such a summary of Arcite would be all but identical to a summary of the still living Palamon. Insistence on the physical detail and the commonplaceness of dying replaces a metaphysical consideration of death, which is given a more forceful expression in Arcite's final lament a few lines later. The destination of his soul is shrugged off in a similarly casual way:

[9] See Charles Muscatine, *Chaucer and the French Tradition* (Berkeley and Los Angeles, 1957) p. 186.

His spirit chaunged hous and wente ther,
As I cam nevere, I kan nat tellen wher.
Therfore I stynte, I nam no divinistre;
Of soules fynde I nat in this registre. 2809–12

This is less a refusal to follow the soul of a pagan to hell, or to open a debate on whether good pagans have a different fate, than an insistence on keeping a focus on the earth. The saints' lives can assume an encompassing benevolent supernatural order; but that is precisely what the Knight's Tale has called into question. The lines are unsettling, and they are meant to be. They extend to the narrator the inability of the characters within the story to find in the universe any order perceptible to reason or to human knowledge.

Interjections of this kind are alien to the mode of courtly romance and philosophic seriousness of the rest of the tale; they disturb the perspective that the genre and the stylistic level of the rest of the work suggest. They serve as a useful reminder, therefore, that such a perspective is only relative. Seen from one angle, love may be all-demanding and all-powerful; seen from another, it is mere stupidity. Emily may be defined through the initial description of her as the quintessential heroine of romance, but there may also be a level at which she is no different from women 'in comune'. Arcite may be given a hero's funeral, but medicine can fail with any man, and, as Egeus points out, there is nothing in the least special or individual about death. It is, at the least, appropriate for the opening tale of the whole work that it should be able to look askance at the perspectives it adopts. If the Knight's Tale sets a standard for the rest, it does not pretend to give a definitive view of the world and those who live in it.

5

Links within the Fragments

If there is still some doubt as to Chaucer's final ordering of the fragments of the *Canterbury Tales*, there is very little as to the arrangement of tales within the fragments. There, the ordering is his, and he arranged them in the way we have them for good reasons. This chapter is concerned with what holds the stories of the various groups together.

We know very little about how Chaucer set about writing the *Canterbury Tales*. There is evidence that he pressed into service some poems that he had originally written as separate works, such as the story of Palamon and Arcite and the life of St. Cecilia. He certainly moved tales from one teller to another, and he probably tried out tales in different combinations. The closeness of some of the relationships between adjacent tales also makes it likely that he wrote some stories specifically to follow on from each other. We cannot appreciate the *Canterbury Tales* unless we can attempt to understand why Chaucer sets up the groups of stories in the way he does; and such an understanding casts a great deal of light not only on the work itself but on Chaucer's poetic methods – his mind and art.[1]

There is, however, no single pattern to follow throughout the *Tales*. Poetic and generic contrasts are always important, but so are similarities. Some fragments are linked primarily by plot motif, others by theme. Generalisation is impossible, and misleading: each tale is sharply individualised, and its individuality is highlighted by the precision of its contrast with the next story.

---

[1] There have been some fine recent studies of some of the fragments of the Canterbury Tales, and these are cited under the appropriate sections below. Mention should be made here of two books that look at the wider relationships between the tales, Trevor Whittock's *A Reading of the Canterbury Tales* (Cambridge, 1968), and P. M. Kean's *Chaucer and the Making of English Poetry* Vol. II: *The Art of Narrative* (London, 1972).

Fragment I(A): Knight, Miller, Reeve, Cook

Harry Bailey has the pilgrims draw lots to settle who should begin the story-telling; and

> Were it by aventure, or sort, or cas,
> The sothe is this, the cut fil to the Knyght.   844–5

Whether the Host fixed the result is an unanswerable question, and irrelevant to the main issues. Chaucer wants the Knight's Tale to come first, and the Knight is the appropriate person to tell it, both socially (in the fiction of the pilgrimage) and rhetorically (in the matching of narrator to generic perspective).

The nature of the tale at once sets off the story-telling from the framework. The General Prologue had claimed to work at the level of journalism, of reported observable fact, of

> al the condicioun
> Of eche of hem, so as it semed me,
> And whiche they weren, and of what degree,
> And eek in what array that they were inne.   38–41

The Knight's Tale transports its audience to a different realm of experience altogether – to the worlds of art and imagination. The precise reference to time and place, April at the Tabard Inn in Southwark, is replaced by the exotic world of ancient Greece. The General Prologue's concern with surface appearances is superseded by a questioning of the meaning of life, and the details of the Miller's nose or the Cook's running sore by a study of the metaphysical context of all human action. The cook who makes his appearance in the Knight's Tale (2020) is there not as a type of his profession nor as an individual but as an example of 'the infortune of Marte'.

One way for Chaucer to differentiate the General Prologue from the story-telling would have been to substitute narrative for the static series of portraits. This of course happens; but the first tale itself contains three portraits, of Emily, Lygurge and Emetreus. Their presence serves not to assimilate the Tale to the Prologue but to heighten the differences. Emily is described as much symbolically, by association with the spring, flowers, angels, as visually: when an apparently visual image is given, it turns out to be something different –

> Emelye, that fairer was to sene
> Than is the lylie upon his stalke grene . . .   1035–6

The point of comparison is not the observable, physical detail of the green stalk, but of beauty in the abstract; and the lily brings in too associations of purity and chastity. Emily is sometimes accused of being merely a conventional heroine after the vigour and liveliness of the Prologue portraits: but what a convention, when it is handled like this! She is established at once as the ultimate in ladies of romance, and so the devotion that Palamon and Arcite feel for her needs no further explanation or justification. The imagery and associations surrounding Emily are unparalleled in the naturalistic world of the Prologue. The same is true of the two warriors. Their attributes are rich and exotic, and selected to fit the tale's scheme of rival planetary influences.[2] Beyond that they are two-dimensional, and need to be so: their function in the tale is a structural and rhetorical one, to give outward form to the opposing forces and to add to the ornamentation of surface opulence. Any potential for individual characterisation would detract from that.

The Knight's Tale tells the story of two lovers who are rivals for a single lady. Both are young, for youth and love go together: Theseus too had been love's servant 'in my tyme' (1814). Love in old age is possible –

> A man moot ben a fool, or yong or oold   1812

– but the folly is more apparent than the appropriateness. The proper sphere of old age is in counsel:

> In elde is bothe wysdom and usage;
> Men may the olde atrenne, and noght atrede.   2448–9

Palamon and Arcite follow all the conventions of quintessential courtly loving. They fall in love with Emily at first sight, and their passion is potentially fatal:

> The fresshe beautee sleeth me sodeynly
> Of hire that rometh in the yonder place,
> And but I have hir mercy and hir grace,
> That I may seen hire atte leeste weye,
> I nam but deed; ther is namoore to seye.   1118–22

That this is more than hyperbole is demonstrated by Arcite's illness when he is exiled from the sight of her.

The tale that follows turns all this inside out. The Host invites the lordly Monk to follow on, but the Miller insists on interrupting; and his tale 'quites' the Knight's brilliantly – and in a way which is entirely Chaucerian and minimally naturalistic or dramatic. The

---

[2] See Douglas Brooks and Alastair Fowler, 'The meaning of Chaucer's *Knight's Tale*', *Medium Aevum* XXXIX (1970) 123–46, esp. pp. 130–4.

Knight's romance had encompassed within itself one opposing genre, tragedy; the Miller counters with another generic anti-type, the fabliau. The opening formula, 'Whilom ther was –', is almost identical to the Knight's; after that, nothing is the same, but many things are instantly recognisable because they have already appeared, if in a different form, in the Knight's Tale.

The setting is not 'far away and long ago', but contemporary Oxford, portrayed in remarkably accurate detail.[3] If the sources of the Knight's Tale are exclusively literary and philosophical, the sources for the Miller's lie not only in some hypothetical fabliau but in the physical phenomena of Oxford life – in the layout of the town, the building works at Osney Abbey, a student's need for lodgings, swearing by the local saint, cat-holes and kneading-troughs. The plot itself is at least as impossible as the plot of the Knight's Tale, but the accumulation of authentic detail gives the tale an entirely artificial aura of plausibility.

Nicholas, unlike the Clerk of Oxenford of the General Prologue, prefers his *sautrie* to his books. Despite knowing about 'deerne love', he has a room

> Allone, withouten any compaignye 3204

– a line that last occurred in Arcite's final agonized meditation on death. By the time the carpenter's young wife is introduced, immediately after the opening description of Nicholas, part of the plot is already predictable. From the start, the inappropriateness of her marriage is emphasised:

> She was wylde and yong, and he was old . . .
> Men sholde wedden after hire estaat,
> For youthe and elde is often at debaat. 3225, 3229–30

In contrast to the ideal of the wisdom of the old mentioned in the Knight's Tale, John the carpenter's 'wit was rude' – a fact amply demonstrated in the course of the tale.

The description of Emily laid down an elevated pattern of ideal female beauty. She was presented throughout in terms of the most spiritual of the five senses, sight and hearing; she is associated with lilies, roses, May, the sunrise, an angel. Strip both heroines of their external attributes of garlands or clothing and they might look very similar; but the impression Alisoun makes could hardly be more different. Emily's hair is yellow; Alisoun's face shines more brightly than the gold of hard cash. The first simile used for Emily is the lily; for

---

[3] See the study by J. A. W. Bennett, *Chaucer at Oxford and at Cambridge* (Oxford, 1974), chs I, II.

Alisoun, a weasel. Barnyard imagery throngs her portrait. She is softer than wool, sings more loudly than a swallow (a comparison of dubious complimentariness),

> she koude skippe and make game,
> As any kyde or calf folwynge his dame, 3259–60

she is skittish 'as is a joly colt'. These animals are a world away from the lions and boars of the Knight's Tale. If Emily was fairer to see than the lily, with all its symbolic associations, the equivalent lines for Alisoun are suspicious in the extreme:

> She was ful moore blisful on to see
> Than is the newe pere-jonette tree. 3247–8

The mere mention of a pear-tree seems to have been sufficient to raise a snigger in the Middle Ages, and the associations barely touched on here are made explicit in the Merchant's Tale.

It is not only what Alisoun looks like and sounds like that characterises her. Chaucer also says what she smelled, tasted and felt like, in a way that puts the audience into extraordinarily close physical contact with her: one would need to poke her to find that she is

> Softer than the wolle is of a wether, 3249

or take a bite to discover

> Hir mouth was sweete as bragot or the meeth,
> Or hoord of apples leyd in hey or heeth. 3261–2

She is intoxicating, tempting – and everyone who comes into contact with her falls instantly. She is 'upright as a bolt', but 'upright' in Middle English also means 'flat on one's back', and is used with this explicitly sexual meaning in the following tale.[4] In addition to all this, her clothes are described in fine detail, but the description keeps passing through to what is underneath them: 'hir body gent and smal', 'hir lendes'. The description does not follow the prescription for the rhetorical *effictio* of starting at the top and working downwards.[5] It starts somewhere around the middle; moves up to her face; comes back to the middle –

> By hir girdel heeng a purs of lether; 3250

[4] I 4194, 4266.
[5] Kevin S. Kiernan, 'The art of the descending catalogue, and a fresh look at Alisoun', *Chaucer Review* X (1975–6) 1–16.

returns to her collar; descends to her feet and works back up her legs –

> Hir shoes were laced on hir legges hye;   3267

and finishes at last in the inevitable way:

> She was a prymerole, a piggesnye,
> For any lord to leggen in his bedde,
> Or yet for any good yeman to wedde.   3268–70

It is hardly surprising that marriage comes as an afterthought. In contrast, Emily's unattained virginity made her all the more inaccessible.

The progress of Nicholas's courtship follows predictably from this. There is no prison or walled garden; he merely waylays Alisoun on the landing,

> And prively he caughte hire by the queynte,
> And seyde, 'Ywis, but if ich have my wille,
> For deerne love of thee, lemman, I spille.'
> And heeld hire harde by the haunchebones,
> And seyde, 'Lemman, love me al atones,
> Or I wol dyen, also God me save!'   3276–81

Whether or not 'spill' and 'die' are intended as *doubles-entendres*,[6] there is no doubt that Nicholas's threat of death is not to be taken as seriously as Palamon's, and he certainly would not mistake this woman for a goddess. He knows what he wants, and it is not worship from a distance.

The parody of the Knight's Tale requires two lovers. Fond as he is of Alisoun, the carpenter is scarcely presented as a rival in the sexual stakes, though the addition of yet another man to the tale is not accidental. The parish clerk Absolon is also introduced by way of a formal description. With his golden curls and grey eyes he might approximate to the courtly ideal of masculine beauty; but the effect is delightfully spoiled by extra details – his hair 'strouted as a fanne large and brode', his eyes are 'greye as goos' (the correct alliterating phrase, 'grey as glass', is used for the Prioress's eyes, and for one of the miller's daughters few good features in the Reeve's Tale). He is dressed up to the minute in fashion, 'with Poules wyndow carven on his shoos'. He is fond of taverns, and barmaids; and last but not least significant,

---

[6] The words were commonly used with a sexual double meaning in the sixteenth century; the evidence for such an implication in the fourteenth century depends on lines such as those quoted, which could be no more than the misapplication of courtly hyperbole.

> He was somdeel squaymous
> Of fartyng.   3337–8

We first see him in action in church, censing the wives of the parish, and Alisoun in particular. He is so impassioned by her that he refuses to take the offertory, 'for curteisie' – a curious application of a good courtly term, almost as curious as Alisoun's appeal to Nicholas to 'Do wey youre handes, for youre curteisye!' Absolon woos her with serenades, alcohol, cake and bribery; he even resorts to the love-language of the Song of Songs.[7]

In the Knight's Tale, the plot is resolved by the action of the gods – the planetary deities. In the Miller's Tale, despite Nicholas's claims, it is not really astrological knowledge that enables him to predict a flood, nor does God actually intend to repeat the Noah episode with the carpenter and his wife escaping in their kneading-troughs. The supernatural in this tale is a non-starter. Everything happens on the level of the commonplace and everyday, however extraordinary the events of the plot may be.

The reduction in level pervades every aspect of the tale. Instead of the months and seasons with their rich associations, it is the days of the week that are stressed.[8] Absolon, like Arcite, has a premonition of the future which he misinterprets, but there is no vision of Mercury, and the true meaning of the omen is rather less dignified than death:

> My mouth hath icched al this longe day;
> That is a signe of kissyng atte leeste.   3682–3

Instead of the lovers' rivalry being fought out with all the panoply of chivalry, it is resolved in the crudest way possible. Alisoun is far from being an impartial observer, as Emily is at the tournament; she is sexually committed to Nicholas from the start, and has some very unspiritual ideas about discouraging Absolon. The poetic level too is a brilliant contrast to the Knight's Tale. In an oral reading of the two tales, the Miller's goes at almost twice the speed of the Knight's, line for line: the French and Latin elements in the vocabulary of the Knight's Tale are largely replaced by light Germanic monosyllables, the weighty set speeches by colloquial exclamations and even the rhythms of folk verse:

---

[7] R. E. Kaske, 'The *Canticum Canticorum* in the Miller's Tale', *Studies in Philology* LIX (1962) 479–500.

[8] The days are only specified at one point in the Knight's Tale, with the lovers' prayers on a Monday and the tournament the next day; the climax of the Miller's Tale is similarly timed, from the preparations of Monday to the events of early Tuesday morning. John Hirsh suggests a background in popular superstition in answer to his title question 'Why does the Miller's Tale take place on a Monday?', *English Language Notes* XIII (1975) 86–90.

'What! Nicholay! what, how! what, looke adoun!
Awak, and thenk on Cristes passioun!
I crouche thee from elves and fro wightes.'
Therwith the nyght-spel seyde he anon-rightes
On four halves of the hous aboute,
And on the thresshfold of the dore withoute:
'Jhesu Crist and seinte Benedight,
Blesse this hous from every wikked wight,
For nyghtes verye, the white *pater-noster*!
Where wentestow, seinte Petres soster?' 3477–86

The vocabulary drops markedly in social and moral level: 'wenche' and 'lemman' replace 'lady', and the lexical difference between them is one that Chaucer stresses several times in the *Canterbury Tales*:

I am a gentil womman and no wenche IV 2202

Ther nys no difference, trewely,
Betwixe a wyf that is of heigh degree,
If of hir body dishonest she bee,
And a povre wenche, oother than this –
If it so be that they werke bothe amys –
But that the gentile, in estaat above,
She shal be cleped his lady, as in love;
And for that oother is a povre womman,
She shal be cleped his wenche or his lemman.
And God it woot, myn owene deere brother,
Men leyn that oon as lowe as lith that oother. IX 212–22

If the words are the same morally, in tone they belong to different worlds. Alisoun is 'so gay a popelote or swich a wenche'; she could never be a lady.

The greatest contrast with the Knight's Tale is that the Miller's remains a story. It is that rare thing, a mediaeval tale with no further meaning whatsoever. Fabliaux commonly have morals, even if they are rather limited in application; but at the end of the Miller's Tale, where the summarising *moralitas* should appear, there is only a recapitulation of the narrative:

Thus swyved was this carpenteris wyf,
For al his kepyng and his jalousye;
And Absolon hath kist hir nether ye;
And Nicholas is scalded in the towte.
This tale is doon, and God save al the rowte! 3850–4

Instead of the lovers' constant and unfulfilled efforts to fathom the mysteries of human life, John the carpenter recommends ignorance:

'Men sholde nat knowe of Goddes pryvetee.
Ye, blessed be alwey a lewed man
That noght but oonly his bileve kan!
So ferde another clerk with astromye;
He walked in the feeldes, for to prye
Upon the sterres, what ther sholde bifalle,
Til he was in a marle-pit yfalle;
He saugh nat that.'   3454–61

There is no sense of any order beyond the everyday world, and the carpenter is a gullible fool for thinking that there might be, that God might intervene in earthly affairs. 'The drenchyng in the see so wan' may be Saturn's province, but God is not going to do the same. That the innocent suffered while the guilty went free had troubled Palamon deeply; as in so much comedy, in the Miller's Tale it is the fool, not the knave, who comes off worst. John ends as a target of general mockery, with a broken arm, while Alisoun goes scot free. If the tale does have any meaning beyond the surface narrative, it can only emerge in relation to the Knight's Tale: there is nothing at all in the story in isolation. In 'quiting' the preceding tale it offers a rival reading of the world – a world of cheerfully amoral disorder, with no metaphysical depth whatsoever.[9]

The Reeve is even more insistent that he will 'quite' the tale just ended, and in a more aggressive fashion:

Leveful is with force force of-showve.   3912

As a carpenter, he feels insulted by the Miller's story, so he will return the insult with a tale against millers. The Reeve, like the Friar and Summoner later, uses fiction as an anti-personnel weapon. Such an abuse of the 'correct' functions of literature says less about the character of the Reeve than about the weapon he chooses – the fabliau. The level of insult belongs with the most non-idealist genre. Fabliaux are *cherles tales*, and the churls who tell them are the least courteous of the pilgrims. Moreover, the chief characters of the fabliaux are drawn from the same lower- or middle-class social level as their tellers, so it is easy for one pilgrim to insert another into his tale. It matters less that the tales told by the Reeve and Summoner express their characters, than that the level of the genre they are given defines their characters. The use of the fabliau for an insult-match not only demonstrates the dramatic conception of the pilgrimage, but also defines the genre in a brilliantly unexpected way.

[9] This argument is forcefully put by Morton W. Bloomfield, 'The Miller's Tale – an unBoethian interpretation', in Mandel and Rosenberg pp. 205–11.

The ways in which the Reeve's Tale 'quites' the Miller's are also more than merely dramatic. It would seem much more likely that Chaucer had the two tales in mind as a pair – one Oxford student sleeps with one woman, two Cambridge students sleep with two – than that he looked for tales dramatically appropriate to the Miller and the Reeve. That Oswald is a carpenter was, in the General Prologue, one of the least important things about him: the couplet giving the information (613–14) is entirely detachable from its context, and could even have been added as an afterthought to provide the grounding for the scheme of personal rivalry in which Chaucer roots the contrasting tales. Certainly the quarrel in the link between the Reeve and Miller accounts for very little of the element of requital in the tale.

The first 'quiting' was primarily generic: romance, with all the elevation of style and ideals that that implies, *versus* fabliau, treated not merely at a low level but as a close parody of the high. The Reeve's Tale, by contrast, pays back the Miller's on the same generic level:

> I shal hym quite anoon;
> Right in his cherles termes wol I speke.   3916–17

If the Knight never in his life spoke 'vileynye' to anyone, and tells a courtly romance, the Reeve will use the genre at the opposite end of the spectrum, fabliau, precisely for the purposes of insult. The competition will now be fought on equal terms, in equivalent university towns; but the Reeve will push ahead by sheer advantage of numbers, both because he has two students successful, and because in deflowering the miller's daughter as well as cuckolding him his tale kicks his rival twice, where John the carpenter only suffered once, through his wife. Physical injury is repaid on equal terms. John knocks himself out and breaks his arm, Symkyn is beaten over the head and left lying; but the students run off with the cake, thus depriving the miller of the profit he had hoped to make, and so Symkyn suffers materially as well as physically.

If the linking of the tales works primarily at the level of equivalence, there are inversions too. John is a mere fool, Symkyn is a knave, so there is perhaps a little more poetic justice in the Reeve's Tale. The two students however come out of the affair better off than before, not only with their flour and the cake made from it but with their conquest of the women, while the rivals of the Miller's Tale receive their share of damage. In the Miller's Tale it was Nicholas, with his parody of courtly love speech, and Absolon, with his affectation of 'curteisie', who laid a claim, however minimal, to social pretensions. In the Reeve's Tale the miller and his wife insist on their rank:

> A wyf he hadde, ycomen of noble kyn;
> The person of the toun hir fader was.
> With hire he yaf ful many a panne of bras,
> For that Symkyn sholde in his blood allye.
> She was yfostred in a nonnerye;
> For Symkyn wolde no wyf, as he sayde,
> But she were wel ynorissed and a mayde,
> To saven his estaat of yomanrye.   3942–9

It is a devastating attack, carried out in the same tones of approving neutrality, on some of Chaucer's favourite targets of the General Prologue – social climbing, the corruption of the clergy, the substitution of financial for ethical values. The parson also has great ambitions for his granddaughter,

> to bestowe hire hye
> Into som worthy blood of auncetrye,   3981–2

despite her less than perfect looks. The narrator, however, calls her a 'wenche': he is not in the least taken in. The students, by contrast, are provincials, speaking in northern dialect, and their education does not prevent the miller from looking down on them intellectually too:

> 'By my thrift, yet shal I blere hir ye,
> For al the sleighte in hir philosophye.'   4049–50

He refers to them as 'children' (4098), and speaks of their 'art' as if it were mere infant make-believe, that could turn the tiny house into an enormous one by mere imagination. After all this it is hardly surprising that his principal outrage at what happens to his daughter is not moral but social, at the insult to her rank:[10]

> 'Who dorste be so boold to disparage
> My doghter, that is come of swich lynage?'   4271–2

The injury to his snobbery is as great as the damage to his head.

There is never any doubt as to the true level of the Reeve's Tale. Symkyn's social pretensions are presented as hollow from the start, and the stylistic level of the tale is the same as the Miller's, though without the dimensions of mock-courtliness. The plots depend equally on the fine details of domestic setting, on the height of the 'shot-wyndowe' or the arrangement of the beds. There is plenty of animal imagery in the Reeve's Tale too. The miller is as proud as a peacock, his wife 'pert as is a pye'; his skull is 'as piled as an ape' (a significant detail for the plot, since its whiteness in the dark leads his wife to hit

---

[10] The point is made by Muscatine, p. 204.

it). There is a reference to beast-fable, 'as whilom to the wolf thus spak the mare' (4055); and so on. Animal sexuality in this tale is literal as well as metaphorical. The clerks' horse runs off the moment he is untied to pursue the wild mares in the fen,

> Forth with 'wehee,' thurgh thikke and thurghe thenne. 4066

If there was ever any doubt about the nature of Alisoun's shriek of delight,

> 'Tehee!' quod she, and clapte the wyndow to, 3740

this resolves it: it is the mating-call of the sexually aroused animal.

The Reeve, like the Miller, concludes with a plot summary; but he adds a brief proverbial *moralitas* as well:

> Hym thar nat wene wel that yvele dooth;
> A gylour shal hymself bigyled be. 4320–1

The Cook promptly adds another to cap it:

> Wel seyde Salomon in his langage,
> 'Ne bryng nat every man into thyn hous';
> For herberwynge by nyght is perilous.
> Wel oghte a man avysed for to be
> Whom that he broghte into his pryvetee. 4330–4

He offers not to 'quite' the Reeve's tale, but to follow it up. Symkyn

> hadde a jape of malice in the derk.
> But God forbede that we stynte heere;
> And therfore, if ye vouche-sauf to heere
> A tale of me, that am a povre man,
> I wol yow telle, as well as evere I kan,
> A litel jape that fil in oure citee. 4338–43

The Cook's tale, clearly, is to be another fabliau; and from the final lines of the sixty or so we possess, we gather that the number of sexual encounters, already doubled by the Reeve from the Miller's total, is going to rise sharply:

> A wyf that heeld for contenance
> A shoppe, and swyved for hir sustenance. 4421–2

There is no way of telling whether this would have been a major theme of the tale, but the moral drop from casual affair to prostitution certainly continues the decline in idealism from the heights of the Knight's Tale.

'Of this Cokes tale maked Chaucer na more', declares the scribe of the Hengwrt manuscript, and there is no reason to doubt his word. One can only speculate as to the reasons. To overgo the physical crudity of the Miller's and Reeve's Tales, as the reference to whoring suggests it might, the plot would need to be very crude – perhaps too much so for Chaucer's taste. It may be that to give three fabliaux in a row threatened a monotony of tone that he clearly designs the *Canterbury Tales* to avoid. There is also a curious element in the treatment of the story that he might have encountered some difficulty in sustaining. The Cook's sententiousness is already apparent in the prologue to the tale, and this element is continued in the narration. The tale opens with a description of the apprentice Perkyn Revelour; once the action gets under way, every detail is underpinned with a proverb or maxim or moral generalisation:

> Sikerly a prentys revelour
> That haunteth dys, riot or paramour,
> His maister shal it in his shoppe abye.   4391–3

> Revel and trouthe, as in a lowe degree,
> They been ful wrothe al day, as men may see.   4397–8

> A proverbe that seith this same word,
> 'Wel bet is roten appul out of hoord
> Than that it rotie al the remenaunt.'
> So fareth it by a riotous servaunt:
> It is ful lasse harm to lete hym pace,
> Than he shende alle the servantz in the place.   4405–10

> Ther is no theef withoute a lowke,
> That helpeth hym to wasten and to sowke
> Of that he brybe kan or borwe may.   4415–17

The only other tale in the whole collection that contains such a density of *sententiae* is the moral treatise *Melibee*. A fabliau treated in the same fashion would have been a very odd beast indeed.

Fragment II(B¹): The Man of Law's Tale

To study links between tales becomes something of a spurious exercise when a fragment consists of a single tale only. There are none the less a few things to be said about the Man of Law's Tale and its positioning and function in the *Canterbury Tales*.

As has been said above, Chaucer may once have intended the Introduction of the Man of Law's Tale to preface all the story-telling; but the tale he apparently had in mind for the Man of Law at that point was one in prose, possibly the *Melibee*. There is no evidence that the tale of Custance was ever meant to come first. The manuscripts, with remarkable consistency,[11] place it after Fragment I and the Cook's Tale, whether the tale ascribed to the Cook is the Chaucerian fragment or the *Tale of Gamelyn* that was sometimes inserted in its place. The Introduction to the Man of Law's Tale does not link up with anything that has gone before, and is presumably an unrevised relic from an earlier stage of compilation; but the consistency of its placing suggests that there may be some authority behind it, possibly Chaucer's. It is not fixed into this position as firmly as the tales within the fragments are, however. There is none of the precise linking between this story and the tales of the preceding group such as the Miller's shows with the Knight's or Reeve's. A break between groups involves not only a lack of dramatic connection in the framework but a break in the thematic thread.

The Man of Law's Tale is the story of Custance, daughter of the Emperor of Rome. She is married to the pagan sultan of Syria, widowed on her wedding day by her mother-in-law's jealousy and cast out to sea in a little boat. She comes ashore in Northumberland, heals a blind man, and after a false accusation of murder and God's intervention on her behalf she is married to the king, Alla. He is converted to Christianity; she bears a child, but her latest jealous mother-in-law writes to the king informing him that the baby is a monster, and has Custance and her child again cast out to sea. On discovering what has happened, Alla kills his mother, and eventually goes to Rome to do penance. Custance has meanwhile also arrived there, after suffering an attempted (but of course frustrated) rape. Through recognising Custance in the child, Alla is reunited with his wife; after his eventual death, she settles in Rome with her father, to live 'in vertu and in hooly almus-dede'.

If one reason for Chaucer's abandoning the Cook's Tale may have been that the sequence of stories was getting stuck in a single genre and plot pattern, the Man of Law's Tale certainly makes a new start. After the ever more sexually active women of the first fragment comes the saintly Emperor's daughter, twice married but sleeping with only one husband, and even that requires her to 'leye a lite hir hoolynesse aside' (713). After the vagaries of Fortune and the frenzied human disorder of the preceding tales comes a story that insists throughout on the providential control of events. The irrational, capricious action of the gods that makes Arcite's horse fall – an act that is, in human terms, a bitterly ironic accident – is replaced by the miracle of God's

---

[11] Hengwrt would appear to be an exception, but it has a misplaced quire at this point: see Doyle and Parkes in their introduction to Ruggiers' facsimile of Hengwrt p. xxiii.

hand striking the false accuser dead, or by Christ, the Virgin and Custance between them throwing her would-be rapist overboard,

And in the see he dreynte for vengeance.   923

In this reading of the world, there is no room for chance or accident or final injustice. Providence, not Saturn with his 'drenchyng in the see', is in control here. Custance may suffer, but only the guilty drown.

The tale has a wide geographical sweep similar to the romance, and its repeated structural sequences are also reminiscent of the Knight's Tale. It is not itself a romance, however: like the Clerk's Tale, it belongs at the point where romance shades into saint's life, as a kind of secular hagiography. Saints' lives are exemplary, providing a pattern of behaviour and belief for sinful mankind to strive to emulate; and the heroines of these tales offer similar patterns of perfection. Their virtues are constantly stressed, and a long list of Custance's is given when she is first mentioned, including humility, courtesy and holiness. Chaucer may have changed her name from the 'Constaunce' of his source in order to lessen her allegorical implications and to give a wider picture of goodness than the single epithet of constancy would suggest (though in Trivet's chronicle she is named after her father, Tiberius Constantine). The tale has the potential for turning into a morality, but Chaucer keeps it firmly in a more literal mode. It fulfils its exemplary function, not through the overt didacticism of personification, but by stimulating piety through pathos.

The Man of Law's Tale is rhetorically designed for pathetic effect. Lengthy passages of exclamation, apostrophe and lament punctuate the often perfunctorily narrated action, and the rhyme royal in which the tale is written (as are the other tales of high pathos, the Clerk's and Prioress's) makes such rhetorical elaboration easy to introduce. To give a single example: when Custance is about to leave home for her first marriage, the lines

The day is comen of hir departynge   260

and

To shippe is brought this woful faire mayde   316

could easily follow each other, in sense and syntax; the intervening fifty lines are taken up with laments from the narrator and from Custance, with a verse-long simile of epic content to describe the weeping in the background, and with three stanzas of apostrophe addressed to her father and to various planetary and zodiacal spheres and bodies. The passage is typical: the focus of the tale is not on the narrative action, but on the audience's emotional response. Their correct reaction is indeed often built into the narrative, for 'the comune voys of every man' is given a kind of choric function in the tale. It is the 'peple' that recognize Custance's virtues (155–69, 624), who love her on sight (532), and who weep at her sufferings (288–93, 820).

The interjections of the narrator also specify the audience's response. They are to condemn vice:

> O Sowdanesse, roote of iniquitee!   358

They are to pity innocent suffering, remembering that no one is beyond the reach of Fortune:

> O queenes, lyvynge in prosperitee,
> Duchesses, and ye ladyes everichone,
> Haveth som routhe on hire adversitee!   652–4

And they are guided into an appropriate mood of pious wonder:

> Who kepte hire fro the drenchyng in the see?
> Who kepte Jonas in the fisshes mawe
> Til he was spouted up at Nynyvee?
> Wel may men knowe it was no wight but he
> That kepte peple Ebrayk from hir drenchynge,
> With drye feet thurghout the see passynge.   485–90

In the Man of Law's Tale, all the lines framed syntactically as questions are rhetorical ones, assuming a single answer. There are none of the metaphysical dilemmas of the Knight's Tale. The sequence of questions is designed to inculcate an unquestioning piety, and that, along with pity and a general air of sententiousness, defines the tone of the tale. It could hardly be more different from the tales of the first fragment, whether the romance or the fabliaux. In the fabliaux, piety was irrelevant, pity excluded, and sententiousness, at least before the Cook's Tale, almost totally ignored in favour of getting on with the story.

What happens after the Man of Law's Tale is the greatest textual dilemma posed by the whole work. The Ellesmere manuscript omits the epilogue, and this may indicate that Chaucer intended the passage to be cancelled. In some manuscripts the epilogue introduces the Squire's Tale, despite its patent inappropriateness. Whoever it is that offers the next tale, promising,

> My joly body schal a tale telle,   1185

it is fairly clearly not one of the 'gentils'. One late and unauthoritative manuscript proposes the Shipman, and this, combined with a single uncertain geographical reference, led many editors to bring forward Fragment VII, or B^2 – the 'Bradshaw shift'. The phrase 'my joly body' sounds a little like the Wife of Bath, who once told the Shipman's Tale. Ellesmere, despite omitting the epilogue, follows it up with the Wife of Bath's present Prologue and Tale.

That the Wife's Prologue and Tale follow on splendidly from the story of Custance is beyond doubt. The holy, chaste wife is followed by the five-times-married expert in the art of matrimony; even the Man of Law's list in his Introduction of the 'noble wyves' written about by Chaucer is balanced by the 'wykked wyves' of the Wife's Prologue. Custance's lament,

> Wommen are born to thraldom and penance,
> And to been under mannes governance,   286–7

could hardly receive a more decisive reply than the Wife gives. In view of all this, Lee Sheridan Cox has argued that the Wife of Bath's Prologue and Tale were written to replace the Shipman's Tale as an answer to the Man of Law's:[12] they certainly constitute a decisive statement on husbandly submission. It is also true that the Wife's five marriages numerically overgo Custance's two, rather as the sexual encounters of the Reeve's Tale multiply those of the Miller's; and the hag's discourse on patient poverty at the end of the tale does match the Man of Law's Prologue on the evils of being poor. All this may be no more than another example of the '*ex post facto* resonances that occur after a given order has been adopted' that Donaldson warns of;[13] but the Ellesmere order does make sense, and in a Chaucerian kind of way. At the very least, one can say this: that the Man of Law's Tale opens out new areas of human and literary potential in the *Canterbury Tales*, areas of virtue, perfection and devotion, images of marriage and of suffering, that many tales take up in reflecting or contrasting ways.

Fragment III(D): The Wife of Bath (twice), Friar and Summoner

> 'This is a long preamble of a tale!'   831

exclaims the Friar when the Wife of Bath, after eight hundred lines of disquisition on anti-feminism and the nature of marriage, announces that she is about to begin her story. He is quite right: the

---

[12] Lee Sheridan Cox, 'A question of order in the Canterbury Tales', *Chaucer Review* I (1966–7) 228–52.
[13] See p. 62 above.

Wife manages to get a double share in the *Tales*. Critics have tend
to accord her the same measure – and general readers too. The Wife
is probably the first pilgrim who springs to mind when one thinks of
the *Canterbury Tales*, and the existence of the 'marriage group' is the
one critical theory that everyone will know about the work.

Chaucer, however, does not write a 'marriage group' – he does not,
that is, write it *as* a group. That there are connections between the
Wife's, Clerk's, Merchant's and Franklin's tales is undeniable, and
Chaucer makes several explicit cross-references to underline the relationship. But he did not associate them in a single fragment: there
are other connections to be made, too, not only between those four
tales and the rest of the work, but between the Wife of Bath's tale and
the two that follow it. By and large, the tales of the marriage group
look back to the Wife's Prologue; the stories of the Friar and Summoner link up with her Tale.

There is an admirable study of the relationship between these three
by Penn R. Szittya,[14] and the following account inevitably overlaps
his – the points to be made on the matter are, after all, the points
Chaucer makes in the text.

The tales of Fragment III form a triad structurally very similar to
the completed tales of the first fragment. Both groups start with a
romance, follow it with a tale of contrasting genre that parodies the
plot and the ideals of the romance, and conclude with a tale that has
generic, dramatic and thematic relations with the second story. The
Miller's Tale acts as a hinge between the Knight's and Reeve's, the
Friar's between the Wife's and the Summoner's. The dramatic relationships between the tales and their tellers are more developed in
the second group. There is no reason in the narrative of the framework
for the Miller to pick up from the Knight; that the Reeve is a carpenter
is not of critical importance – it is only when he reminds us of the fact
that we can read with hindsight the insult he has found in the Miller's
Tale – and once his own tale is under way the pilgrim Miller is
supplanted by Symkyn. The quarrel between the tellers of the third
fragment is given rather more prominence. It starts before the Wife
has even begun her own tale, when the Friar comments on her long
'preamble'. The Summoner reacts coarsely to his interjection, and they
both promise to tell tales against each other's profession. The Wife's
tale interrupts the quarrel, both dramatically (as the Host silences
the rivals to give her a chance to be heard) and thematically, since

---

[14] 'The Green Yeoman as Loathly Lady: the Friar's parody of the Wife of Bath's Tale',
PMLA XC (1975) 386–94. Szittya also argues that the Friar's Tale is designed partly
as an insult to the Wife, but despite his persuasive style I am not altogether convinced:
it is true that the hag is there re-shaped as the devil, but the connection with the Wife
is getting a little tenuous by that time.

her tale, of the knight who marries an old hag in return for information as to what women most desire, has in itself nothing to do with
the insult-match that precedes it. She does, however, manage to get
in an insult of her own at the very start of the tale, in revenge for the
Friar's interruption:

> Ther as wont to walken was an elf,
> Ther walketh now the lymytour hymself . . .
> Wommen may go now saufly up and doun.
> In every bussh or under every tree
> Ther is noon oother incubus but he,
> And he ne wol doon hem but dishonour.   III 873–4, 878–81

After that, the story leaves behind its dramatic context – except for
the fact that, more than any other tale in the whole work, it is psychologically as well as rhetorically appropriate for its teller. The theme
of women's sovereignty and the hag's recovery of youth and beauty
have an obvious appropriateness for the wife who has spent her entire
matrimonial career in establishing domination over her husbands,
and who can lament,

> I have had my world as in my tyme.
> But age, allas! that al wole envenyme,
> Hath me biraft my beautee and my pith.   473–5

Although her Prologue has been devoted to an exposition of the 'wo
that is in mariage', it is entirely right that this inexhaustible practi-
tioner of marriage should conclude her tale with an image of the
wedded state as 'blisse'. Even the detail of the writing is at times
specially adapted for her, in a way almost unique in the *Tales*, as the
formula 'wives and maidens' is twice given an important qualification:

> Ful many a noble wyf, and many a mayde,
> And many a wydwe, for that they been wise   1026–7

> In al that court ne was ther wyf, ne mayde,
> Ne wydwe . . .   1043–4

Her disquisition on how women are best won (929 ff.) is also put into
the first person – it is, after all, a subject on which she is the highest
authority.

One might have expected Chaucer to give the Wife a fabliau, to
follow up the unashamedly sexual emphasis of her Prologue. That was
indeed apparently his original intention, as the first-person reference
to women in the Shipman's fabliau suggests. The Shipman's Tale,
however, with its stress on sexual trickery and financial motives, was

perhaps too similar to the Prologue. In changing tales, Chaucer also changes the Wife's character. In her Prologue she is colloquial, has a short way with moral abstraction, and perpetually refers to an animal level of imagery, even if often to deny the comparisons –

> I holde a mouses herte nat worth a leek
> That hath but oon hole for to sterte to.   572–3

Her tale introduces an unexpected note of idealism. With the fabliau, she would have been portrayed as a cynic; given her present tale, she is presented as an incurable romantic.

The particular form of romance that Chaucer selects for the Wife is rhetorically appropriate for her lower social level. It has none of the epic or metaphysical reach of the Knight's Tale. It is set 'in th'olde dayes of the Kyng Arthour' – and Arthurian romance, according to the Nun's Priest, is especially suited to women's credulity:

> This storie is also trewe, I undertake,
> As is the book of Launcelot de Lake,
> That wommen holde in ful greet reverence.   VII 3211–13

[handwritten marginal note: a romance that started as a fabliau — with rape.]

The Wife's tale is explicitly a fairy story:

> Al was this land fulfild of fayerye.   859

It is a much more popular kind of romance than the Knight's. Like many fairy stories it also dispenses entirely with names: neither the knight nor the hag, nor even the queen, is ever named, and it is effectively locationless. Unlike the fairy story, however, this romance maintains a discursive interest in ideals: good may be vindicated in folktales, but it would be hard to find any parallel outside the context of moral or courtly works for the hag's disquisition on the true nature of *gentillesse*.

The plot of the Wife's tale is initiated by a rape – the ultimate assertion of masculine *maistrie*. Arthur condemns the knight to death; but at the entreaty of 'the queene and othere ladyes mo' he hands him over to them 'al at hir wille'. Theseus, similarly entreated after his condemnation of Palamon and Arcite, had granted mercy but had still kept judgment in his own hands; Arthur's action here is governed not by political wisdom but by the demands of the theme of the tale. The knight is sent off to find

> What thyng is it that wommen moost desiren,   905

and Chaucer (or in this case, the Wife) gives a long list of possible answers: riches, honour, 'jolynesse', clothes, 'luste abedde', flattery,

And oftetyme to be wydwe and wedde.   928

Only when the knight is riding 'under a forest syde' and sees, first the
dance of twenty-four ladies – fairies, presumably – who disappear, and
then the ugly old woman, is he told the true answer, revealed only
when he returns to the court:

> Wommen desiren to have sovereynetee
> As wel over hir housbond as hir love,
> And for to been in maistrie hym above.   1038–40

In payment for the information, the knight has formally pledged his
'trouthe' to do whatever the hag requires of him; and she demands his
hand in marriage. The wedding celebrations are described with a
rhetorical deflation that is the precise opposite of the *occupationes* on
the ceremonial of the Knight's Tale:

> I seye ther nas no joye ne feeste at al.   1078

The drop in level is also marked by the single animal image of the
whole tale, as the knight hides himself like an owl. When they are in
bed he is provoked into pointing out the hag's ugliness, age and low
rank; and she responds with a hundred-line discourse, taking up a
quarter of the tale, on the inward nature of true nobility and the value
of poverty.

> Looke who that is moost vertuous alway,
> Pryvee and apert, and moost entendeth ay
> To do the gentil dedes that he kan;
> Taak hym for the grettist gentil man.
> Crist wole we clayme of hym oure gentillesse,
> Nat of oure eldres for hire old richesse.   1113–18

Only when the theoretical basis of true worth has been thus established will Chaucer go on to give the happy ending. Not only does the
knight hand over to his wife the decision as to whether she will be
ugly and chaste, or beautiful and let him take the consequences; but
in addition, as a result of getting the 'maistrie', she goes on to say

> 'Dooth with my lyf and deth right as yow lest.' . . .
> And she obeyed hym in every thyng
> That myghte doon hym plesance or likyng.   1248, 1255–6

They live happily ever after, 'in parfit joye': a joy achieved not, as one
might have expected from the dramatic context, through wifely sovereignty, but through mutual obedience and respect. It is as if the
story has changed key with the great speech on *gentillesse*, so that the

tale itself now acknowledges a higher level of idealism than the opening had seemed able to encompass.

It is an idealism that is rapidly brought down to earth by the Friar's Tale, just as the Knight's is by the Miller's. This story is not a fabliau, though it is sometimes described as such; the level of animal imagery, almost entirely absent since the Wife's Prologue, makes a forceful return, but it occurs here generally in the thematically appropriate form of images of hunting and taking prey.[15] It is more of a moral *exemplum*, a cautionary tale, like the Pardoner's tale, though aimed less against a single vice than against a single profession. In its lack of names it has the archetypal quality of a morality, and also mirrors the preceding tale. The treatment of its plot, of a summoner carried off to Hell by the Devil in response to an old woman's curse, also gives it some claim to be the first English ghost story.

The plot of the Friar's Tale, like the Wife's, gets under way when the protagonist is journeying 'under a forest syde'. The motifs of both journey and forest might seem too commonplace to be worth commenting on, but in fact, widespread as they are in mediaeval literature in general, they are distinctly unusual in Chaucer. He very rarely makes a journey the structural basis of a work: the framework of the *Canterbury Tales* would seem to be the overwhelming exception, but given the perfunctory way in which he treats the road to Canterbury, it is an exception more apparent than real. The forest, too, ubiquitous in most mediaeval romance, rarely appears in Chaucer. (The wood of the *Book of the Duchess*, with its neatly spaced trees, is a different, though related, phenomenon.) The symbolic associations of the forest are with wilderness, savagery, everything that is the opposite of human society and reason; perhaps even with chaos.[16] Chaucer's rare use of forest settings looks almost like reluctance, a parallel to his reluctance to metamorphose man into beast. Certainly there is always something sinister or anti-human about his forests. In the Knight's Tale the lovers have their combat there, a combat that is the perversion of the surface friendliness of their arming; and Theseus stops it in order to substitute the ordered tournament, fought by rules and with a judge. In the Pardoner's Tale the rioters find Death in a grove. In the Wife's and Friar's tales the knight and summoner find a supernatural figure who will change their destiny; in the Friar's Tale it is a devil. Knight and summoner alike meet their destiny as they jour-

---

[15] See the discussion in Janette Richardson, *Blameth Nat Me: A Study of Imagery in Chaucer's Fabliaux* (Mouton Studies in English Literature 58, The Hague, 1970) ch. 4.

[16] Winthrop Wetherbee suggests an association between the Chartrian philosophers' use of the term *silva* for uncreated matter and the extensive use of the forest setting in romance: see his *Platonism and Poetry in the Twelfth Century* (Princeton, 1972), esp. pp. 158–61, 170–2, 226.

ney, and beside a forest; and the exact parallelism of phrase underlines the parallelism of situation. In the Wife's tale,

> it happed hym to ryde,
> In al this care, under a forest syde;   989–90

in the Friar's, it

> happed that he saugh bifore hym ryde
> A gay yeman, under a forest syde.   1379–80

The knight pledges his word to the hag:

> 'Plight me thy trouthe heere in myn hand,' quod she;   1009

and in so doing he commits himself to lifelong partnership. Summoner and devil also

> Everych in ootheres hand his trouthe leith,
> For to be sworne bretheren til they deye.   1404–5

If the knight's marriage leads to 'blisse', however, the summoner's sworn brotherhood leads him to damnation. The working out of both plots depends on the force of the spoken word, twice over. In the Wife's tale, the series of events set in motion by the initial plighting of troth is completed when the knight must give his wife her own way, and mean it:

> 'As yow liketh, it suffiseth me.'
> 'Thanne have I gete of yow maistrie,' quod she,
> 'Syn I may chese and governe as me lest?'
> 'Ye, certes, wyf,' quod he, 'I holde it best.'   1235–8

Only then can she assume her form of youth and beauty, and the knight find his heaven. In the Friar's Tale, devil and summoner agree to share their takings – if 'sovereignty' is the ultimate desire of the Wife's Tale, 'wynnyng' is the supreme good in the Friar's. The only Hell the Summoner of the General Prologue had been able to envisage was a financial one.[17] After these agreements, the climax of the story depends on two curses. The first is hurled by the carter to his horses, but it is not meant, so the devil cannot carry off the animals. With the second, the widow damns the summoner with all her heart; and the devil, like the Wife's hag, makes quite sure the words are intended before he will act upon them:

---

[17] 'Purs is the ercedekenes helle', I 658.

Misses the point. Sum.
has chance to repent. He damns
himself.

'Unto the devel blak and rough of hewe
Yeve I thy body and my panne also!'
And whan the devel herde hire cursen so
Upon hir knees, he seyde in this manere,
'Now, Mabely, myn owene mooder deere,
Is this youre wyl in ernest that ye seye?'
'The devel,' quod she, 'so fecche hym er he deye!' 1622–8

In the context too of persistence in evil

'Curs wol slee,' as Chaucer had commented in the course of the initial description of the Summoner. The devil, now referred to as 'this foule feend', and his trim yeomanly shape presumably dropped, duly carries his victim off to Hell.

The Summoner has even more right than the Reeve to feel aggrieved, since the Friar's Tale, unlike the Miller's, is specifically intended as a personal insult. He responds, like the Reeve, in the 'cherles termes' of the fabliau. The tale makes some claim to be a moral tale instead, with an inset sermon on the vices of anger and drunkenness, but the claim is as hypocritical as the sermon. If the Friar had told of the wicked practices and ultimate damnation of a summoner who bore a strong resemblance to the Summoner of the General Prologue, the Summoner will expose the practices of a friar who bears an even closer likeness to Friar Huberd. They share a fondness for middle-class establishments, agreeable women and smooth talk; both are skilful at wheedling money, and are only out for what they can get. If the climax of the Summoner's Tale is more earthly – and earthy – than that of the Friar's, he makes up for it in his Prologue, as he tells of a friar's vision of the final resting-place of his brothers in the devil's arse. This little story bears an obvious relationship to the conclusion of his Tale, where a fart has to be divided among a whole convent of friars.

The Friar's and Summoner's Tales parallel each other, not only in the way in which they vilify the rival profession, but in theme. The Friar, his summoner, the pilgrim Summoner and his Friar John all have many of the same vices, notably avarice, anger, and a weakness for alcohol, and in telling tales against each other the narrators are both also damning themselves. Both characters within the tales get a very different kind of reward from the one they had expected: not money, but damnation, or the fart. Both tales use the motif of brotherhood in a way that turns its conventional associations inside out. The devil and summoner become sworn brothers, undertaking to share their spoils, and so the summoner damns himself; Thomas in the Summoner's Tale is 'brother' to Friar John as a lay member of the fraternity,[18] and it is because of that relationship that the friar de-

---

[18] III 1944, 2089, 2126.

mands all that Thomas has to give. Friar John, like the summoner, is trapped by an oath: Thomas asks him to swear that he will divide the gift equally among his fellows, and he complies just as the knight and the summoner had done in the two earlier tales of the fragment:

> 'I swere it,' quod this frere, 'by my feith!'
> And therwithal his hand in his he leith.   2137–8

The preceding tales had worked out their plots through speeches expressing intention: the knight must agree wholeheartedly to allow his wife sovereignty, the old woman curses the summoner. The climax of the Summoner's Tale depends on an equally fully intended communication, though this time it is non-verbal.

> The rumblynge of a fart, and every soun,
> Nis but of eir reverberacioun.   2233–4

Words and rude noises are physically indistinguishable. Friar John is paid back for his earlier determination to find in a gloss whatever the text will not reveal; this time, since the text has no semantic context, there can be no gloss, only the bare fact. There is too the same poetic justice linking the dénouement to the earlier oath as in the preceding tales. Friar John had protested to Thomas,

> 'What is a ferthyng worth parted in twelve?'   1967

and Thomas's response provides a punning retort. One might add that the Summoner's Tale numerically surpasses the Friar's even more decisively than the Reeve's does the Miller's. The Friar despatches a single summoner to Hell; the Summoner gets a whole convent of friars, thirteen in all, ranged around his wheel.

The idea of text and gloss also looks back through the Friar's Tale to the Wife's Prologue. She started decisively with the lines,

> Experience, though noon auctoritee
> Were in this world, is right ynogh for me.   1–2

If she goes on to marshal an astonishing number of authorities, it is usually only to dismiss them out of hand, text and gloss and all, as in her short treatment of St. Timothy on women's dress (I Tim.ii.9):

> After thy text, ne after thy rubriche,
> I wol nat wirche as muchel as a gnat.   346–7

When the authorities of Jankyn's anthology of wicked wives get too much for her, she refutes them even more simply by ripping the book.

In the tale she tells, authority and experience are not at odds but reinforce each other. The authoritative answer given by the hag brings about the happy ending when put into practice, when she is given 'maistrie'; and all the authorities she cites in her speech on *gentillesse* to prove that appearances count for little, are justified when she turns beautiful and virtuous. The Friar continues the theme: the fiend promises the summoner, in answer to his questions about devils, that he shall soon have more than professorial knowledge of them, not academically through authority but from practical experience.

> Thou shalt herafterward, my brother deere,
> Come there thee nedeth nat of me to leere.
> For thou shalt, by thyn owene experience,
> Konne in a chayer rede of this sentence
> Bet than Virgile, while he was on lyve,
> Or Dant also.   1515–20

At the end of his tale he threatens the pilgrim Summoner with more authorities on Hell. The Summoner's Tale reduces the debate on authority *versus* experience to a very low point. For Friar John, authorities – text and gloss – are there merely to be used for the purposes of extortion; and all the moral *exempla* he tells against anger are undermined (as the whole tale itself is, and as the Pardoner's Tale is later) by the fact that he is the character most guilty of it. The experiential claims of the world are all-important, and authority and text are subservient to those. The problem that Thomas sets the friars is, appropriately, not an abstract one answerable by reference to authority, as were the questions raised by the Wife or by the summoner in the Friar's Tale, but a very down-to-earth matter indeed.[19] Even this, however, is treated as an academic problem – a problem in 'arsmetrike', though one unparalleled in the history of the subject (2222–3).

As at the end of the first fragment, Chaucer may have found difficulty in following on. The three stories show a steady debasement on all fronts: the courtly relationship of *trouthe* and integrity has descended through making a pact with the devil to the sordid physicality of the fart; authority has become a cover for self-interest; the discourse on Christian *gentillesse* has been replaced by the insulting personal moral of the Friar's Tale urging repentance as a way of avoiding damnation, especially for summoners, and the entirely self-interested preaching of Friar John. The Summoner makes no attempt at all to give a concluding moral. He ends,

[19] See W. G. East, 'By preeve which that is demonstratif', *Chaucer Review* XII (1977–8) 78–82.

My tale is doon; we been almost at toune,   2294

and the line sounds like a deliberate signing off on Chaucer's part.

What was the new start to be? The opening triad of romance and fabliaux is followed by a rhyme royal tale of secular hagiography, the tale of Custance, and the ordering may perhaps go back to Chaucer. It is probable that he intended to repeat the pattern here, this time using the story of Griselda. Almost all the manuscripts follow the Summoner's Tale with the Clerk's; and there is also internal evidence this time that this order may be right, since the Clerk's tale, with its closing references to the Wife of Bath, cannot be far separated from hers, and in addition its moral picks up from the end of the Friar's Tale:

He may nat tempte yow over your myght.   1661

The Friar's Tale barely justifies such a moral; it is in the Clerk's Tale that testing becomes the chief issue.

Fragment IV(E): Clerk and Merchant

The Clerk's and Merchant's tales stand in a different relationship to each other from the tales in the groups discussed above, though it is a relationship found again in all the two-tale fragments. There is little plot parody, and no dramatic grounding in mutual insult; instead they are related through precise thematic contrast.

The collocation of the stories of Griselda and May demonstrates this relationship more clearly than any. The brilliant juxtaposition of the tales of the patient and the unfaithful wife has indeed tended to overshadow not only the relationships that the stories have with other tales in the work, but even the remarkable solidity of each tale in its own right. It becomes quite hard to think of the Clerk's Tale in isolation from the Wife of Bath's or the Merchant's. There is evidence, however – abundant evidence, as these rather hypothetical matters go – that it only came to Chaucer's mind late to include the stanzas that link the Clerk's Tale explicitly with the Wife, or to follow it with the Merchant's; on the evidence of manuscript arrangement, indeed, there is more reason for putting the Clerk's Tale (without its Envoy) into the same fragment as the Summoner's than for linking it with the Merchant's. Number of manuscripts is not everything, however, and there is no reason to doubt that the connection of the two tales found in the *a* order of manuscripts represents Chaucer's final intentions.

In terms of the drama of the pilgrimage, the Clerk's tale is a response to the Wife of Bath's charge,

It's nothing

It is an impossible
That any clerk wol speke good of wyves,
But if it be of hooly seintes lyves.   III 688–90

Griselda, perfect as she is, is not a saint; Chaucer gives the Clerk a
tale that gives the lie to the assertion, and yet, in speaking 'good of
wyves', it manages to be the most colossal insult to the Wife herself.
The Clerk's model wife could hardly be more different from Alisoun
of Bath. If the Reeve or Summoner could return a professional insult
in their tales, the Clerk is doing a similar thing against the Wife's
Prologue: her fifth husband and the villain of the piece had, after all,
been an Oxford clerk as well. There is a point, none the less, when he
admits the charge even while his own compliment to women belies it:

Though clerkes preise wommen but a lite,
Ther kan no man in humblesse hym acquite
As womman kan, ne kan been half so trewe
As wommen been, but it be falle of newe.   IV 935–8

That there may be a race of 'archewyves' who do not fit the pattern is
a fact reserved for the Envoy; the tale itself is untouched by any such
considerations. In the great debate in the *Canterbury Tales* on anti-
feminism, the Clerk's Tale, far more than the Wife's Prologue, is a
statement for the defence.

It is a remarkable tale in all kinds of ways. It is one of the few that
cite a literary source (appropriately enough for the academic clerk).
Its metrical form, in rhyme royal stanzas, is the same as that of the
other tales of pathos, the Man of Law's, Prioress's and Second Nun's;
but its manner of writing is much more restrained. There are none of
the verse-long apostrophes of the tale of Custance; the outbursts from
the narrator are all the more forceful for their undemonstrative
sobriety:

Nedelees, God woot, he thoghte hire for t'affraye.

He hadde assayed hire ynogh bifore,
And foond hire evere good; what neded it
Hire for to tempte, and alwey moore and moore,
Though some men preise it for a subtil wit?   455–9

Imagery, rhetorical figures, even adjectives, are used sparingly. Circumstantial details are minimal, but when they occur they often carry
a weight of association, even symbolism, that makes them stand out:
the 'oxes stalle' by the threshold where Griselda sets down her
water-pot picks up from the lines

> hye God somtyme senden kan
> His grace into a litel oxes stalle.   206–7

She sits as meekly 'as a lamb' when her daughter is taken from her, and the comparison is religious, not animal. A number of phrases associate her with the Virgin:[20] her humility, her kneeling to hear her 'lordes wille' (294), lines such as

> She from hevene sent was, as men wende,
> Peple to save and every wrong t'amende.   440–1

The onlookers, as in the tale of Custance, are given a choric function: we see Griselda more often through their eyes, as in the lines just quoted, than through Walter's, and the narrator's description of her virtues culminates in the confirmation of their reaction to her:

> Ech hire lovede that looked in hir face.   413

An almost identical line is used of Custance; the rhetorical understatement of the Clerk's Tale makes the line here considerably more powerful. The asceticism of treatment extends to vocabulary as well. As Muscatine noted, 'The language of the poem verges on monotone in its semantic restraint.'[21] The adjectives are almost all expressive of moral quality: *humble, benigne, verray, feithful, wifely, trewe, sad, vertuous, pacient*; or on the other side, a sinister set suggesting evil without often stating it: *drery, suspecious, despitous, ugly*, or, at the worst, *crueel* and *wikke*. The extensive use of negatives also strengthens the stylistic understatement: Griselda will not disobey, or grieve, or weep. The tone of pathos comes above all, however, from the literary skill that simply allows the story to speak for itself.

> Mekely she to the sergeant preyde,
> So as he was a worthy gentil man,
> That she moste kisse hire child er that it deyde.
> And in hir barm this litel child she leyde
> With ful sad face, and gan the child to blisse,
> And lulled it, and after gan it kisse.   548–53

The complex irony behind the phrase 'worthy gentil man' – an irony that Griselda herself seems unaware of – is swallowed up in the pathos of the episode. The risk of sentimentality at such a point is enormous; Chaucer avoids it simply because the emotions he is appealing to are

---

[20] See Francis Lee Utley, 'Five genres in the *Clerk's Tale*', *Chaucer Review* VI (1971–2) 198–228, esp. 217–27, and Alfred L. Kellogg, 'The evolution of the "Clerk's Tale": a study in connotation', in *Chaucer, Langland, Arthur: Essays in Middle English Literature* (New Jersey, 1972) pp. 276–329, esp. pp. 298–302.
[21] Muscatine p. 195.

so thoroughly justified by the events of the story. The restraint of style focuses attention on the unnatural restraint of Griselda's own feelings; it is at once compassionate and appalled.

The Clerk's Tale is one of the most disturbing in the *Canterbury Tales*. The appeals to pity in the Man of Law's Tale had been at their most turgid when Custance walks down to the sea carrying her child; but at least the moral issues there were clear and comforting – she is an innocent suffering at the hands of the wicked, and God will protect His own. In the Clerk's Tale, maternal love must give way to matrimonial love; Griselda must acquiesce in apparent evil willingly and cheerfully for the sake of her obedience to her husband. She has indeed formally sworn absolute obedience before their marriage, in an episode a little like the oaths of the tales of Fragment III: she gives her word and must live by the consequences. This tale, however, seems to take place in a moral void. Griselda's virtue may be complete, but Walter is obsessed – and obsessed not like a fairy-tale tyrant or the villainous pagan of a saint's life, but in a recognisably human way:[22]

> Ther been folk of swich condicion
> That whan they have a certein purpos take,
> They kan nat stynte of hire entencion,
> But, right as they were bounden to a stake,
> They wol nat of that firste purpos slake.   701–5

The most disturbing thing about the tale is that, for all the moral of the ending, it is not allegorical. If 'patience' etymologically means endurance and suffering, Griselda's suffering goes beyond all moral abstraction; and there is nothing in the moral world to which Walter can correspond.

The *moralitas*, when it comes, looks as if it ought to solve the problem by suggesting a parabolic level perceptible beyond the events of the narrative:

> Sith a womman was so pacient
> Unto a mortal man, wel moore us oghte
> Receyven al in gree that God us sent.   1149–51

But it is not enough of an answer. The most direct moral reading of the tale is explicitly rejected:

> This storie is seyd, nat for that wyves sholde
> Folwen Grisilde as in humylitee,
> For it were inportable, though they wolde   1142–4

[22] The point is forcefully made by A. C. Spearing, *Criticism and Medieval Poetry* (2nd ed., London, 1972) p. 97.

– both psychologically and morally intolerable, *inportable*, one feels. But the parabolic reading of the tale implies some kind of equation of God and Walter, such as is utterly at odds with any providential interpretation of the universe. If the narrator has stressed one thing, it is that Walter's testing of his wife was 'nedelees'. At the end he appears to be about to answer the question as to God's reasons for 'preevyng' mankind: He

> suffreth us, as for oure exercise,
> With sharpe scourges of adversitee
> Ful ofte to be bete in sondry wise;
> Nat for to knowe oure wyl, for certes he,
> Er we were born, knew al oure freletee.   1156–60

After 'nat for –' one expects 'but for –'; but it never comes.[23] The conclusion is merely,

> For oure beste is al his governaunce.   1161

The tale of Griselda too had had a 'happy ending', with herself restored to her place as wife and her children returned to her; but an earlier moment holds a much more compulsive grasp on the imagination, when Griselda, discovering her children are alive, faints while holding them so tightly

> That with greet sleighte and greet difficultee
> The children from hire arm they gonne arace.   1102–3

The strength of that embrace reflects the force of the emotions she has been suppressing; and it is not an image of overwhelming delight and relief, but of the extremity of suffering. After that, the ways of Providence become all the more inexplicable.

Then comes a complete change of tone, mood, even verse form:

> Grisilde is deed, and eek hire pacience,
> And both atones buryed in Ytaille.   1177–8

The Envoy is sung 'for the Wyves love of Bathe', and it is an outrageous recommendation of everything the Wife exemplified in her Prologue:

[23] Chaucer's handling of his material at this juncture gives a markedly different emphasis from his principal sources (Petrarch's Latin and its French translation as *Le Livre Griseldis*) despite a superficial similarity. The sources say that Griselda's example is unfollowable, not *inportable*, 'intolerable', but *vix imitabilis* or *a paine ensuivable*; and they also provide the expected 'but for –' clause: 'ut nobis nostra fragilitas notis ac domesticis indicijs innotescat', 'pour que par jugemens clers et evidens recongnoissions et veons nostre fragile humanité' (Bryan and Dempster pp. 330–1).

> Lat noon humylitee youre tonge naille,
> Ne lat no clerk have cause or diligence
> To write of yow a storie of swich mervaille
> As of Grisildis pacient and kynde.   1184–7

The curious fact remains that in spite of all this, in spite of Alisoun and Griselda being diametrically opposite types of wifehood, the outlook finally presented by the Wife's and Clerk's tales is astonishingly close. If the hag in the Wife's tale, having become beautiful and achieved sovereignty over her husband, then 'obeyed hym in every thyng' in a kind of mutual exchange of service, so the Clerk's tale stresses that Walter's insistence on dominance is unnatural, and Griselda herself is allowed her one word of protest when she pleads with her husband not to subject his new wife to the 'tormentynge' that she herself has undergone. The hag's hundred-line speech on the irrelevance of high birth to true Christian *gentillesse* and the value of patient poverty is a little beside the point in that tale; Griselda is the perfect embodiment of the ideas.

> Bountee comth al of God, nat of the streen
> Of which they been engendred and ybore.   IV 157–8

Wife and Clerk appear to send their stories off in different directions, but the lines of meaning that they follow curve back in to complete a single circle.

The Merchant's Prologue picks up from the last line of the Clerk's Envoy – 'wepyng and waylyng, care and oother sorwe'. As the Clerk's fable had countered the Wife's experience, so it will in its turn be answered by the experience of the Merchant – or rather, by a tale of similar fictional experience, since he has had quite enough of his own 'soore' to want to talk about it further. The plot of the story, and many of its narrative motifs, are a close parody of the Knight's Tale.[24] By putting it next to the Clerk's, Chaucer brings to prominence different elements in it, especially, and famously, the whole question of the nature of marriage. Its relationship with the Clerk's Tale, or even the Wife's, is primarily anecdotal: they give two accounts of marriage, the Merchant gives a third. The precision with which many tales pick up abstract moral themes from each other, as the Clerk picks up the questions of sovereignty and *gentillesse* from the Wife, is largely missing here; and the story closest to it in the text that gives a parallel plot comes later, in the form of the Franklin's Tale. None the less, the Clerk's Tale and the Merchant's do have a congruence – or a deliberate incongruence – that goes well beyond the rival perspectives on marriage.

---

[24] See above, pp. 67–8.

The closest parallels between the tales occur at the beginning: after that they tend to part company, on the surface at least. In the Clerk's Tale, Walter is long unmarried and is urged by his people to take a wife and beget an heir before he grows old. They assure him that marriage is a

> blisful yok
> Of soveraynetee, noght of servyse,   113–14

but he persists in seeing matrimony as loss of liberty and as 'servage'. In fact, of course, it is Griselda who must be the totally submissive partner, and he makes her swear obedience:

> 'Eek when I sey "ye," ne say nat "nay." '   355

He refuses his subjects' offer to choose for him a wife of high birth, preferring the poor and virtuous Griselda. In the Merchant's Tale, January, after a lifetime of lechery, decides to find 'a yong wyf and a feir' – no mention of virtue –

> On which he myghte engendren hym an heir.   1272

His method of choosing his prospective bride relies entirely on external qualities: when he goes to bed at night he imagines 'many fair shap and many a fair visage', and the superficiality of such a survey is stressed by Chaucer's simile for the whole process:

> As whoso tooke a mirour, polisshed bryght,
> And sette it in a commune market-place,
> Thanne sholde he se ful many a figure pace
> By his mirour; and in the same wyse
> Gan Januarie inwith his thoght devyse
> Of maydens whiche that dwelten hym bisyde.   1582–7

The mirror in the market-place is as loaded a simile as is Emily's lily, though its import is directly opposite: May is something common, and something to be purchased.

Such an image represents a sharp drop from the idealised portrayal of marriage found at the opening of the tale. There, marriage is described as

> thilke blisful lyf
> That is bitwixe an housbonde and his wyf.   1259–60

Notions of sovereignty and service are subsumed in an image of order:

> A wedded man in his estaat
> Lyveth a lyf blisful and ordinaat
> Under this yok of mariage ybounde.   1283-5

There are even echoes of St. Paul's mystical vision of ultimate beatitude:

> The blisse which that is bitwixe hem tweye
> Ther may no tonge telle, or herte thynke.   1340-2

Nowhere else in the *Tales* is marriage presented as such an ideal state. Within this high vision, however, plenty of warning notes are sounded. A wife is God's gift, but she may last 'wel lenger than thee list'. The very choice of words and imagery often brings its own qualification along with it. 'Paradise' is a favourite term, and the first wife was Eve, created·to be

> mannes help and his confort,
> His paradys terrestre, and his disport   1331-2

– but it is a rather more dangerous comparison than the association of Griselda with the Virgin. Moreover, this ideal vision of marriage parts company totally with reality:

> She seith nat ones 'nay,' whan he seith 'ye.'   1345

Even the Clerk had acknowledged that wives were not really like that. Griselda may swear that her 'werk' and 'thoght' will match each other, but May is all too ready to say one thing and do something completely different – swear her faithfulness while signalling to Damian, or assert her intention of healing January's blindness while up the pear-tree. The opening discussion of the nature of marriage turns into a debate when January's friends Placebo and Justinus line up their arguments, authorities and (in Justinus' case) experience on opposite sides. January dismisses their authorities –

> Straw for thy Senek, and for thy proverbes!   1567

– and does exactly what he wants. He, moreover, is not even going to learn from his experience; and at the end, women's ability to fool their husbands receives divine sanction from Proserpina herself.

Griselda is so explicitly an exemplar of virtue that it is easy to accept the shift at the end of the Clerk's Tale from the literal to the parabolic mode, however difficult it may be to accept the particular meaning offered. The Merchant's Tale is in no way exemplary, even though it functions as further evidence in the greater debate on the nature of marriage, women, and ultimately the nature of good action.

It does none the less contain an anomalous allegorical strain in the names Chaucer chooses. In most of the tales he either names the characters (as in the Knight's and Miller's, right down to Gerveys the smith) or else avoids naming them (as in the Wife's, Friar's and Pardoner's tales); only rarely do the names suggest an allegorical function in the characters. January and May, however, are trapped in their rôles as old husband and young wife, frigid winter and erotic spring (rôles echoed in Chaucer's choice of Pluto and Proserpina at the end of the tale).[25] Placebo and Justinus have their arguments defined and judged in advance by their names, Placebo as the flatterer and yes-man, Justinus as the one who is right. The alarming thing is that these suggestions of moral import beyond the story never add up to anything. They suggest a pattern of coherent allegory, but never in fact provide one. The Miller's Tale could rest in the sufficiency of a cheerfully amoral narrative; the Merchant's Tale perpetually raises moral questions or expectations which it answers cynically or fails to fulfil.

The Clerk's Tale is disturbing because it is a story at odds with its own meaning. Virtue must serve an apparently wicked cause; and *matter* and *sentence*, the human development of the narrative and the *moralitas* the story is called on to serve, are never reconciled. There is almost as great a tonal misfit as in the story of Paletinus and his hanging-tree in the *Gesta Romanorum*. The Merchant's Tale is disorienting because of a similar displacement, though it is grounded in different elements of the work. It is primarily a generic displacement: the tale is a fabliau dressed up as a romance. The initial ideal view of human relationships gives way to licit and illicit sex of the crudest kind; Hymen and Venus may dance at the wedding, but May tears up Damian's note and drops the pieces in the privy. Romance elements in the story are debased by the way they are handled: the gods indulge in quarrelling and trickery; the love-garden comes complete with a reference to Priapus, the god of other things besides gardens; 'fresshe May' appears more stale with every action. Noble human virtues such as *pitee* and *gentillesse* become a high-sounding cover for self-interest:

> Lo, pitee renneth soone in gentil herte,   1986

is the comment (perhaps from the narrator, perhaps from May herself) on May's decision to throw over moral values and her marriage vows and pursue her affair with Damian. Animal imagery returns along

---

[25] See Whittock p. 160. Emerson Brown jr. suggests that Damian may be so named for similar contextual reasons, in 'The Merchant's Tale: why is May called "Mayus"?', *Chaucer Review* II (1967–8) 273–7. St. Damian was one of the patron saints of physicians, whose powers of healing included restoring sight; in the Sarum Breviary, Latin verses on the calendar page note, 'Mayus amat medicos.'

with animal action: January is 'coltish', 'ful of jargon as a flekked pye', with bristles like a houndfish; Damian fawns like a dog and acts like an adder; May is compared to animals in their edible form, to pike and veal. The strong layer of Christian reference in the tale is equally devalued. The paradise of marriage, and the paradisal garden, both contain their serpent, and their Eve; the garden substitutes a pear tree, with all its sexual associations, for the apple. St. Paul's mystic vision is debunked, along with that other supreme mystical text, the Song of Songs. January perverts this first by applying it literally, reducing its allegorical function as the highest expression of the love of Christ and the Church back to bare sexuality, and blind sexuality at that:

> Rys up, my wyf, my love, my lady free!
> The turtles voys is herd, my dowve sweete;
> The wynter is goon with alle his reynes weete . . .
> The gardyn is enclosed al aboute . . .
> No spot of thee ne knew I al my lyf. 2138–46

The *hortus conclusus* is often used as a symbol of the Virgin, and immaculateness is her attribute; they could hardly be less appropriate for May.[26] The narrator delivers the *coup de grace* to the speech by dismissing even the poetry:

> Swiche olde lewed wordes used he, 2149

and the narrative moves on at once, to the manoeuvrings to get Damian into the garden 'enclosed al aboute' by means of his duplicate key. Mystical allegory and sexual *double-entendre* are running dangerously close. As in romance, the tale ends with everyone happy, but this is itself a further perversion. May and Damian get what they want, but that is as crudely animal as anything in the *Canterbury Tales*. January is cured of his blindness and, one gathers, lives happily ever after; but his mental blindness is thicker than ever. If the ending of the story of Griselda failed to make up for the earlier suffering, there was at least a kind of satisfying justice in it, of virtue rewarded; here folly is duly rewarded, but January does not even realise that his bliss is a sham. The high ideals and the 'happy' ending of the Merchant's Tale all prove to be mere delusions.

In its conflation of high and low style, idealism and cynicism, Christian and animal, romance and fabliau, the Merchant's Tale is one of the virtuoso pieces of the *Canterbury Tales*. Brilliant as it is in itself, it becomes far richer in context. It is one of the most allusive stories

---

[26] Kellogg also compares Daniel xiii 20; see 'Susannah and the "Merchant's Tale"' (1960), reprinted in *Chaucer, Langland, Arthur* pp. 330–8.

in the whole collection, surpassed only by the Nun's Priest's. In level
it belongs with the fabliaux, but it looks back to the Knight's Tale in
plot and in its use of high style, and of associated conventions such as
gods and gardens. Its treatment of marriage picks up from the Wife
of Bath and Clerk. Its concern with the nature of blindness looks
across to the Second Nun and Canon's Yeoman. Its plot structure is
repeated and resolved in the Franklin's Tale. It contrasts strongly
with the explicitly religious tales in its treatment of Christian ideals;
but some of the most explicit (and baffling) links between the Parson's
Tale and the rest of the *Canterbury Tales* are located in this story.[27]
If Chaucer did decide on its placing only late in his scheme, this very
multiplicity of reference may be why: it offers too many possibilities.
It is followed in this arrangement, however, with a tale that has little
overt connection, the Squire's.

Fragment V(F): Squire and Franklin

The Squire's Tale has evoked a good deal of bewilderment among the
critics who have concerned themselves with it, but not bewilderment
of the deeply unsettling kind of the Clerk's or Merchant's Tales. It is
one of the few tales that have been felt to be badly written – an
unwelcome distinction that it shares with the Monk's Tale and the
prose tracts. Various reasons have been suggested for this: that it may
have been written early in Chaucer's career, and therefore shows his
youthful naïveté and artistic inexperience; or that the youthful
naïveté and artistic inexperience may be not Chaucer's but the
Squire's, who is the only young pilgrim on the journey, and so in style
as well as subject the tale is made appropriate for its teller.[28] Both
explanations appear unlikely. In his early work, such as the *Book of
the Duchess*, Chaucer does have moments of rhetorical clumsiness, but
not of the kind that call attention to themselves, as happens in this
tale: the most overworked rhetorical figure here is the modesty *topos*,
the disclaimer of artistic skill. If the disclaimers are not Chaucer's but
the Squire's – D. A. Pearsall comments, 'He has so much to be modest
about'[29] – then the process is still a very odd one. When Chaucer wants
to write bad poetry, as he does in *Sir Thopas*, the results can be quite
brilliant; but to write a sub-standard tale merely for dramatic purposes

---

[27] For examples, see pp. 203–4, 216 below.
[28] See e.g. Eleanor Prescott Hammond, *Chaucer: A Bibliographical Manual* (New
York, 1908) p. 250; Brewer, *Chaucerian Poetic* p. 9 n. 1; Marie Neville, 'The function of
the *Squire's Tale* in the Canterbury scheme', *JEGP* L (1951) 167–79; D. A. Pearsall,
'The Squire as story-teller', *University of Toronto Quarterly* XXXIV (1964–5) 82–92. On
the fallacy of equating poor quality with early work, see Robert O. Payne, *The Key of
Remembrance: A Study of Chaucer's Poetics* (New Haven, 1963) p. 151.
[29] Pearsall p. 84.

would seem perverse. If he can put superb poetry into the mouth of the Miller, there is no reason for him to make the Squire second best. The Squire indeed is the only pilgrim – apart from Chaucer – who has any literary pretensions:

> He koude songes make and wel endite. I 95

In view of what Chaucer does with his own tales, this might be suspicious; but it is hardly stressed enough to make an ironic point.

The reason for these peculiarities may perhaps lie not in the author or the narrator, but in the tale itself. If the stress on the difficulty of telling the tale has worried some critics, others have found a congruence between the story and the style that removes any problems. The Squire's Tale is a romance, like the Knight's; but all the romances of the *Canterbury Tales* are carefully differentiated. The Squire's is an interlaced romance – or rather, part of one, since it breaks off at the start of its third section. It shows every sign, too, of not being the more sophisticated kind of *entrelacement* described by Rosemond Tuve,[30] but of sheer multiplication of incident. The first part introduces Cambyuskan (perhaps a form of Genghis Khan) and a 'strange knight' who arrives at a feast bearing four magic gifts: for the king, a flying brass steed, and a sword that will cut any armour and heal the wounds it makes; and for his daughter Canacee, a mirror that shows coming adversity and distinguishes friend from foe and true lovers from false, and a ring that enables its wearer to know the virtues of herbs and understand the language of birds. In the second part, Canacee, who alone has no hangover after the previous night's feast, walks in the park and, by the virtue of her ring, hears and understands the lament of a falcon who has been betrayed in love by a false tercelet. This section concludes with an outline of what is to come: the king's son Cambalo will help the falcon to recover her love; there will be marvellous 'aventures' and 'batailles'. In addition,

> First wol I telle yow of Cambyuskan,
> That in his tyme many a citee wan;
> And after wol I speke of Algarsif,
> How that he wan Theodora to his wif,
> For whom ful ofte in greet peril he was,
> Ne hadde he ben holpen by the steede of bras;
> And after wol I speke of Cambalo,
> That faught in lystes with the bretheren two
> For Canacee er that he myghte hire wynne. 661–9

Three lines later the tale breaks off in mid-clause.

---

[30] See above, pp. 70–1.

There has been as much debate over whether Chaucer interrupts the tale deliberately as over the question of whether it is poorly written or a brilliant imitation of poor writing. The generic nature of the tale perhaps answers both questions. For all the recent critical attempts to rehabilitate the interlaced romance, the fact remains that most examples of the form are shapeless monsters of inordinate bulk. The tale must surely be interrupted deliberately: that is why the plot outline of the next half-dozen instalments is given, so that Chaucer can indicate the nature of the creature without actually having to write the rest. There is no room in the tight structuring of the *Tales* for an interlaced romance of full size, but by breaking it off short he can still include the form in his encyclopaedia of kinds. The interruption is made to serve more than a merely practical purpose, too. Chaucer makes a virtue of necessity. The Squire's Tale, like all the other tales, is a good one of its own particular kind; but Chaucer is implicitly passing aesthetic judgment on the whole genre.

As with the other stories, the tale defines, even creates, its own narrator. The elaboration of interlaced romance requires someone of high social rank as teller, on the principle of rhetorical decorum; and it requires too someone with an insatiable appetite for the marvellous, for adventures, for chivalry and sentiment, above all for plenty of things happening. The young and enthusiastic squire is posited by the nature of the tale itself. The naïve eagerness follows; and the terms in which it is expressed are instructive. Denying his own ability to do justice to the story, the Squire declares,

> He moste han knowen love and his servyse,
> And been a feestlych man as fressh as May,
> That sholde yow devysen swich array.   280–2

The lines are a self-portrait: the Squire himself is a 'lovyere', 'servysable' and 'as fressh as is the month of May'. Like the speeches that rise up to Fame's palace, this tale by its very nature forms its own speaker, and forms him in the image of the Squire. The Squire does, however, answer his own question as to just who could describe 'swich array', with its dancing and its love-glances:

> No man but Launcelot, and he is deed.   287

The line serves to relate both the action and style of the tale to the French romances of Lancelot, which were also often interlaced in structure, and which portrayed a world divorced from immediate human experience. Chaucer seems to have been little attracted by such romance. His only venture into Arthurian territory is the Wife of Bath's Tale, and there Arthur is relegated to the world of folktale; and the Nun's Priest firmly defines stories of Lancelot as fantasy.

A third question often raised in connection with the Squire's Tale, along with those on its quality and on the reasons for its incompleteness, is why it stands where it does, apparently interrupting the marriage group. This is something of an artificial problem: the theme of sovereignty in marriage is only one of the more obtrusive of the many interwoven thematic relationships in the work, and there is no reason why all the stories on that subject should come together, any more than do those on the love-triangle or the sufferings of the innocent. The Wife of Bath's Tale has its own relationships to the Friar's and Summoner's that are quite different from its links with the Clerk's and Merchant's; and the Squire's Tale is equally closely tied to the Franklin's.[31] As throughout the work, the links between fragments are less strong, or at least rely less on fine detail, than the links between the tales within a fragment. If the scheme for following the Merchant's Tale with the Squire's does go back to Chaucer, presumably he had in mind the same kind of balancing of character within a tale and within the pilgrimage as happens with the Miller and Symkyn, John the carpenter and Oswald the Reeve, the Friar and the Summoner. The Merchant's Tale had an amorous squire as one of its main characters; the amorous pilgrim Squire, who, as the Host points out in the Introduction to his tale, knows as much about love as anybody, will be given his right of reply. As one of the *gentils*, not one of the *cherles*, he ignores the opportunity of 'quiting' at a personal level; but his performance does at least rescue squires from the low level to which they had fallen, in preparation for the squire Aurelius' contest in *gentillesse* in the Franklin's Tale.

As part of the drama of the pilgrimage, the paired fabliaux had been linked by mutual insult. Fragment V is the only place in the work where two romances are juxtaposed; and they are linked by compliment. If the Merchant's Tale had presented a distasteful picture of a squire, the Franklin's Tale makes up for it; and the words of the Franklin to the Squire are as effusively complimentary as the exchanges between Friar and Summoner are insulting. 'Quiting' is used not in the sense of paying back but of living up to a personal or social standard:

> 'In feith, Squier, thow hast thee wel yquit
> And gentilly.' 673–4

---

[31] The relationships are studied, though along different lines from those I follow here, by Harry Berger, jr., in 'The F-fragment of the *Canterbury Tales*', *Chaucer Review* I (1966–7) 88–102, 135–56.

The Franklin's fictional squire within his tale is portrayed as exactly the same type as the pilgrim Squire: Aurelius

> fressher was and jolyer of array,
> As to my doom, than is the month of May.
> He syngeth, daunceth, passynge any man
> That is, or was, sith that the world began.
> Therwith he was, if men sholde hym discryve,
> Oon of the beste farynge man on lyve;
> Yong, strong, right vertuous, and riche, and wys,
> And wel biloved, and holden in greet prys.   927–34

Symkyn is a cruel parody of the Miller; Aurelius is the Squire raised to a higher degree of superlatives.

In the speech in which the Franklin addresses the Squire, he praises his 'wit', his eloquence, his 'vertu', and, by implication, his 'gentillesse'. Over the question of literary standard the praise is slightly barbed, with qualifications such as 'considerynge thy youthe', or

> 'As to my doom, ther is noon that is heere
> Of eloquence that shal be thy peere,
> If that thou lyve.'   677–9

Chaucer does not carry the compliment so far as to make any great claims for the story that has just been told. It has been argued that the Franklin's words to the Squire sound as if they are meant to follow a completed tale;[32] but 'thow hast thee wel yquit' could at least as well be an interruption, indicating that the Squire has done quite enough to fulfil the requirements of the story-telling, and the rest of the speech makes good sense as an effusively tactful cover for the break. The Franklin's speech gives a dramatic impetus to a generic necessity: Chaucer will turn his need to cut the tale short to advantage for his scheme of relationships. He will demonstrate courtesy and *gentillesse* in the goodwill that the Franklin generates, so that the narrative of the pilgrimage reflects the ideals of the tales. He will contrast the looseness of the interlaced romance with the tautness and concentration of the Breton lai, which is a kind of mini-romance focusing on a single action. He will take up themes from the Squire's Tale, especially the question of the relationship of gentle blood to gentle deeds, and handle them with a profundity that the earlier story completely missed. In addition, the Franklin's Tale looks back to many of the earlier tales: to the Knight's, in its exploration of the nature of Providence or the motif of the girl with two lovers; to the Wife's, in its exposition of sovereignty in marriage and of the nature of *gentillesse*;

---

[32] E.g. by Neville p. 168.

and, above all, to the Merchant's, of which it is in many respects a twin – though the Merchant's Tale is a deformed creature, the Franklin's ideal.

The romance is the literary form that stresses the perfectibility of man. In the late fourteenth century there was an increasing questioning as to whether such perfection was attainable – whether because of human fallibility, as in *Sir Gawain and the Green Knight*, or because of the conditions of the mutable world, which finally prevent a work such as *Troilus and Criseyde* from being a romance at all. Perfect virtue remains a valid ideal none the less: it is only the cynicism of the pseudo-romance of the Merchant's Tale that sees it as mere delusion. The Franklin's Tale is the story in the *Canterbury Tales* that comes closest to fulfilling that ideal.

The curious modern reluctance to take virtue seriously, and the equally curious belief that Chaucer must always be ironic, have led to a widespread reading of the Franklin's Tale as something rather different. The Franklin, by this account, is a social climber, acutely conscious of his inferiority to the Knight and Squire, and therefore obsessed with *gentillesse*. The main theme of his tale, the nature of virtuous action, can therefore be discounted as expressing a personal psychological quirk. As the Host says to him, 'Straw for youre gentillesse!' (695). The very fact that Chaucer gives Harry Bailey such words is an indication that there are other ways of looking at the matter: the Host is a singularly unreliable commentator. The argument is in any case circular: the insistence on *gentillesse* in the tale 'proves' the Franklin's obsession, and since he is obsessed his insistence need not be taken seriously. This is not Chaucer's method, however. Even in sections where the narrator is notoriously fallible – the Pardoner's Tale, for instance – the story itself remains untouched. The Pardoner may tell it to extract money, but the tale becomes all the more powerful an indictment of avarice because of that. In the same way, even if the Franklin did have a false view of *gentillesse*, his tale would be unaffected, or even strengthened, by it. There is, however, little evidence for this kind of psychological relationship of tale to teller. As is normal in the *Tales*, the primary fit is one of decorum. The romance is one of the major genres of mediaeval literature and comes in many forms, each demanding a different teller if Chaucer is to use them; but the social range of the General Prologue does not allow for too many aristocrats. In terms of social rank it is entirely appropriate that the Franklin, who is described by the romance term *vavasour*,[33]

---

[33] Roy J. Pearcy, 'Chaucer's Franklin and the literary Vavasour', *Chaucer Review* VIII (1973–4) 33–59. Pearcy concludes that the Franklin is not a social climber 'but the figural representative of an age wistfully asserting spiritual allegiance with an antique chivalric world whose values are rapidly becoming anachronistic' (p. 53).

should be given a romance to tell along with the Knight and Squire. Its particular form and content are also entirely appropriate for him. Its theme – a theme already sounded strongly by the Wife, Clerk and Squire – that virtue is independent of blood, and that the low-born can be as *gentil* as the aristocrat, is best suited to the man of middle rank, where it can sound neither pious nor envious. (It is, incidentally, another answer to the charge of social climbing that the Franklin is just as prepared to associate *gentillesse* with his clerk as with his knight.) In scope the tale is less epic (like the Knight's) or exotic (like the Squire's) than domestic, and therefore eminently fitting for the man whose virtues are shown in the details of local and domestic life: he is a great 'housholdere', generous with his hospitality and fond of good food and wine;[34] he is a justice of the peace, and has been a sherriff and a member of Parliament. If any psychological detail from his life is carried over into the tale, it is his generosity of spirit, his concern to find the best solution, his optimistic temperament (he is 'sangwyn'), and his magician's concern (1210–12) that the meal should be ready for his guests.

Having it both ways

?

More important than the tale's link with the Franklin is its connection with the preceding story. Their relationship of mutual goodwill exemplifies the theme of the Franklin's Tale; and if there is nothing explicitly complimentary to the Franklin in the Squire's Tale (as there is plenty that is explicitly insulting to the Summoner in the Friar's), it is at least the one tale in which the virtue of hospitality is stressed. Cambyuskan, like the Franklin, is fond of food and wine and eager to share it. One need not deduce from this that the Franklin takes it as a personal compliment – to invent a fictional character's unspoken thoughts when the author does not give the slightest hint of them is fantasy, not criticism – but it is perhaps enough to start the train of thought; and it makes it appropriate in the thematic structure of the work for Chaucer to have the Franklin respond as he does.

The tales are also contrasted generically, and poetically. The Squire's perpetual apologies for his shortcomings, and his prolix insistence that 'for fulsomnesse of his prolixitee' he must get on with the narrative (401–8), are replaced by the Franklin's much more socially graceful declaration of modesty:

> But, sires, by cause I am a burel man,
> At my bigynnyng first I yow biseche,

---

[34] Another charge sometimes levelled against the Franklin is that he exemplifies the sin of gluttony. In contrast with the Monk, however, the stress falls on the fact that the Franklin *shares* his food: the Monk could never be described as St. Julian, patron saint of hospitality. D. W. Robertson (who accuses the Franklin of avarice as well as self-indulgence) gives the counter-argument: see 'Chaucer's Franklin and his Tale' (1974) reprinted in *Essays in Medieval Culture* (Princeton, 1980) pp. 273–90, esp. pp. 278–9.

Have me excused of my rude speche . . .
Colours ne knowe I none, withouten drede,
But swiche colours as growen in the mede,
Or elles swiche as men dye or peynte.
Colours of rethoryk been to me queynte.   716–18, 723–6

His apology, it turns out, is entirely unnecessary: the tale is beauti-
fully told, and with no shortage of rhetorical colours. In form, too, it
is everything that the Squire's is not. There has been much debate as
to why Chaucer calls the tale a Breton lai: whether it is to demonstrate
the Franklin's old-fashioned provincialism, or whether Chaucer's immediate source may have been neither the *Filocolo* nor the *Decameron*
but a French lai that has been lost without trace.[35] The nature of the
genre itself offers a more immediate explanation. In its handling of
narrative and of romance motifs, the typical Breton lai is diametrically
opposed to the interlaced romance. It is short; it concentrates on a
single action, not the sprawling multiplicity of character and incident
of the interlace; and its emphasis falls not on narrative but on human
emotion. These are the characteristics of both the Anglo-French *Lais*
of Marie de France and of the English lais of the Auchinleck manuscript and elsewhere; they are also, supremely, the characteristics of
the Franklin's Tale. If the story is not a Breton lai by origin, Chaucer
will provide the excuse for the classification by giving it a setting in
Brittany; and Boccaccio's story has the potential for narrative and
thematic transformation into the typical pattern of the lai.

The main narrative element of the Squire's Tale was the four magic
gifts; the main area of emotional or moral comment had to do not with
people but with birds. The concerns of the Franklin's Tale are very
solidly human. The tale opens with the courtship and marriage of
Dorigen and Arveragus: she is touched by 'pitee', impressed by his
'worthynesse', and through *gentillesse* they establish a relationship in
which each obeys the other. Arveragus goes abroad to maintain his
chivalric honour in the larger world; in his absence, the squire
Aurelius confesses his love for her. She is horrified and rejects him,
but tries to soften his despair by promising to love him if he will
remove the rocks that threaten to wreck her husband's ship on his
return. After two years of languishing, Aurelius enlists the help of a
magician to remove the rocks. Dorigen confesses to her husband what
she has done; and he sends her to fulfil her vow. Aurelius, however,
refuses to take advantage of Arveragus' *gentillesse*, and sends her
back unharmed; and the magician in his turn, a clerk of Orleans,
releases Aurelius from the thousand pounds promised to him,
declaring,

[35] See Bryan and Dempster p. 385 and the references cited there.

> God forbede, for his blisful myght,
> But if a clerk koude doon a gentil dede
> As wel as any of yow, it is no drede!   1610–12

Not the least interesting thing in all this is how very unimportant the disappearance of the rocks is. Chaucer never claims that they actually vanish –

> For a wyke or tweye,
> It *semed* that alle the rokkes were aweye   1295–6

– and nobody ever actually goes to look. The Squire's Tale could not progress at all without its element of the marvellous and the supernatural; here, all the emphasis falls on how the characters react. The dilemma of the plot is resolved, not through magic, but because the irruption of the supernatural into the ordinary world makes everyone behave with a fineness that goes, not beyond the human – the point of the story is that all men have the same potential for noble action – but certainly beyond the commonplace.

The tales of the Wife of Bath and the Clerk had stressed the positive aspect of the independence of virtue from noble blood: that *gentillesse* could be found in the low-born. The Merchant's Tale by implication denied that *gentillesse* could be found anywhere – phrases such as 'this gentil May' deprive the term of all meaning. The falcon in the Squire's Tale seems quite surprised that high blood and virtue are separate. 'Pitee renneth soone in gentil herte' (479), 'gentil herte kitheth gentillesse' (483), but that is no defence against hypocrisy: the tercelet 'semed welle of alle gentillesse' (505),

> And kepeth in semblaunt alle his observaunces
> That sownen into gentillesse of love.   516–17

When it comes to the point, however – when the tercelet sees and falls for a kite, a less noble bird – 'though he were gentil born'

> No gentillesse of blood ne may hem bynde.   620

The falcon had loved the tercelet 'for the trouthe I demed in his herte' (563), and they had exchanged vows. The tercelet, however, like Arveragus after his own marriage, has to leave her to maintain his honour in the larger world; and in betraying her for the kite,

> He hath his trouthe falsed in this wyse.   627

'Trouthe' is a key word of the Franklin's Tale too. Dorigen swears her 'trouthe' to be a 'humble trewe wyf' to Arveragus; never suspecting any clash between the oaths, she makes a similar promise to Aurelius:[36]

> I seye, whan ye han maad the coost so clene
> Of rokkes that ther nys no stoon ysene,
> Thanne wol I love yow best of any man,
> Have heer my trouthe, in al that evere I kan.   995–8

The second promise seems to presage disaster; but in fact it is the insistence on keeping *trouthe*, the readiness to stand by one's pledged word, that brings about the happy ending, just as in the Wife of Bath's Tale. Arveragus sends his wife to Aurelius with the words – spoken weeping –

> Trouthe is the hyeste thyng that man may kepe.   1479

There is nothing easy in following the dictates of ideal virtue: but his example inspires Aurelius and the clerk to act with equal magnanimity.

To compare this story with the Squire's at this point may seem odd when the subjects and tones are so different, but the close similarities of plot and even of phrasing insist on the comparison. Breaking of 'trouthe' destroys the apparent bliss of the falcon's love and prevents her mate from returning to her; keeping of 'trouthe' in the Franklin's Tale ensures that in the end

> Arveragus and Dorigen his wyf
> In sovereyn blisse leden forth hir lyf.   1551–2

If the Franklin interrupts the Squire's Tale, there is also an important sense in which he completes it. Supernatural intervention in the ordinary world and human relationships are both re-defined, and set

---

[36] Dorigen's apparent willingness to break her marriage vow, and to keep her word to Aurelius rather than her husband, has been the subject of critical censure, notably by Alan T. Gaylord, 'The promises in the Franklin's Tale', *ELH* XXXI (1964) 331–65. The criticism can be rejected, I believe, on three grounds. First, neither folktales nor Breton lais necessarily follow strict Christian ethics: see Kathryn Hume, 'Why Chaucer calls the *Franklin's Tale* a Breton lai', *Philological Quarterly* LI (1972) 365–79. Secondly, there is a clash in the tale between acting by the letter and acting by the spirit. Acting by the spirit is higher; but the letter is none the less binding. Dorigen must stand by the literal interpretation of her promise to Aurelius precisely because she has a lesser relationship with him; her relationship with her husband is one of emotional fidelity transcending spoken promises, or even sexual fidelity. The end of the *Morte Darthur* would serve as an analogy: Arthur can see beyond strict legalism to a higher magnanimity, but he is none the less legally bound to support Gawain in a technically just quarrel regardless of the cost. In addition, it is Arveragus who releases Dorigen from her *trouthe*, just as the clerk releases Aurelius.

in a plot that makes sense of them. Magic, the Franklin insists, even 'magyk natureel', is a perversion in the ordered Christian world (1261–93), with no more value than illusory wish-fulfilment. It is only in 'apparaunce' that Aurelius can dance with his lady. The way to bring about a permanently happy ending to a story of unhappy love is simply through human virtue. Given the Franklin's Tale, the Squire's does not need to be finished. The narrative may be incomplete, but its themes are taken over and concluded with a profundity that the Squire's Tale itself could never have achieved.

Fragment VI(C): Physician and Pardoner

The fragment containing the Physician's and Pardoner's Tales always occurs in the manuscripts immediately before Fragment VII(B²), but only the Ellesmere manuscript and its associated group place it after the Franklin's. The arrangement is not unsatisfactory: the Physician's Tale is an exemplary story of female chastity of exactly the kind referred to by Dorigen in her lengthy lament.[37] Whether this reflects Chaucer's ordering, or whether one is finding one more example of Donaldson's *ex post facto* resonances, remains a matter for conjecture; but allowing for the incomplete state of the *Tales*, the Ellesmere placing is probably the best there could be.

The Physician's and Pardoner's Tales are in some respects anti-types of each other, giving exemplary portrayals of virtue and sin. In terms of plot motif, they are unexpectedly close, being the only two tales of the whole work to be concerned with violent death deliberately inflicted (martyrdoms and *tragedies* excluded, and also Arcite's 'accidental' death). The tales portray in turn the gifts of Nature and of Fortune.[38] Virginia, the heroine of the Physician's Tale, is outstandingly beautiful,

> For Nature hath with sovereyn diligence
> Yformed hire in so greet excellence.   9–10

The rioters of the Pardoner's Tale, having come upon the heap of gold, exult that

> This tresor hath Fortune unto us yiven.   779

---

[37] See Peter G. Beidler, 'The pairing of the *Franklin's Tale* and the *Physician's Tale*', *Chaucer Review* III (1968–9) 275–9.

[38] See Gerhard Joseph, 'The gifts of nature, fortune and grace in the *Physician's, Pardoner's* and *Parson's Tale*', *Chaucer Review* IX (1974–5) 237–45; R. Michael Haines, 'Fortune, nature, and grace in Fragment C', *Chaucer Review* X (1975–6) 220–35; and Paul G. Ruggiers, *The Art of the Canterbury Tales* (Madison, 1965) pp. 122–3.

In the link connecting the tales, the Host comments on this pairing, though he sees the two sorts of gifts not as being contrasted with each other but as both leading equally to disaster:

> I seye al day that men may see
> That yiftes of Fortune and of Nature
> Been cause of deeth to many a creature . . .
> Of bothe yiftes that I speke of now
> Men han ful ofte moore for harm than prow. 294–6, 299–300

It is the kind of platitude that Chaucer delights in giving to the Host; he hints at, without apparently being aware of, the deeper questions raised by the juxtaposition of the tales, notably the fact that the virtuous are just as likely to come to an unpleasant end as are the sinful.

The Physician's Tale is a short tale of suffering virtue. Virginius' chaste and beautiful daughter is seen and desired by the wicked judge Apius; he procures a man to lay a false claim that she is his slave, stolen away when a child, and Virginius, to prevent her falling into Apius' hands, kills her. The people rise against Apius, he is imprisoned and commits suicide. The origin of the story goes back to Livy, though Chaucer's primary source was the *Roman de la Rose*; as in the *Roman*, Chaucer does not specify any location for the story, and the pagan setting implied by his mention of a temple is modified later by Virginia's acquaintance with the story of Jephtha and her apostrophes to God. The tale therefore becomes a kind of secular hagiography, a pious as well as an exemplary work. It has often been compared to the stories of the *Legend of Good Women* (the legend of Lucretia, who also prefers death to dishonoured life, is a particularly close parallel); but the shift of emphasis towards piety makes it tonally different, and its placing next to the Pardoner's Tale qualifies it further to make an effect impossible in the single-moral series of the *Legend*.

Each tale starts with a brief mention of its protagonists – Virginia, the three rioters – and then proceeds with a long analysis of their virtues or vices, often very precisely contrasted. Virginia conducts herself

> With alle humylitee and abstinence,
> With alle attemperaunce and pacience,
> With mesure eek of beryng and array.
> Discreet she was in answeryng alway. 45–8

The revellers eat and drink 'over hir myght', 'by superfluytee abhominable'; they swear, and laugh at each other's oaths; and in the course of the tale their pride, impatience, indiscretion and 'vileynye' in speech and action are abundantly demonstrated. Virginia avoids every place that might conduce to vice:

> She hath ful ofte tyme syk hire feyned,
> For that she wolde fleen the compaignye
> Where likly was to treten of folye,
> As is at feestes, revels, and at daunces.   62–5

Such a setting is precisely suited to the rioters:

> In Flaundres whilom was a compaignye
> Of yonge folk that haunteden folye,
> As riot, hasard, stywes, and tavernes,
> Wher as with harpes, lutes, and gyternes,
> They daunce and pleyen at dees bothe day and nyght.   463–7

Virginia avoids sloth and alcohol, and therefore unchastity: she is

> everе in bisynesse
> To dryve hire out of ydel slogardye.
> Bacus hadde of hir mouth right no maistrie;
> For wyn and youthe dooth Venus encrease.   56–9

The rioters are perpetually idle, and given over to drunkenness and lechery:

> Luxurie is in wyn and dronkenesse.   484

The two tales speak with one voice on the things that corrupt the young; but Virginia has kept herself uncorrupted. Many juxtaposed stories in the *Canterbury Tales* contrast virtue and vice – the Clerk's and Merchant's; the Second Nun's and Canon's Yeoman's; also the Man of Law's and the fabliaux of Fragment I, if that arrangement is Chaucerian. The Physician's and Pardoner's Tales are one of the most striking instances, especially striking because of the closely similar descriptions of the two states, and because both stories have not only an exemplary but something approaching an allegorical quality.

None of the characters is a moral personification; but the handling of both stories has similarities with the allegorical mode of the morality play. The Physician's Tale was indeed turned into one in the later sixteenth century, as *Apius and Virginia*, 'wherein is lively expressed a rare example of the vertue of Chastitie'.[39] There are good family reasons for Virginia's being called as she is – her father Virginius is named in the second line of the tale – but the name clearly has a

---

[39] From the title page of the 1575 edition, reproduced in *Tudor Interludes* ed. Peter Happé (Harmondsworth, 1972) p. 271. The play, by 'R.B.', dates from the 1560s.

morally defining function within the story too. Virginia herself is not named until her father has decided that he must kill her:

> 'Doghter,' quod he, 'Virginia, by thy name,
> Ther been two weyes, outher deeth or shame,
> That thou most suffre.'   213–15

Her identity, even her existence, is unimaginable without her virginity:

> O gemme of chastitee, in pacience
> Take thou thy deeth,   223–4

and it is on those terms that she accepts willingly:

> Blissed be God, that I shal dye a mayde!   248

The moment of naming is often crucial in mediaeval literature – especially in romance (the naming of Perceval in Chretien de Troyes' *Conte del Graal* is a fine example), but also in works such as the *Divine Comedy*, where Dante's name is heard only once, as the first word spoken by Beatrice. The completion of the heroine's full identity by giving her her name in the Physician's Tale shows exactly the same technique, and within the lesser terms of the story it is just as momentous.

The Pardoner's Tale, by contrast, gains much of its morality-like quality from its lack of proper names. The opening line identifies the setting as Flanders, for no very obvious reason; it might have something to do with the fame of Dutch drinking habits. In any case, the location is unimportant: by the time the story gets under way, after almost two hundred lines in which the Pardoner expatiates on the viciousness of vice, geographical setting has been forgotten. It does matter that the story should start from a particular place, should be recognisable in terms of literal action; but after that it moves into a more sinister world where meanings unsensed by the rioters underlie the landscape – the gold is to be found in a 'grove', with its associations of disorder and chaos, reached by a 'croked way'.[40] The three rioters are never named. They are differentiated by neutral terms, 'that oon', 'that oother'; or by age, 'the yongeste'; or, more significantly, by their degree of sinfulness – 'the proudeste', 'the worste', 'this cursed man'. It is part of their morality function that they should not be identifiable as *other* people: they are, potentially, the audience, and the theme of the sermon, *Radix malorum est cupiditas*, 'Love of money is the root of all evil', is aimed at the listeners through their potential exempli-

---

[40] VI 761–2; see above p. 129.

fication in the rioters. The lack of proper names is indeed stressed in the tale. When the revellers hear a bell ring as it is carried before a corpse, they send to know the man's name:

> 'Axe redily
> What cors is this that passeth heer forby;
> And looke that thou reporte his name weel.'   667–9

The name is never given, for the corpse is an Everyman figure. As in the famous passage in Donne's *Devotions*, there is no need to seek to know for whom the bell tolls: it tolls for them. Instead, the man's slayer is named – the one name given in the whole tale.

> Ther cam a privee theef men clepeth Deeth.   675

The central theme of the tale is not in fact love of money; it is the nature of death – death who strikes the reveller as he sits drinking, who carries off a thousand together in times of pestilence, who can be found in the form of the pile of gold under a tree, and yet who will spare the old, the maimed and the sorrowing. The Old Man who longs to die is a figure familiar from the mediaeval iconography of death, where skeletons seize the young and beautiful and ignore the elderly beggars who stretch out their hands to be taken. The Old Man, 'povre' as he is, yearns to exchange the last of his worldly goods, the chest in his chamber, for a shroud; death to him would be a 'grace'. Through their desire for riches the young men find only agonising death, and the 'fair grace' that they believe they have found in the treasure is bitterly ironic.

The Pardoner's Tale is an extraordinarily compelling piece of writing – one of the finest pieces of short fiction ever composed.[41] As such it illustrates particularly well the autonomy of each tale of the Canterbury series; but even here the tale derives extra richness from its setting in the wider context of the pilgrimage. Like the Canterbury journey itself, the Pardoner's Tale is a quest: the pilgrimage is a quest for salvation, the rioters embark on a quest for death. In many of its plot motifs and thematic concerns it is related not only to the Physician's Tale but to other tales at greater distance: to the Wife's and Friar's in its episode of meeting one's fate by the wayside in a forest, to the Knight's and Friar's in its concern with sworn brotherhood. Its concern with the nature of true 'felicitee', however negatively expressed here, is one of the major themes recurring throughout the work. The most immediate context for the Pardoner's Tale, however, is the Pardoner himself. Chaucer's characterisation of the tale's nar-

---

[41] Mention should be made here of Ian Bishop, 'The narrative art of *The Pardoner's Tale*', *Medium Aevum* XXXVI (1967) 15–24.

rator does not alter the story, but it does affect the way it is written and our understanding of it – the long diatribe against drunkenness and gluttony, for instance, is inseparable from the fact that the Pardoner insists on stopping at an 'alestake' to eat and drink before he can begin his story. It also alters our understanding of what a tale can do, of the uses, or in this case the abuses, of literature.

There is a rather odd passage at the beginning of the Physician's Tale on the importance of having good governesses for 'lordes doghtres'. As good a qualification as honesty for such a profession is experience in all the 'olde daunce', on the principle that one should set a thief to catch a thief – or (Chaucer's own analogy) that poachers make the best gamekeepers. Too indulgent an approach is disastrous, for

> Under a shepherde softe and necligent
> The wolf hath many a sheep and lamb torent.   101–2

The passage is explicitly irrelevant to Virginia, who 'so kepte hirself hir neded no maistresse', and it has sometimes been explained by reference to historical circumstances relating to the family of John of Gaunt.[42] There is no need to look so far for a context for the passage, however. In terms of Fragment VI, it is less a digression than an introduction. The Pardoner himself, the avaricious drinker who preaches against drunkenness and avarice, is an active poacher who has set himself up as gamekeeper, a wolf who fleeces the laity under the guise of pastoral care.

Worst of all, he knows exactly what he is doing:

> I preche agayn that same vice
> Which that I use, and that is avarice.   427–8

He knows all about the moral justifications for fiction: instruction is best conveyed by *exempla*, for the unlearned enjoy stories –

> Thanne telle I hem ensamples many oon
> Of olde stories longe tyme agoon.
> For lewed peple loven tales olde.   435–7

The authors of legendaries or of vernacular Bible collections such as the *Cursor Mundi* had given exactly the same reason for their compilations. Their primary purpose, however, was to teach men by example of the good. The Pardoner claims to be able to make people repent of avarice,

---

[42] See Robinson's note on line 72 ff.: John of Gaunt's mistress (and eventual third wife), Katherine Swynford, was also the governess of his legitimate daughters.

> But that is nat my principal entente;
> I preche nothyng but for coveitise.   432–3

The morality of the story, from his point of view, is primarily a way to fill his pockets. The Pardoner's Tale fulfils its traditional literary purpose of both delighting – 'lewed peple loven tales olde' – and teaching, for it brings people to repentance; that literature can bring more practical rewards too is a factor omitted from the classic formulation. The Pardoner wrecks the easy distinction between corrupting tales and stories conducive to virtue:

> Though myself be a ful vicious man,
> A moral tale yet I yow telle kan.   459–60

Poetry and ethics were closely related in mediaeval literary theory:[43] the theoretical justification for literature was indeed entirely ethical, never aesthetic. In terms of the aesthetic judgment that Chaucer invites his readers to bring to the tales when he sets up the storytelling as a competition, the Pardoner's Tale ranks very high. Ethically, it serves God and Mammon with impressive even-handedness.

If a vicious man can tell a moral story, there is still one important respect in which the Pardoner's Tale differs from the moral stories told by many of the other pilgrims, the Physician included. The tales of Custance and Griselda and Virginia all concentrate on virtue; it may be no defence against suffering, or against the wickedness of pagan stepmothers and lecherous judges, but at least those tales essentially portray goodness. Vision of that kind is not available to the wicked themselves. The Pardoner's first inclination is to tell 'ribaudye', *No* but the *gentils* demand 'som moral thyng' instead. Even his 'honest' story, however, is devoid of virtue. The Pardoner, and also the Friar, are ecclesiastics who abuse their religious function for their own ends; both are fond of wenching, and are prepared to wring money out of the poorest widow; both abuse their powers of absolution. The tales they tell are also very similar: of sinful men who go out questing and commit themselves to sworn brotherhood that leads them to death and damnation. In the Friar's Tale there is a momentary glimpse of something approaching virtue, in the ordinary fallible humanity of the carter who blesses his horses when they have dragged the cart out of the mire; in the Pardoner's Tale there is not even that. The Pardoner, by profession, should open the way to salvation; but in his vision of the world there is nothing but evil.

---

[43] See Allen and Moritz p. 66.   *The old man*

Peculiarly unsatisfactory

Fragment VII(B²): The Tales of the Shipman, the Prioress,
Chaucer, the Monk and the Nun's Priest

The six tales of Fragment VII make up the longest group in the
Canterbury Tales. The fragment might therefore be expected to illustrate Chaucer's methods of interlinking the tales most clearly; and
the presence of his own tales among the six further suggests that the
level of artistic self-consciousness in the section will be particularly
high, however derogatorily or ironically Chaucer may present himself.
These hopes are magnificently fulfilled, though in few of the ways one
might have expected.

At first glance, the fragment is more diffuse, and each tale more
prone to head off in its own direction regardless of the others, than
any other section of the *Canterbury Tales*. The generic diversity of the
tales is immediately striking: the Shipman's fabliau of the wife who
has an affair with a monk, the Prioress's miracle of the Virgin in
which a small boy is murdered by the Jews and miraculously sings
the *Alma redemptoris mater*, the debased popular romance of *Sir Thopas*, the moralistic tract of *Melibee*, the Monk's tragedies, the Nun's
Priest's beast-fable of Chauntecleer and Pertelote. The prosodic medium as well as the genre is changed for each tale: riding rhyme for
the first and last tales, the Shipman's and the Nun's Priest's; rhyme
royal for the Prioress; prose for the tract; an eight-line stanza for the
Monk; tail-rhyme stanzas of an increasingly undisciplined kind for *Sir
Thopas*, for which the sprawling manuscript layout adds one more
joke to all the rest provided by the tale. Such diversity makes the risk
of overall structural incoherence particularly acute; and where in
other fragments Chaucer binds together contrasting stories by echoes
of plot or theme – the Miller's fabliau as parody of the Knight's
romance and so on – there is comparatively little of that here. Both
the child of the Prioress's Tale and 'child' Thopas set their love on a
heavenly or supernatural woman – the Virgin and the Elf-queen;[44]
the Nun's Priest's Tale has a generous potential for turning into a
tragedy of Fortune of the kind that the Monk has been telling; but
while such links may be interesting, they are hardly the centre of
interest.

Instead, the series turns into a debate on literature, its methods and
functions and status. Alan T. Gaylord has indeed suggested the name
'the Literature Group' for this fragment.[45] Unlike the debate over
sovereignty in marriage, the discussion here is not projected back into

[44] See Mary Hamel, 'And now for something completely different: the relationship
between the *Prioress's Tale* and the *Rime of Sir Thopas*', *Chaucer Review* XIV (1979–
80) 251–9.

[45] In a fascinating article in *PMLA* LXXXII (1967) 226–35, '*Sentence* and *Solaas* in
Fragment VII of the *Canterbury Tales*: Harry Bailey as horseback editor', p. 227.

the pilgrims' consciousness. They often make some slight comment on
the theoretical nature of the tale they are going to tell, or Harry
Bailey is given a response that expresses his own ideas of what a story
could or should be, but the range and depth of debate belongs to the
author alone. The pilgrim Chaucer has no more idea than the Host of
what is really going on in *Sir Thopas,* nor does the Monk see his
anthology of tragedies as an epitome of the kind of story-collection
that the *Canterbury Tales* as a whole is not. The discussion of the
nature of literature goes far beyond defining in miniature what the
work itself is, however, although that inevitably comes into it: the
encyclopaedic emphasis in the *Tales* draws all literary experience
within its range, and so the analysis given in this section has implications for the whole work. Any final understanding of the *Canterbury
Tales* must take into account the discussion of poetry contained in this
fragment. Other sections of the *Tales* explore the potential contained
in different genres, with their different perspectives on experience; in
this group, the generic diversity is more marked than anywhere else
in the work, but the limitations of each genre are also shown up as
they are not elsewhere. Chaucer constantly tests the relationship of
meaning and style, from its most formal and technical aspects to a
questioning of the nature and function of rhetoric. He examines from
many angles the rôle of literary and semantic tradition and convention. The relation of matter to meaning, *sentence,* which is an issue
throughout the *Tales,* is explicitly brought to the fore here, and the
formulation that literature should teach and delight, contain 'som
murthe or som doctryne', or both, is tested against the experience of
actual tales. Chaucer even raises such basic questions as the status of
language.

The Shipman's Tale might seem a singularly unlikely place to find
matters of such far-reaching literary import. It is the story, once
apparently assigned to the Wife of Bath, of how a merchant's wife
agrees to sleep with a monk in return for a hundred franks, which the
monk borrows off her husband and then declares he has repaid to the
wife. The social class of the characters is higher than in the other
fabliaux, and the tone rises a little accordingly: there is less overt
bawdiness than in the Miller's or Reeve's Tales, and the animal
imagery is less obtrusive. Both are there, none the less; and there is
a clear equation made between animal and female flesh when the
monk, Daun John, asks the merchant for a loan so that he can buy
'beestes'. The Host too sees the tale as taking place on precisely that
level of animality:

> 'The monke putte in the mannes hood an ape,
> And in his wyves eek, By Seint Austyn!'   440–1

Animal instinct in the Miller's Tale had at least brought freshness and spontaneity with it; here the equation made is between sex and money. The wife barters her favours for the hundred franks, and at the end informs her husband that she will pay him back in the same way. The tale has a potential for cynicism as great as the Merchant's, both in the plot and in the way words such as 'gentil' or 'honour' are used in a debased sense; but the tone is not cynical. There are no ideals, and so there can be no disillusionment. All the characters seem entirely happy with the bargain they have struck, and if the merchant does not know quite what has been going on he is not blinded in the way January is. Everybody gets what they want; that there might be higher things to be wanted is an issue never raised.

The Shipman's Tale is not just a high-class fabliau: there are more subversive implications too in the way Chaucer handles the story. The world of the Miller's Tale was one of cheerful amorality; and even in the fabliaux less bursting with vitality, there is a sense of poetic justice in the way the plots work out – the Reeve's Symkyn suffers the social and pecuniary loss he deserves, the Summoner's Friar gets the gift he asked for. John the carpenter may not be a knave, but he is that figure equally the butt of comedy, the fool. The fabliau, in other words, tends to work by its own scheme of morality; but not the Shipman's Tale. The merchant is upright, generous, and unsuspecting, demonstrably not guilty of the impotence and meanness his wife charges him with. Half the fun of the other fabliaux lies in their conscious breaking of moral and social norms; here, that the wife sells her favours and the monk cheats her of the price passes without causing a ripple on the surface. The other fabliaux depend on the listeners' consciousness of accepted morality; here neither the characters in the tale nor the narrator seem aware of any such thing, and the audience is invited simply to appreciate a set of clever tricks culminating in a happy ending. Of all the fabliaux in the *Canterbury Tales*, this is the only one to be totally amoral, for the contrasting moral context has disappeared.

It has disappeared, that is, from within this particular tale. The reason why Chaucer re-assigned the tale to the apparently inappropriate Shipman may be that he, like so many of the other pilgrims who tell tales artistically brilliant of their kind but of less than perfect significance, is professionally superlative but less than perfect as a human being – witness his lack of 'nyce conscience', and his custom of drowning the men he overcomes in the course of what seems to be a career, or a side-line, of piracy. There is some point, perhaps, in following his tale with the Prioress's, for whom 'al was conscience and tendre herte'. A tale in which morality is totally absent is followed by one in which spiritual standards dominate. That there might be a world of the spirit, even a world of emotion, is a consideration that never impinges on the Shipman's Tale; in the Prioress's, there is nothing else.

The tales are each so completely self-enclosed that the contrast remains an unspoken effect of the juxtaposition. It is never hinted at in the words of the text – unless it is suggested by the difference in tone of Harry Bailey's guffawing reaction to the Shipman ('The monke putte in the mannes hood an ape') and his elaborately deferential politeness to the Prioress:

> 'My lady Prioresse, by youre leve,
> So that I wiste I sholde yow nat greve,
> I wolde demen that ye tellen sholde
> A tale next, if so were that ye wolde.
> Now wol ye vouche sauf, my lady deere?'   446–51

Language in the indicative is a totally different social and moral phenomenon from language in the subjunctive. The change of key between the tales – tales which show a more complete contrast in genre, subject and style than any pair outside this fragment – is accomplished in the link between them; but the level of semantic and linguistic consciousness Chaucer shows in his choice of words for the Host points to another element in the tales beyond that of simple contrast, for both tales are concerned, though in different ways, with the status of words.

Puns are not as rare in Chaucer as was once supposed, but it is certainly unusual to find a work that depends on them; the plot climax of the Shipman's Tale is worked out through precisely these means. The wife gets herself out of the fix she is in by promising to repay her husband by his scoring the debt on her 'taille', in both its sexual sense and its meaning of 'tally' – the worlds of sex and finance are again equated. The same happens with words such as 'dettour', 'paye' and 'wedde' (when the wife offers her 'joly body' 'to wedde', as security for a loan and for the purposes of sex): the merchant understands primarily the financial meaning, she the sexual implication. There are a number of other puns or equivocal meanings at work in the story. 'Cosyn' and 'cosynage' very soon cease strictly to denote kinship and acquire a secondary sense of 'cozen', 'cozenage' – a word not elsewhere attested in Middle English but familiar enough, in a bilingual culture, from French.[46] It is certainly hard to believe that Chaucer did not

---

[46] Cf. Cotgrave's definition of French *cousiner* (1611) as 'to clayme kindred for aduantage, or particular ends; as he, who to saue charges in trauelling, goes from house to house, as cosin to the owner of euerie one'. The etymology is probably false: see OED *cozen* (where this passage is quoted). There is a discussion of the uses of the *double-entendre* in the Shipman's Tale in David H. Abraham, 'Cosyn and Cosynage: pun and structure in the *Shipman's Tale*', *Chaucer Review* XI (1976–7) 319–27; and see also V. J. Scattergood, 'The originality of the *Shipman's Tale*', ibid. pp. 210–31, esp. pp. 216–17.

have the other meaning in mind in lines such as Daun John's final farewell to the merchant,

> 'Grete wel oure dame, myn owene nece sweete,
> And fare wel, deere cosyn, til we meete!' 363–4

The lines have much more of the sting of a parting shot if the second meaning is borne in mind; and there is an appropriate additional irony in the wife's comment to her husband that she believed the monk had given her the money

> For cosynage, and eek for beele cheere. 409

The second phrase, 'beele cheere', means different things to the wife and the merchant – she means sex, she intends him to understand hospitality and kindness; and while the term is not actually a pun, there are other words and phrases similarly used to carry two levels of meaning at once. 'Honour' (179, 408) is one such word, when the wife twice declares her expense on clothes is for her husband's honour; its moral connotations in this story tend to come second to its social implications. 'Good' is another, when the merchant asks his wife before he leaves and again at the very end to 'kepe our good', 'keep bet my good': she is disposing of what is rightfully his in ways he never dreams of.

The process of undermining the fixed status of language, coupled with the unspoken critique of the assumptions of the tale, may be the reason why Chaucer puts the Shipman's Tale into this group. The Prioress's Tale also displays a concern for the function of language, though in a totally different way suited to the totally different genre. Here, the concern is with the inadequacy of earthly language to express the spiritual. The prayer to the Virgin in the Prologue sets out the problem:

> Lady, thy bountee, thy magnificence,
> Thy vertu, and thy grete humylitee,
> Ther may no tonge expresse in no science . . . 474–6

> My konnyng is so wayk, o blisful Queene,
> For to declare thy grete worthynesse,
> That I ne may the weighte nat susteene;
> But as a child of twelf month oold, or lesse,
> That kan unnethes any word expresse,
> Right so fare I, and therfore I yow preye,
> Gydeth my song that I shal of yow seye. 481–7

The theme of the tale picks up a similar idea: the 'litel clergeon', seven years old, can of course speak, unlike the twelve-month-old, but he cannot understand Latin. In learning the *Ave Maria* and the *Alma Redemptoris Mater* he is using a language of which he understands the spiritual, not the verbal, import:

> The swetnesse hath his herte perced so
> Of Cristes mooder that, to hire to preye,
> He kan nat stynte of syngyng by the weye.   555–7

His life beyond earth, in Heaven, is envisioned as a place of spiritual singing to 'the white Lamb celestial'. Just as the Prioress asks for the Virgin's guidance in her own 'song', so after his murder it is by her intervention that the boy continues to sing, until the 'greyn' she has laid on his tongue is removed. None of the analogues to the story contains a grain, and there has been some discussion as to what Chaucer meant by it.[47] The obvious sense would be of a grain of wheat or something equivalent; and it is at least possible that in choosing the miraculous object Chaucer did not wish to exclude the meaning of 'grain' as used in the commonplace metaphor for literature as grain and chaff. The Virgin's gift would then be an analogy for the true spiritual meaning within the narrative of the tale. It is true that in the story as it stands there is no hint of any such meaning; but hypothetical as the suggestion must be, Chaucer's apparently deliberate, and original, choice of the term, and his setting of the tale in a context in which discussion of narrative and meaning becomes increasingly important, makes it not implausible. This is, after all, the fragment that ends with the injunction,

> Taketh the fruyt, and lat the chaf be stille.   3443

The clergeon's grain may stand for spiritual understanding beyond the 'chaff' of words.

If the Nun's Priest's line points to problems within the tale it concludes, the Prioress's Tale raises a good many questions of its own. The grain is primarily literal, not allegorical or analogical;[48] and the story too is primarily narrative, whatever spiritual implications – or, in distinctly second place, linguistic implications – may emerge from it. Like all the tales, it is both self-sufficient and affected by its context. As a miracle of the Virgin (a genre recognised at the end, when it is referred to as a 'miracle'), it is impressively good, and the other Middle English examples of the form fall way below it. The same story as told

[47] Robinson favours a pearl: see his note to VII 662.

[48] On the whole question of allegory in Chaucer, cf. Brewer, *Chaucerian Poetic*, p. 7: 'Unless there is explicit, internal evidence to the contrary, the face value of a 'naked text' should be accepted, whether secular or devotional.'

in the Vernon collection of miracles,[49] for instance, is a clumsy affair in four-stress couplets with none of Chaucer's skilled pacing or rhetorical control of audience response. The rhyme royal stanzas give the tale a level of poetic dignity and seriousness. As in the other tales where this verse form is used for a story of pathos, especially the Man of Law's, the stanza is admirably adapted to apostrophes: 'O martir, sowded to virginitee', 'O grete God, that parfournest thy laude/By mouth of innocentz', 'O yonge Hugh of Lyncoln'. Here too they are designed less as addresses to the person specified than as ways of stirring the appropriate emotions in the listeners. The semantic range of adjectives is also directed towards evoking the pathos of the story: *sely, tendre, innocent, pitous, sweete,* and, above all, *litel* – 'a litel clergeon', 'hir litel sone', 'this litel child, his litel book lernynge', and so on throughout the tale. At this point one begins to wonder whether the aim of writing a particularly good miracle of the Virgin has not tipped over into something else. Chaucer's mastery of pathos is abundantly demonstrated by the Clerk's Tale; but here the pathos tends to take over, becoming dangerously close to sentimentality.

The treatment of evil is as crude as the treatment of virtue is sentimental. It is entirely in accordance with popular literary and religious convention that the Jews should be the villains of the piece: like Saracens, or modern invaders from Mars, they are sufficiently exotic not to need to be accorded full humanity. However, while the easy anti-Semitism of

> Oure firste foo, the serpent Sathanas,
> That hath in Jues herte his waspes nest 558–9

may be normal for the genre, there is a complacency in the use of the convention that ignores all the hard questions raised elsewhere about evil. It also seems unnecessary that a cess-pit should have to be defined:

> Where as thise Jewes purgen hire entraille; 573

and there is an unsettling contrast between the sentiment expended on the child's murder and the mother's grief, on the one hand, and the abruptness of the Jews' brutal punishment:

> With wilde hors he dide hem drawe,
> And after that he heng hem by the lawe. 633–4

('Draw' here presumably means 'drag along', not 'tear to pieces').

---

[49] In Bryan and Dempster pp. 470–4; the whole collection of miracles is found in *Minor Poems of the Vernon MS* Vol. I ed. Carl Horstmann (EETS O.S. 98, 1892) pp. 138–67. Chaucer's precise source is unknown.

It has been customary to attribute these features of the tale to the Prioress; and certainly the sentimentality is exactly suited to the woman who will weep over a trapped mouse, even if that habit raises significant questions about the status of the emotion generated within the tale. That the Pardoner is a vicious man who tells a moral tale does not in one sense affect his tale at all; the treatment of the Prioress's Tale is perhaps more subversive. Just as the exemplary story against avarice is exactly suited rhetorically and in terms of social function to a pardoner, so the miracle of the Virgin, with its inevitable generic stress on female mercy and popular piety, is appropriate to a female and unlearned prioress; that this Prioress is more feminine than most, and equally unlearned, says as much about the genre as about herself. The genre, as so often, tends to define its own teller; and the peculiarities that emerge in the course of the telling of this tale may be due as much to the nature of the genre as to the psychology of the narrator. The placing of the tale between a fabliau and a popular romance tends to endow them all with the same quality of *fiction* – pious fiction in this instance, no doubt, but just as fabular in terms of narrative action. There is no clear poetic or semantic way of distinguishing romance marvel from religious miracle. The villainy of the Jews and their brutal death is sensationalism masquerading as piety. All this goes beyond anything that may be ascribed to the Prioress: Chaucer is allowing certain features inherent in the genre to emerge, and they are not all equally spiritually edifying. It is however impossible to pick out such features in this way without losing the delicate balance Chaucer achieves. The Prioress's Tale is not a parody, nor self-destructive; rather, by raising the genre to its highest level and demonstrating its full potential, Chaucer also manages to suggest its dangers and its limitations.

Generic limitation becomes the very subject of the next tale, *Sir Thopas*. The poetic poverty of the piece is emphasised by the fact that the link that binds it to the preceding tale continues the Prioress's rhyme royal – the only link not to be written in riding rhyme. The miracle has left the company 'sobre', and the Host asks the pilgrim Chaucer to tell 'a tale of myrthe' to liven things up. His offer of 'a rym I lerned longe agoon' is welcomed by the master of ceremonies, and he proceeds to tell *Sir Thopas*. The poem describes itself in the third line as being a tale 'of myrthe and of solas'; it never claims to have any *sentence*, and the Host clearly finds little enjoyment in it either. It is the one tale in the whole series deliberately written badly, and it is at that level that Harry Bailey responds. The appreciation of the genius of its badness is reserved for the literal audience, not the fictional one, just as the skill behind it is the real Chaucer's, the bumbling doggerel his fictional pilgrim's.

If the first two tales of the fragment show up the dangers of their particular literary kinds and the limitations of vision imposed by generic perspective, *Sir Thopas* is a kind of poetry that should not be written at all. It is parody of a deadly accuracy: the bulk of its analogues demonstrates abundantly how very close Chaucer's piece is to other verse being perpetrated in the fourteenth century.[50] To give a single example, if Sir Thopas spurs ('prikyng') his steed till it sweats enough to be wrung out, Sir Amis, in *Amis and Amiloun*,

> priked þe stede, þat him bare,
> Boþe niȝt and day.
> So long he priked wiþ-outen abod,
> þe stede, þat he on rode,
> In a fer cuntray
> Was ouercomen and fel doun ded.

Chaucer makes the debt to popular romances explicit, comparing *Sir Thopas* to their heroes – Horn Child, Ypotys, Beves of Hamtoun, Guy of Warwick, Lybeaus Desconus, Pleyndamour, Sir Percyvell. All the romance conventions that Chaucer gets right in the other romances of the *Canterbury Tales* are wrong here. The supposedly exotic setting is in Flanders, on the most convenient bourgeois trade route (and last heard of in the anti-romance Pardoner's Tale), and Chaucer moreover gives us his hero's exact address: 'at Poperyng, in the place'. Lower-class or belittling details perpetually intrude: Sir Thopas not only hunts and hawks but wrestles for rams, presumably at country fairs; the 'wilde best' at large in the forest turn out to be deer and hares; the herbs growing in the forest are those associated with kitchen gardens. The narrative line lacks any sign of coherence or internal logic: Sir Thopas' frantic spurring and his love for an elf-queen are equally unmotivated. The supernatural is fatally lacking in interest, so much so that the giant Sir Olifaunt has to be endowed with three heads four stanzas after his first appearance, in a desperate attempt to keep things exciting. Even the most heroic elements are wrong. The first meeting with the giant comes to nothing because Sir Thopas does not have his armour with him and cannot fight without it. In the section on the arming of the hero, an episode of near-epic import in most works, Chaucer starts in effect with Sir Thopas's underpants.[51] His warhorse ambles, in the lady's pace designed especially for those riding sidesaddle.

[50] See Laura H. Loomis's chapter in Bryan and Dempster pp. 486–559. The quotation from *Amis* is from p. 511.

[51] There is an admirable analysis of this episode by Derek Brewer, 'The arming of the warrior in European literature and Chaucer', in *Chaucerian Problems and Perspectives: Essays Presented to Paul E. Beichner* ed. Edward Vasta and Zacharias P. Thundy (Notre Dame, 1979) pp. 221–43, esp. p. 238.

The poetry is as bad as the handling of romance conventions. The stanza form gets increasingly out of hand as the First Fit progresses. The manuscript layout demonstrates this particularly clearly: *Sir Thopas* becomes a visual joke as well as a poetic one. We are accustomed from printed editions to thinking of *Sir Thopas* as a *narrow* poem, but in manuscript it sprawls across the entire page. Tail-rhyme stanzas were customarily written with the couplets on the left, their rhymes joined by a brace (}), and the short lines to the right, again with the rhymes joined by a brace. The additional even shorter lines introduced into *Sir Thopas* add a third column further to the right, with horizontal lines running out to the braces all over the place. The final effect in most of the early manuscripts, especially Ellesmere, looks rather like the schedule for a tennis tournament for an inconvenient number of players, complete with byes.

The reference in the poem to its division into fits (888) is unique in Chaucer, and again serves as a mark of poetic inadequacy: everywhere else in his works the Latin *pars* or *liber* is used to indicate sections. Chaucer apparently intended *Sir Thopas* to be divided into three fits (the heading 'The Second Fit' is editorial). His second and third sections, marked in the manuscripts with larger capitals, begin with new appeals to the audience, once to them to listen (833) and once to 'holde youre mouth, *par charitee*' (891). It sounds from the increasing desperation as if the poetaster is aware that he is likely to lose their attention. The fits in *Sir Thopas* are too short to serve much practical purpose, but they do help to give the illusion that the poem is interminably long. The first section runs for eighteen stanzas, the second for nine, and there are four and a half in the third before the Host interrupts: whether or not the precise halving is intentional, it does show the narrative structure getting into deep trouble.

Vocabulary and rhymes suffer as much as plot and stanza structure. Many words appear in *Sir Thopas* that are never used elsewhere by Chaucer: *verrayment, auntrous, launcegay, payndemayn* and so on – words that lie outside his normal lexical range, and that have associations of archaism, provincialism and cliché; words, above all, that are the language of a poetic totally alien to his own. Other words are twisted to fit the exigencies of rhyme: 'plas' and 'gras' (in the sense of 'grace') lose their normal -ce ending when required. Rhetorical *topoi* and imagery are both mishandled. The description of the hero from head to foot is so anxious not to miss anything out that

> He hadde a semely nose   729

is given not only a line to itself but the emphatic concluding line of the stanza. A sequence of similes works from the more effective to the less:

This assumes that the persona
of Chaucer are entirely separate. ??

Links within Fragments 171

His brydel as the sonne shoon,
Or as the moone light.   879–80

One could continue the list for the length of the poem: there is not a single line in it that can be taken at face value.

Sir Thopas is the one story of the *Canterbury Tales* that is completely different for the pilgrim audience and the real, for the poet and the narrator. Within the work, they see 'rym dogerel' and nothing else, and the pilgrim Chaucer's defence that it is 'the beste rym I kan' gets a brief retort from the Host:

> Thy drasty rymyng is nat worth a toord!   930

That popular romance is parodied to the point of destruction shows the high level of Chaucer's artistic consciousness and the precision of his understanding of the form; it also demonstrates the literary sophistication of his audience, who are certainly meant to appreciate the joke. The way *Sir Thopas* has to be read on two entirely different levels is particularly interesting so far as the discussion of the nature of literature in this section is concerned. The levels are moreover mutually exclusive in many respects: on one interpretation the Host's verdict is right, but read differently the tale emerges as a brilliantly witty artistic *tour de force*. The 'rym dogerel' is also a virtuoso performance. The degree of artistic sophistication in both author and audience can make two completely different poems from exactly the same text.

After the débâcle of *Sir Thopas*, the Host forbids Chaucer to rhyme any more, and invites him to try in 'geeste' – apparently Chaucer's term for alliterative verse – or prose instead,

> In which ther be som murthe or som doctryne.   935

It is interesting that he sees mirth and doctrine as alternatives at this point. Chaucer agrees to tell 'a litel thyng in prose'; the irony of the adjective can hardly be missed in the light of what follows. He does not promise any 'murthe'; his tale will be 'a moral tale vertuous'. This is the tale of *Melibee*, which is a close translation of the French version of Albertanus of Brescia's *Liber Consolationis et Consilii*. The fact that the treatise is a translation, and not the kind of free adaptation and re-creation that Chaucer normally makes of his sources, must affect our reading of the lines that follow:

> Al be it told somtyme in sondry wyse
> Of sondry folk, as I shal yow devyse.
> As thus: ye woot that every Evaungelist,
> That telleth us the peyne of Jhesu Crist,

Ne seith nat alle thyng as his felawe dooth;
But nathelees hir sentence is al sooth,
And alle acorden as in hire sentence,
Al be ther in hir tellyng difference . . .

Therfore, lordynges alle, I yow biseche,
If that yow thynke I varie as in my speche,
As thus, though that I telle somwhat moore
Of proverbes than ye had herd bifoore
Comprehended in this litel tretys heere,
To enforce with th'effect of my mateere,
And though I nat the same wordes seye
As ye han herd, yet to yow alle I preye
Blameth me nat; for as in my sentence,
Shul ye nowher fynden difference
Fro the sentence of this tretys lyte
After the which this murye tale I write.   941–8, 953–64

The sentiments expressed here are unexceptionable, and the difference between surface narrative or subject-matter and *sentence* admirably described. The whole speech is, however, uniquely irrelevant to the 'tretys' that follows, for Chaucer there is exceptionally faithful to his original. Apart from some stylistic elaboration, and the addition (discussed below) of one name, there is no more 'difference' to be found in the words than in the meaning. The pilgrim Chaucer disclaims responsibility for precisely the wrong thing. He could well claim that the words are not his in the first place; but he apologises instead for not preserving them.

Irrelevant as the analysis of words and meanings may be here, it does bear closely on the larger discussion of literature in this fragment. The Shipman's Tale demonstrates the way in which the sliding meanings of words can alter one's perception of event; the Prioress declares the inadequacy of words to express meaning; *Sir Thopas* defines itself partly by its lexical range; the Nun's Priest's Tale too is to take up the question of words and their function. In the *Melibee*, the most striking thing about the relationship between words and meaning is their disproportion. The *sentence* threatens to be buried under a torrent of verbosity.[52] The bulk of the treatise consists of conversation, mostly dialogue between Melibee and his wife Dame Prudence, though also with sections of advice from counsellors and such; and the method of discourse is to amass rival proverbs and *sententiae*, as Chaucer warns in his introductory speech. The key question under discussion is the rightness of revenge, but action is all but non-existent; it is the debate that matters. If the Wife of Bath has little sympathy for the

[52] See the interesting discussion in Dolores Palomo, 'What Chaucer really did to *Le Livre de Melibee*', *Philological Quarterly* LIII (1974) 304–20.

authorities she quotes, Dame Prudence's sole function is to cite authorities, sometimes to develop an argument of her own, sometimes to beat down an argument of her husband's by sheer weight of ammunition. *Melibee* substitutes *auctoritee* for *experience*. Words, however, are also shown to be notoriously slippery things, and Prudence has no difficulty in showing Melibee that he has totally misunderstood the sense of something said by accepting its surface meaning:

> And though that Salomon seith that he ne foond nevere womman
> good, it folweth nat therfore that alle wommen ben wikke. 1076

> The wordes of the phisiciens ne sholde nat han been understonden
> in thys wise. 1283

Melibee, more than any other of the *Canterbury Tales*, consists solidly of words, but words alone cannot be trusted.

There has been much debate as to whether Chaucer meant the *Melibee* to be taken seriously. Its subject is clearly a serious one; and the treatise, in its Latin, French and English forms, was widely disseminated and widely read – Chaucer's own translation was sometimes anthologised separately, and on the evidence of manuscript numbers was one of the more popular of the *Tales*.[53] It has found defenders for both its subject and its style: in its seriousness it has been associated with the Parson's Tale as one of the sections of the *Tales* devoid of undercutting irony,[54] and its elaboration of style has been shown to be related to the highest models of European prose writing.[55] Other critics have found it hard to accept that after giving himself the drasty *Sir Thopas* Chaucer could have meant the *Melibee* to be taken entirely seriously, though its length clearly goes beyond what is acceptable as a joke. The brief *Sir Thopas* creates the illusion of interminableness while never in fact losing its hold on one's attention; the *Melibee* seems all too interminable.

There is no need, however, to select one reading of the tale, as serious or ironic, and abandon the other. The *Canterbury Tales* is full of examples of stories that mean one thing in isolation, another in the context of the *Tales*; and *Melibee* is one of these. As a 'moral tale vertuous', it is meant seriously and should be taken so; but its placing

---

[53] See E. T. Donaldson in Brewer, *Writers*, p. 95.

[54] See e.g. Paul G. Ruggiers, 'Serious Chaucer: the *Tale of Melibeus* and the Parson's Tale' in Vasta and Thundy pp. 83–94; Christian K. Zacher, *Curiosity and Pilgrimage: The Literature of Discovery in Fourteenth-Century England* (Baltimore, 1976) pp. 100, 116–19, 126–7.

[55] Margaret Schlauch, 'The art of Chaucer's prose', in *Chaucer and Chaucerians: Critical Studies in Middle English Literature* ed. D. S. Brewer (London, 1966) pp. 140–63; Diane Bornstein, 'Chaucer's *Tale of Melibee* as an example of the *Style Clergial*', *Chaucer Review* XII (1977–8) 236–54.

in this fragment, and in Chaucer's mouth, indicates other qualities in it as well. Like the Pardoner's Tale, it is a moral tale whose context suggests further meanings not contained in the story itself.

The morality of the treatise is largely orthodox – or it would be orthodox if it were not that other tales had presented different views of many of the same matters. That age and wisdom go together, for instance, is not as self-evident as might seem from the authoritative tone adopted here; and Dame Prudence's defence of women is not the decisive answer to her husband that it appears, when the whole tract is set in a continuing debate. 'If that wommen were nat goode,' she argues, 'and hir conseils goode and profitable, oure Lord God of hevene wolde nevere han wroght hem, ne called hem help of man, but rather confusioun of man.'[56] Two tales later Chauntecleer returns to the point:

> *Mulier est hominis confusio,* –
> Madame, the sentence of this Latyn is,
> 'Womman is mannes joye and al his blis.'   3164–6

Looking for precise parallels of this kind in either of the prose tales is like searching haystacks for needles; but given the transformation of the idea in the Nun's Priest's Tale, it would be a brave critic (there are some, none the less) who argued that Chaucer the poet and Chaucer the pilgrim are speaking with one voice here, and that that voice is Dame Prudence's. The tale, as so often, is in one respect autonomous, and on that level it is serious and non-ironic; but that does not mean that Chaucer need fully endorse every word of it.

There is indeed one small but explosive piece of evidence that he does not. It occurs in the very first sentence:

> A yong man called Melibeus, myghty and riche, bigat upon his wyf, that
> called was Prudence, a doghter which that called was Sophie.   967

It is Chaucer's only significant addition to his source that he names the daughter. 'Sophie' means 'wisdom'; and the name suggests the possibility of an allegorical reading of the scanty narrative that serves to introduce the debate in the rest of the treatise. Melibeus is away one day when 'thre of his olde foes' break into his house

> and wounded his doghter with fyve mortal woundes in fyve sondry places,
> – this is to seyn, in hir feet, in hire handes, in hir erys, in hir nose, and
> in hire mouth, – and leften hire for deed, and wenten awey.   971–2

The slight concern for story here is demonstrated by the fact that we

---

[56] See 1163–4, 1056–110; quotation from 1105–6.

are never told whether she recovers; but an allegorical interpretation raises problems. The three foes who mortally injure one's wisdom through the five senses[57] are the world, the flesh and the devil. The identification is made explicit later when Prudence herself gives an allegorical reading of the action:

> The three enemys of mankynde, that is to seyn, the flessh, the feend, and the world, thou hast suffred hem entre in to thyn herte wilfully by the wyndowes of thy body, and hast nat defended thyself suffisantly agayns hire assautes and hire temptaciouns, so that hey han wounded thy soule in fyve places; this is to seyn, the deedly synnes that been entred into thyn herte by thy fyve wittes. 1421–4

For Prudence this is only a moral analogy – 'in the same manere ... thy three enemys been entred into thyn house by the wyndowes, and han ywounded thy doghter in the forseyde manere'; but by naming the daughter at the very beginning Chaucer suggests that an allegorical reading should have primacy. The trouble with this is that it makes nonsense of the rest of the work. If the three foes really are the world, the flesh and the devil, then the last thing that Prudence should do is to make peace with them. Chaucer's insistence that changing the words makes no difference to the *sentence* is palpably false; the addition of one name has the potential to alter the tale completely. The contradiction was latent in Albertanus' original treatise, but Chaucer brings it to the surface. *Forced*

If the content of the treatise can be at once serious and yet contain a hint of subversion, the rhetoric of the piece is similarly double-edged. The demonstration that stylistically the tract is written in accordance with the best models of prose must be accepted; but that need not mean that Chaucer fully endorses such standards, any more than the fact that *Sir Thopas* faithfully reflects the stylistic model of the popular romance means that he endorses that. *Sir Thopas*, however, is written to be bad, and the very length of the *Melibee* would seem to rule out such a possibility here. The style is acceptable if it is taken in isolation, just as the content of the treatise is; it is only its contrast with the stylistic conciseness of the other tales that reminds one that there are different ways of writing, just as differences of genre are a reminder that there are different ways of thinking. Chaucer never wrote great prose; some of the vernacular mystical writings more or less contemporary with him, such as the *Cloud of Unknowing*, show

---

[57] One would expect 'eyes' rather than 'feet', and the Latin original, and some manuscripts of the French, read *oculis*, *yeux*; other French manuscripts erroneously read *piez* (see Bryan and Dempster p. 568, note to line 14). Chaucer may have found the reading satisfactory because of the connection of the sin associated with sight, curiosity, with wandering by the way; on the connection see Zacher chapter 2.

Come! Melibee has meaning & Prudence points out. And Prudence!

a control of rhythm and syntax far superior to anything he achieved. Many of the high-style features of the *Melibee* prevent Chaucer from coming close to anything of that kind. Repetition and synonymy, parallelism of words and phrases, amplifications, the use of established metrical patterns, all get in the way of his concentrating on the point at issue. The principle behind the style of *Melibee* – and it is a tendency exaggerated from the original – is never to use one word where two will do. Almost every sentence contains at least one paired set of words, many contain several:

> And therfore *deere and benygne* lady, we *preien yow and biseke yow* as mekely as we *konne and mowen* . . .   1743

It is hard to believe that the same poet who has just shown himself so brilliantly aware, in *Sir Thopas*, of the redundancy of filler lines ('As I yow telle in good certeyn') should not be equally aware of the redundancy of much of *Melibee*: 'as for to speke proprely', 'this is to seyn', 'as to the point that Tullius clepeth "causes", which that is the laste point', and so on. This is not taken to the point of parody, however, as it is in the 'rym dogerel': *Melibee* is, again, too long for a parody. It seems more likely that Chaucer is passing an implied comment on such a style – a style officially admirable – by the very fact of juxtaposing it with the romance. *Sir Thopas* is too demotically low to be stylistically acceptable; there is an implication that *Melibee* is too pedantically elaborate. Both tales contribute to the debate on what the nature of literature is, or should be.

The Host, with his usual critical perversity, reacts to the *Melibee* as if it were an exemplary tale in the literal mode, with Prudence as the model of what a wife ought to be – which is everything his own wife is not. If Prudence fights for peace with massed ranks of proverbs, Goodelief takes a more concrete line of argument:

> Whan I bete my knaves,
> She bryngeth me forth the grete clobbed staves,
> And crieth, 'Slee the dogges everichoon,
> And brek hem, both bak and every boon!'   1897–900

The passage is a delightful illustration of how little the real world conforms to the injunctions of the treatise; and in its vitality and its colloquial directness it is a superb contrast, of a kind that does not work entirely to Goodelief's disadvantage, with the bloodless platitudes of orthodox wisdom expounded at such length in the tract.

The Monk, who is called on next, is an enthusiast for story-telling. He promises 'a tale, or two, or three'; and his first idea, of recounting the life of St. Edward, is immediately replaced by an even better one, telling the hundred tragedies he has in his cell. He is as forthcoming with literary theory as he is with sheer quantity of tales. He gives a definition of *tragedie* by content and prosodic medium:

> Tragedie is to seyn a certeyn storie,
> As olde bookes maken us memorie,
> Of hym that stood in greet prosperitee,
> And is yfallen out of heigh degree
> Into myserie, and endeth wrecchedly.
> And they ben versified communely
> Of six feet, which men clepen *exametron*.
> In prose eek been endited many oon,
> And eek in meetre, in many a sondry wyse. 1973–81

The reference to metre may be Chaucer's way of directing attention to the verse form that follows – a technically difficult form, unique in his work, of an eight-line, three-rhyme stanza. The Monk also shows himself aware of the problems of ordering a story-collection, as he apologises for confusing the chronological order of his tragedies: the apology is doubly ironic since the chronology is more or less correct apart from the textual problem of where to place the series of 'modern instances'.

The Monk's Tale is the sort of story-collection that consists of a prologue followed by an unlimited series of tales that share a single tone, a single genre, a single narrative pattern, and a single moral. The prologue stanza declares what all four are to be (italicised in order):

> I wol *biwaille*, in manere of *tragedie*,
> The harm of hem that stoode in heigh degree,
> And *fillen* so that ther nas no remedie
> To brynge hem out of hir adversitee.
> For certein, whan that Fortune list to flee,
> Ther may no man the cours of hire withholde.
> *Lat no man truste on blynd prosperitee*;
> Be war by thise ensamples trewe and olde. 1991–8

The separate stories follow, starting with individual stanzas for Lucifer and Adam, then longer sections on Samson, Hercules, Nebuchadnezzar and other assorted Biblical, Classical and historical figures. No attempt is made to draw any moral distinction between the sufferings of the evil and the innocent; Nero and Holofernes rub shoulders with Hugelyn and his three infant children. Hugelyn is entirely the victim of Fortune, contributing nothing to his own downfall: he is imprisoned on the strength of a 'fals suggestioun', and there is no hint in Chaucer's version that the Ugolino of his source, Dante's *Divine*

Dante puts him in Hell

Comedy, was to be found in Hell. Chaucer's retelling of the story is the high point of the Monk's Tale. The *tragedie* has the spareness and understated pathos of the Clerk's Tale:

> And on a day bifel that in that hour
> Whan that his mete wont was to be broght,
> The gayler shette the dores of the tour.
> He herde it wel, but he spak right noght,
> And in his herte anon ther fil a thoght
> That they for hunger wolde doon hym dyen.
> 'Allas!' quod he, 'allas, that I was wroght!'
> Therwith the teeris fillen from his yen.
>
> His yonge sone, that thre yeer was of age,
> Unto hym seyde, 'Fader, why do ye wepe?
> Whanne wol the gayler bryngen oure potage?
> Is ther no morsel breed that ye do kepe?
> I am so hungry that I may nat slepe.
> Now wolde God that I myghte slepen evere!
> Thanne sholde nat hunger in my wombe crepe;
> Ther is no thyng, save breed, that me were levere.'   2423–38

The chilling contrast of the father's realisation of the true situation and the child's ignorance undercuts any possibility of a sentimental appeal to a ready-made emotion. The portrayal of innocence, however – and of positive virtue, in the children's offer to let their father eat their own flesh – makes the easy *moralitas* of the turning of the wheel of Fortune shockingly inadequate, even immoral. The point is emphasised by the poetic skill of this section: that it stands out so far in quality above the dreary functional narration of the other biographies makes the insufficiency of the given moral all the more obvious.

The Monk's Tale is interrupted, like the Squire's and *Sir Thopas*; but unlike them it is not broken off in mid-sentence. The last stanza is complete, and the closing lines have all the quality of final summary that one would associate with an epilogue to the series:

> Tragedies noon oother maner thyng
> Ne kan in syngyng crie ne bewaille
> But that Fortune alwey wol assaille
> With unwar strook the regnes that been proude;
> For whan men trusteth hire, thanne wol she faille,
> And covere hire brighte face with a clowde.   2761–6

The only new idea introduced into this formulation since the prologue stanza is the notion that there is some measure of just retribution in the actions of Fortune, and that is not borne out by the tragedies themselves; apart from this, the lines are mere repetition, and underscore the lack of any development in the series. The Monk's Tale could go on indefinitely – at least to his threatened hundred – without making any progress at all.

The tale is interrupted by the Knight, and his action is backed up by the Host. Both have comments to make on what they have just heard. The Knight criticises the content:

> I seye for me, it is a greet disese,
> Whereas men han been in gret welthe and ese,
> To heeren of hire sodeyn fal, allas!
> And the contrarie is joye and greet solas,
> As whan a man hath been in povre estaat,
> And clymbeth up and wexeth fortunat,
> And there abideth in prosperitee.
> Swich thyng is gladsom, as it thynketh me,
> And of swich thyng were goodly for to telle.   2771–9

The Knight's own tale is sufficient indication that he is not advocating the telling of none but happy stories. His story had balanced Arcite's tragedy with Palamon's romance, his rising to the top of Fortune's wheel and abiding there, 'lyvynge in blisse, in richesse, and in heele' (I 3102). Nor did it draw easy moral lessons from the actions of Fortune; it asked questions about the metaphysical context for man's life at a more profound level. The Knight's interruption marks the climax of the mounting criticism of the genres contained in this fragment. It is his humane width and depth of vision as reflected in his Tale that gives him the right to interrupt, and which shows up the moral poverty of the tragedies. His only other intervention in the action of the pilgrimage was to insist, courteously but firmly, that the Host and Pardoner make peace with each other, and his own refusal to speak *vileynye*, as well as his rank, give him the authority to do so. His authority for interrupting the Monk's Tale, on the other hand, derives not from his rank and character as portrayed in the General Prologue, but from the views expressed in his own tale. The Knight's Tale had served as an introduction to the multifarious themes and styles of the *Canterbury Tales* and set a standard for the rest; it is called on to bear witness to the inadequacy of this lesser story-collection.

The Host's objections are, inevitably, to more superficial matters. He dislikes the perpetual 'biwailling', since it doesn't serve the slightest purpose. He dislikes the elaboration of style:

> This Monk he clappeth lowde.
> He spak how Fortune covered with a clowde
> I noot nevere what.   2781–3

He also dislikes hearing of 'hevynesse', not for the Knight's more considered reasons but because it is a 'peyne' and no fun:

> Swich talkyng is nat worth a boterflye,
> For therinne is ther no desport ne game.   2790–1

This formulation comes close to identifying the enjoyment of literature with escapism. Moreover, the Host declares, it was only the bells on the Monk's bridle that kept him awake, and there is no point in telling any 'sentence' if nobody is listening. After thus brusquely demolishing the tone, style, content and social and moral function of the Monk's stories, he turns to the Nun's Priest to give the next tale.

Dramatically, it is going to be difficult to follow this series of charges. The Host appears to have excluded so much of literature, and made such demands for what remains, that the next speaker is bound to be in trouble. In practice, of course, the Nun's Priest's Tale is a triumph. After the critique of genre and style that the earlier tales of the fragment had shown, this story demonstrates how to get things right, how to transcend generic and rhetorical limitations. If the Monk's Tale is a story-collection that illustrates what the larger collection is not, the Nun's Priest's Tale can be seen as an encapsulation of everything that the *Canterbury Tales* is.[58] The Monk's tragedies imposed a single tone and moral and style; in the beast-fable, everything is relative.

If the Nun's Priest's Tale is the *Canterbury Tales* in miniature, it does in addition bring together many of the themes of plot or idea found in the earlier stories of the group. The two tales immediately preceding, *Melibee* and the Monk's, are the ones most fully called on, in the Nun's Priest's remarks on women's counsel and his survey of the matrimonial relationship of his cock and hen, and in the tale's potential for tragedy and its associated discussion of Fortune and free will.

The *Tale of Melibee* is a demonstration of the limitations (in Melibeus) and the potential (in Dame Prudence) of human rationality as a guide to conduct. That the woman is more rational than the man is only possible because she is more personification than person. Her rôle is to draw on the wisdom of the past, in the shape of authorities and proverbs, in order to evaluate the present and advise on future action: a fully-allegorised Prudence has three eyes, looking to past, present and future.[59] Pertelote is the embodiment less of prudence than of practical common sense: if her husband appears to be suffering from prophetic dreams, she will treat them as nightmares and prescribe laxatives, and even cite Cato in support. The joke lies in the

---

[58] See the Introduction, pp. 5–7 above. In different terms, the point is admirably made by Muscatine pp. 237–43. Other fine studies include those by R. T. Lenaghan, 'The Nun's Priest's fable', *PMLA* LXXVII (1963) 300–7, and Morton W. Bloomfield, 'The wisdom of the Nun's Priest's Tale' in Vasta and Thundy pp. 70–8.

[59] Cf. *Troilus and Criseyde* V. 744–9.

contrast not only between Chauntecleer's understanding of his dreams and his wife's, or between her kind of advice and that given by Prudence, but between animal instinct and human rationality. Animals in beast-fables almost always retain their animal characteristics: their relationship with the human world depends on the way in which human actions are reflected by animal ones. Fox and lamb, for instance, do not need to be altered in nature to be represented as vicious deceiver and innocent victim. Different authors of course have different ways of handling the likeness, and the disparity, between beasts and men; Chaucer manages to emphasise both at the same time. That the cock has seven wives turns him into a great lover; his courtliness of language is punctured only by the gallinaceous detail:

> Of o thyng God hath sent me large grace,
> For whan I se the beautee of youre face,
> Ye been so scarlet reed aboute youre yen,
> It maketh al my drede for to dyen.   3159–62

He is also learned by instinct in complex mathematical and astronomical calculations:

> *By nature* he knew ech ascensioun
> Of the equynoxial in thilke toun . . .[60]

Human reason, on this basis, has to struggle to catch up with beasts. When Chauntecleer comes to marshal his own selection of authorities to support his arguments, on the other hand, he insists that he has *read* them, and even locates the chapters to prove it (3064–5). If his instinct surpasses man's rationality, his book-learning is the equal of theirs; he is literate as well as numerate.

Melibee is set up as a debate, with argument and counter-argument. The Nun's Priest's Tale gently satirises the whole notion of debate. Chauntecleer and Pertelote are not concerned with the logical rights and wrongs of their arguments, with reaching the truth through the exercise of reason; they know what they want before they start, and their arguments are secondary to that conviction. The opening premise of Pertelote's speech on the insignificance of dreams is

> I kan nat love a coward, by my feith!   2911

Chauntecleer's conclusion is even more practical:

> Shortly I seye, as for conclusioun,
> That I shal han of this avisioun

---

[60] VII 2855–6; and for a more elaborate example, see 3191–7.

> Adversitee; and I seye forthermoor,
> That I ne telle of laxatyves no stoor,
> For they been venymous, I woot it weel;
> I hem diffye, I love hem never a deel! 3151–6

His thesis in the debate gets mixed up with his dislike of medicines and both are 'defied' together. Dame Prudence at least knew precisely what she was arguing: she set out clearly, if long-windedly, with a logical progression from one point to the next, why woman is man's help and not his confusion. Chauntecleer, with much greater conviction, argues on both sides at once:

> *In principio,*
> *Mulier est hominis confusio,* –
> Madame, the sentence of this Latyn is,
> 'Womman is mannes joye and al his blis.' 3163–6

Chauntecleer, presumably, is unaware of the contradiction, but Chaucer knows all about it. When he does make an unequivocal statement, he at once disclaims all responsibility for it, through the unusually strongly felt presence of the narrator:

> Wommenes conseils been ful ofte colde;
> Wommanes conseil broghte us first to wo,
> And made Adam fro Paradys to go,
> Ther as he was ful myrie and wel at ese.
> But for I noot to whom it myght displese,
> If I conseil of wommen wolde blame,
> Passe over, for I seyde it in my game.
> Rede auctours, where they trete of such mateere,
> And what they seyn of wommen ye may heere.
> Thise been the cokkes wordes, and nat myne. 3256–65

The lines have a double dramatic function in the *Tales*: Sir John is deferring to the Prioress whose priest he is, to the virago Wife of Bath, and to all those who have approved of the *Tale of Melibee*; he is also parodying the Monk's similar sentiments in the Samson *tragedie* (2092). The lines also serve to undermine the whole idea of getting at truth through argument, and the final line is even more of a palpable lie than such disclaimers usually are. Nobody has so much as pretended this time that the words were Chauntecleer's.

The Host has instructed the Nun's Priest to be 'blithe' and cheer the company up after the Monk's tragedies. The beast-fable includes all the standard ingredients of the tragedies and gives a happy ending as well. Croesus, the last of the Monk's victims, has had a prophetic dream of his downfall, which he misinterprets; Chauntecleer too has his prophetic dream, which he chooses to ignore, even though Croesus is among the *exempla* of true dreams that he cites. There is a hint, as in many of the tragedies, that the cock's downfall is a just retribution – nemesis for his 'pryde', or an example of the 'trecherye' that is the counterpart of greatness in the 'lordes' to whom he is compared. The Monk's outbursts against Fortune are echoed and surpassed:

> O destinee, that mayst nat been eschewed!   3338

And the endlessly repeated moral of the Monk's Tale is flourished again as if it were the most surprising discovery:

> Evere the latter end of joye is wo.
> God woot that worldly joye is soone ago;
> And if a rethor koude faire endite,
> He in a cronycle saufly myghte it write
> As for a sovereyn notabilitee.   3205–9

The Nun's Priest also, however, includes the counter-movement of Fortune: Chauntecleer escapes. (The first tale of the *Decameron* to be told to a set theme, of the prosperity brought by Fortune, is about a man who narrowly escapes hanging.) This is the aspect of life so strikingly absent from the Monk's vision; but even this is presented in his terms, as a fall – the downfall of the fox.

> Lo, how Fortune turneth sodeynly
> The hope and pryde eek of hir enemy!   3403–4

The obvious way to read the tale is as a comedy, as defined by its happy ending; the words of the text claim it to be a double tragedy, of the falls of both cock and fox. There is some truth in both readings. The Knight's Tale had shown Arcite's tragedy juxtaposed with Palamon's bliss, and here Chauntecleer's escape is Daun Russell's downfall. The very structure of the tale supports the terms of the Knight's interruption and denies the Monk's single vision.

The insistence on relativism in everything from the nature of reason to the definition of genre extends to the presentation of the narrator himself. We are made perpetually conscious of his presence in a way that rarely happens outside the confessional prologues. He comes across in two ways. At one level he is the apologist, the implications of whose tale lie quite beyond him, and who will unload responsibility for it on to his own fictional fox; he is the man who uses high rhetoric, but lifts the most striking passages straight out of the standard stylistic textbook. At another level he is entirely conscious of all that is going on. The other tales are full of non-dramatic effects that must be ascribed to Chaucer and not the narrators; once the general rhetorical fit with the teller is achieved, Chaucer has a free hand with the poetry, with the way he uses genre to suggest its own limitations, with his handling of conventions and so on. The Nun's Priest is uniquely self-aware – as self-aware as Chaucer.

It has long been a custom, in schools and universities, to set an essay on the character of the Nun's Priest. It is an interesting exercise because there is no portrait of him in the General Prologue, and so all the evidence has to be deduced from his tale.[61] The attempt is however self-defeating, for what one comes out with is an identikit picture of Chaucer. The Nun's Priest's Tale is given to a man without separate identity precisely because poet and narrator merge. The learning, irony, wit, literary sophistication, rhetorical control, and the multiplicity of perspective all belong to both of them. The tales given to the pilgrim Chaucer effectively eliminate him from the story-telling contest; the tale given to the poet's double, the Nun's Priest, epitomises it.

There is scarcely a single genre or style or theme in the whole work that is not touched on in this tale. If it is primarily a beast-fable, it also has pretensions to beast-epic, and beyond that to epic: it even cites the *Aeneid* as a parallel. If it is mock-heroic, it is mock- everything else too. Its courtliness of love-language relates it to romance, but hens are not courtly heroines. Romance is in any case as fictional as stories of talking beasts:

> This storie is also trewe, I undertake,
> As is the book of Launcelot de Lake,
> That wommen holde in ful greet reverence.   3211–13

The excessive number of Chauntecleer's wives, and the cheerfully open sexuality of the tale, bring it close to fabliau, but if there is such a thing as mock-fabliau, this is it:

> I fele a-nyght your softe syde,
> Al be it that I may not on yow ryde,
> For that oure perche is maad so narwe, allas!   3167–9

---

[61] The only description of the Nun's Priest comes from the Host's words in the Epilogue to his tale, and this is not found in the most authoritative manuscripts. It contains the line,

> Thou woldest ben a trede-foul aright,   3451

which also occurs in the Monk's Prologue. The words have an obvious relevance to the Nun's Priest, as they do not to the Monk, in that they pick up directly from his tale: Harry Bailey indeed adds that the Nun's Priest would need 'seven tymes seventene' hens to keep him occupied. The lines seem genuinely Chaucerian, but there can be little doubt that he cancelled them, so avoiding giving his readers any portrait of the man other than that conveyed by the tale. The Host's reference to the Monk as a 'trede-foul' enhances the dramatic relationship of the two tales.

Note the intrusion of anti-feminism into the tale. Surely not Chaucer's.

It also parodies the preceding debate and tragedies. Like all beast-fables, it is moral and exemplary, though these qualities are handled in such an equivocal fashion that the whole principle of fable as a cover for morality comes under attack. Hagiography is represented in the tale by the summary of the life of St. Kenelm, who, according to legend, was only seven years old at the time of his martyrdom, the same age as the Prioress's infant martyr. The legend however loses its potential seriousness by the very enthusiasm with which Chauntecleer recommends it to his wife:

> By God! I hadde levere than my sherte
> That ye hadde rad his legende, as have I. 3120–1

A cock reading saints' lives is as incongruous as a cock wearing a shirt. There is a level of religious reference in the tale, in the mention of Adam in Paradise or its discussion of divine foreknowledge and predestination, but the story itself is entirely secular in focus. The choice of genre precludes any possible criticism on these grounds. It is almost always earthly wisdom that is taught by beast-fables; and cocks are excluded by nature from any spiritual pilgrimage.

The stylistic range of the tale is equally great, and often equally subversive of the styles it uses. It opens innocuously enough, in a tone of quiet spareness touched up with delightfully irrelevant detail:

> Thre large sowes hadde she, and namo,
> Three keen, and eek a sheep that highte Malle. 2830–1

It can draw on the idiom of popular poetry, in alliterative formulae – 'loken in every lith' – or a line of song, 'My lief is faren in londe'. The whole subject, of the fox seizing the cock and being chased by the housewife with her distaff, is drawn from folksong. Two such poems survive from the fifteenth century, and misericord carvings of the scene show that it was widely known.[62] *Sir Thopas* had demonstrated the debasement of one kind of popular literature; the Nun's Priest's Tale shows the poetic potential of folk traditions. By contrast, there are passages in the language of courtly love (always adapted for the protagonist poultry), and of philosophy; and there is elaborate rhetoric. If some of the rhetoric is confessedly lifted out of the rhetorical hand-

---

[62] The poems are edited by Rossell Hope Robbins in *Secular Lyrics of the XIVth and XVth Centuries* (2nd ed., Oxford, 1955) pp. 43–5. There is no way of proving that they are themselves folksongs: most readers would probably agree that even if they are not, they ought to be, but that hardly constitutes a scholarly argument. Their existence alongside the misericords and the Nun's Priest's Tale does at least strongly indicate some folksong tradition. Misericord carvings are found at Beverley, Ely and Carlisle: see *Wood Carvings in English Churches I: Misericords* by Francis Bond (London, 1910) pp. 36–8.

Punic?

book of Geoffrey of Vinsauf, other passages look suspiciously as if they parody other tales within the work. The Man of Law's Tale associated the Trojan and Phoenician wars to give a parallel for the weeping at Custance's departure from home:

> I trowe at Troye, whan Pirrus brak the wal,
> Or Ilion brende, at Thebes the citee,
> N'at Rome, for the harm thurgh Hanybal
> That Romayns hath venquysshed tymes thre,
> Nas herd swich tendre wepyng for pitee
> As in the chambre was for hire departynge.   II 288–93

The Nun's Priest's Tale uses the same similes for the hens, and develops them even further:

> Certes, swich cry ne lamentacion
> Was nevere of ladyes maad when Ylion
> Was wonne, and Pirrus with his streite swerd,
> Whan he hadde hent kyng Priam by the berd,
> And slayn hym, as seith us *Eneydos*,
> As maden alle the hennes in the clos,
> Whan they had seyn of Chauntecleer the sighte.
> But sovereynly dame Pertelote shrighte
> Ful louder than did Hasdrubales wyf . . .   3355–63

> O woful hennes, right so criden ye,
> As, whan that Nero brende the citee
> Of Rome, cryden senatoures wyves . . .   3369–71

Good

The disparity between Custance's situation and the hens' is almost as striking as between the fowls and the epic heroines they are compared to. The effect goes beyond mock-heroic incongruity, however. We are, perversely, much more interested in Pertelote than Hecuba; and the audience is being satirised too, for their degree of imaginative commitment to what is merely a cock-and-hen story. Equally perversely, the similes do work to enlarge the story to heroic proportions. The *Aeneid* is the authoritative model for epic, and while our rational minds reject the association, Chaucer's hold on the imagination makes it very nearly credible to accept the ruffled hen as the poetic and tragic equivalent of Fortune's ultimate victim. If the Prioress's Prologue had declared the inadequacy of words to express spiritual meaning, the Nun's Priest's Tale demonstrates how rhetoric can be manipulated to endow the most trivial of barnyard events with epic significance. At the other extreme, the analysis of the nature of words that Chaucer sets up in the group of tales gets its *coup de grace* from Chauntecleer's 'Cok! cok!' Words can, after all, be pure sound, and mean nothing at all.

On the other hand, words can be a cover for a deeper truth.

> But ye that holden this tale a folye,
> As of a fox, or of a cok and hen,
> Taketh the moralite, goode men.   3438–40

The injunction is entirely orthodox, and especially where beast-fables are concerned: they are the form that inevitably comes with a *moralitas* attached. It is not in the least clear here, however, just what the 'moralite' is. Several are given at the end: the cock declares that one should not trust in flattery and should keep one's eyes open; the fox adds that one ought to keep one's mouth shut. All this is unexceptionable, but scarcely adequate to the whole tale. There have already been a good number of sententious maxims given in the course of the tale, and they have been equally limited. Chauntecleer triumphantly winds up the first part of his argument on the significance of dreams with the blissfully irrelevant

> Mordre wol out, this my conclusioun.   3057

The narrator's own discovery of the 'sovereyn notabilitee' of earthly mutability is little better; and the question of the nature of woman is resolved in favour of both sides at once. The real trouble, in this tale, with the formulation,

> Taketh the fruyt, and lat the chaf be stille,   3443

is that it shows Chaucer so brilliantly as the poet of the chaff: it is the surface that matters, not the trite little moral fruits that can be extracted from it. One's reaction to those may be like Chauntecleer's,

> He chukketh whan he hath a corn yfounde,   3182

but the point of the story lies elsewhere.

The tale acts as an epitome of the whole work not just because it contains in little so much that is found at large in the other tales, but because it is given a special relationship to the idea of the story-collection. It is probably not chance that made Chaucer select the beast-fable as the tale that gives the collection in miniature, for beast-fables are one of the most widespread forms of story-collection, and are rarely found in isolation; and they are the form in which the two primary functions of literature, *murthe* and *doctryne*, are most closely related. Moreover, while in one sense they represent the simplest kind of children's literature – Vincent of Beauvais' placing of his fables in his educational encyclopaedia indicates that – they were also

But no mention of widow and daughter?
They own the chickens too, brought in at end again.

188   *The Structure of the Canterbury Tales*

recognised as a highly sophisticated rhetorical form.[63] Relativity is therefore built into the genre in all kinds of ways, not least in the balance between the animal world and the humans they almost, but never quite, represent. Morality is, after all, inapplicable to animals;[64] the fox can no more be blamed for eating poultry than the cock for polygamy. The contrast with the fixed morality of the Monk's Tale is complete: this tale recognises the multifariousness of experience and its interpretations to a degree impossible in the literal physical world, devoid of talking animals, generic perspective and literary convention.

good

Fragment VIII(G): The Second Nun and the Canon's Yeoman

> He that wynketh, whan he sholde see,
> Al wilfully, God lat him nevere thee!   VII 3431–2

This couplet from the end of the Nun's Priest's Tale could stand as an epigraph to the fragment containing the Second Nun's and Canon's Yeoman's Tales. They are a contrasting pair about the pursuit of spiritual and worldly ends, God and Mammon, and the dominant image of both tales is of sight and blindness.

The importance of reading the individual stories of the *Canterbury Tales* as part of the larger work is demonstrated particularly clearly in the case of the Second Nun's Tale. According to the Prologue of the *Legend of Good Women*, it was originally written as a separate poem; but read separately, it has little beyond competence to commend it. As Bruce A. Rosenberg remarks in a seminal article on this fragment, 'Only when this life of St. Cecile is read in conjunction with and in the light of the *Canon's Yeoman's Tale* will the Nun's story gain literary stature.'[65] Seen as part of a larger pattern, of the fragment and the whole work, the Second Nun's Tale acquires a richness of meaning from its context that does not emerge from the story taken in isolation. The Canon's Yeoman's two-part tale, of his own experience as alchemical assistant and the parallel adventures of an alchemist like his master, also fits into place in the Canterbury scheme through its pairing with the saint's life. The introduction of a new character into the pilgrimage and the nature of his tale have sometimes been taken as unwelcome digressions in the progress of the

---

[63] Stephen Manning, 'The Nun's Priest's morality and the mediaeval attitude toward fables', *JEGP* LIX (1960) 403–16.

[64] See Jill Mann, 'The *Speculum Stultorum* and the *Nun's Priest's Tale*', *Chaucer Review* IX (1974–5) 262–82, esp. p. 276.

[65] 'The contrary tales of the Second Nun and the Canon's Yeoman', *Chaucer Review* II (1967–8) 278–91, p. 279. See also Joseph E. Grennen, 'Saint Cecilia's "chemical wedding": the unity of the *Canterbury Tales*, Fragment VIII', *JEGP* LXV (1966) 466–81.

Tales;[66] they are in fact closely integrated into the sequence. The fragment portrays dimensions of experience, and perspectives on the world, not provided elsewhere in the work.

It must be admitted that poetically neither piece is Chaucer's best. The rhyme royal stanzas of the saint's life are perpetually being filled out to reach the seven-line total, where the effect in the Clerk's Tale or *Troilus* is more likely to be of compression, with event and syntax being alike packed into the verse form. The handling of the Canon's Yeoman's couplets is also unusually slack, with an abundance of empty formulae – 'as in effect', 'I dar seyn boldely'. Ironically enough, the stylistic slackness appears to be the direct result of what is often cited as Chaucer's greatest virtue: the dramatic use of the speaker's voice. This is the only tale where Chaucer carries this principle through with anything approaching consistency. He does it again with much greater success in the Wife of Bath's and Pardoner's prologues, but the genres of their tales, folktales and sermon *exemplum*, are both impersonal. Both parts of the Canon's Yeoman's Tale, the confessional opening and the tale proper, are at once more colloquial and more empirically plausible than any of the other stories; and they demonstrate very clearly the artistic limits of the speaking voice and of narrative plausibility.[67] It must be borne in mind also that this tale alone is told outside the context of the competition. The Canon's Yeoman talks in order to reveal all about his master and the 'game' of alchemy, not with any aesthetic purpose. He does have an ethical purpose – or rather two: first, to warn his hearers off confidence tricksters of the alchemical variety, 'to th'entente that men may be war therby'; and second, to point out that 'multiplying', the search for the philosopher's stone and for the means of transmuting base metals into gold, is the way to damnation.

The Second Nun's Tale is about the way to salvation. In the Prologue, the narrator (whether the Nun, some earlier male teller to whom the tale was assigned, or simply Chaucer) declares that he or she has translated the life of St. Cecilia

> Lest that the feend thurgh ydelnesse us hente. 7

The point is made at some length, and with sufficient force for it to remain in the mind when the Canon's Yeoman comes to describe the

---

[66] N. F. Blake rejects the whole Canon's Yeoman section as non-Chaucerian, since it is not in the Hengwrt MS; he also argues that the very precision with which it is placed in the journey, being given an explicit reference both to its accompanying tale and to geographical location, casts doubt on its authenticity. It is hard to imagine an imitator supplying its deeper thematic connections with the Second Nun's Tale, however.

[67] See Morton Bloomfield, 'Authenticating realism and the realism of Chaucer' (1964), reprinted in his *Essays and Explorations* (Cambridge, Mass., 1970) pp. 174–98.

'swynk' of alchemy. Writing hagiography is a pious activity that frustrates the devil; alchemy, the Yeoman perpetually insists, is a 'feendly' labour that plays into the devil's hands. Cecilia herself is a type of 'lastynge bisynesse', who

wan thurgh hire merite
The eterneel lyf, and of the feend victorie.   33–4

The devil is ever-present with the alchemists:

Though that the feend noght in oure sighte hym shewe,
I trowe he with us be, that ilke shrewe!   916–17

The Yeoman has no doubt that his master is in league with the fiend, and his invocations to the devil to fetch him are as heartfelt as the old woman's curse in the Friar's Tale.

The Second Nun's Tale is the one saint's life of the *Canterbury Tales*. The most closely similar stories are clearly generically differentiated: the Prioress's Tale is a miracle of the Virgin, the Man of Law's and Clerk's are tales of secular piety, the Physician's an *exemplum* of pagan virtue. For his representative saint, Chaucer chooses another woman, to complete the pattern of Custance, Griselda, Virginia and Dame Prudence as types of female goodness. Together they offset the anti-feminism of the Wife of Bath's Prologue and the Merchant's Tale and the dubious virtue of the women of the early fabliaux. Cecilia contributes to the great debate on sex by more than piety: the distinctive form her sanctity takes is to refuse to sleep with her husband. She tells him that she is protected by an angel; and when he, not unnaturally, expresses incredulity until he may see it, she sends him off to St. Urban to be baptised. On his return he sees the angel, who gives garlands of roses and lilies to Cecilia and himself. His brother Tiburce can smell the garlands, but he is likewise unable to see them until he too has been baptised. The three are brought before the prefect Almachius and ordered to sacrifice. When they refuse, Valerian and Tiburce are beheaded; and a third convert, the officer Maximus, who sees their souls

to hevene glyde
With aungels ful of cleernesse and of light,   402–3

proclaims the faith and is martyred in his turn. After a debate with Almachius, which she decisively wins, Cecilia is put in a 'bath of flambes', but they have no power to hurt her. Almachius tries to have her beheaded instead; but she is still alive after three strokes, and she preaches for a further three days 'with her nekke ycorven' before she too dies.

It is a compelling story, but Chaucer does not allow the potential sensationalism to take over. Instead he has the emphasis fall on a series of related words and themes: words of visual brilliance such as *light, cleere* and *brightnesse*, and themes of worldly blindness against spiritual sight. The pattern of imagery is set up in the stanzas in the Prologue on the interpretation of Cecilia's name. She is 'hevenes lilie', anticipating the lilies of the garland; it also means

> 'Wantyng of blyndnesse,' for hir grete light
> Of sapience, and for hire thewes cleere.   100–1

Just as the heavens are

> swift and round and eek brennynge,
> Right so was faire Cecilie the white
> Ful swift and bisy evere in good werkynge,
> And round and hool in good perseverynge,
> And brennynge evere in charite ful brighte.   114–8

The interpretations are not just appropriate analogies: her name expresses her nature, her identity, not just as Virginia's name marks her out by a single virtue in men's eyes, but as she is seen by God as well as men.

The narrative itself is structured around the same set of images. Secular blindness must give way to spiritual sight, as Valerian sees the angel, Tiburce the angel and the garlands and Maximus the departing souls accompanied by angels. Tiburce can smell the flowers before he can see them: as in the descriptions of Alisoun and Emily, smell is a physical sense, sight is spiritual. The spiritual qualities associated with Cecilia are however fully religious. Emily too was associated with roses and lilies, but the divine meanings behind the images are brought to the fore in this tale; the heroine here is a saint, not the ideal lady of courtly values. The rose garland that Emily weaves for herself is part of her Maying, and so is bound to the cycle of the seasons; the garlands the angel brings are inappropriate for 'this tyme of the yeer' because eternity transcends seasonal change, and they are an emblem of 'the corone of lif that may nat faille'. Emily in the garden is seen by the knights as Chaucer portrays her in his first description of her; earthly vision is inadequate in the spiritual perspective of the saint's life. The eyes of the unbaptised Tiburce 'han no myght to see' the garlands, and Almachius' physical sight is useless, as Cecilia charges:

> 'Ther lakketh no thyng to thyne outter yën
> That thou n'art blynd; for thyng that we seen alle
> That it is stoon, – that men may wel espyen, –

That ilke stoon a god thow wolt it calle.
I rede thee, lat thyn hand upon it falle,
And taste it wel, and stoon thou shalt it fynde,
Syn that thou seest nat with thyne eyen blynde.'   498–504

The earthly senses, sight, touch and taste, are all limited to earthly perception, and cannot move beyond the physical. The idols themselves lack even those senses, being dumb and deaf. The mere possession of sensory faculties is not enough: full humanity demands a consciousness of spirit as well as body, and those who lack that are mere beasts (288). Those who are aware of this spiritual dimension move onto a higher plane of reality:

'In dremes,' quod Valerian, 'han we be
Unto this tyme, brother myn, ywis.
But now at erst in trouthe oure dwellyng is.'   262–4

This 'trouthe' transcends even the ultimate physical fact of death, so that martyrdom is as accident to the substance of the 'cleernesse' and 'light' of heaven.

Burning, like sight, has two meanings in the tale, physical and spiritual, and again one shades into the other, the literal sense becoming a metaphor for the spiritual truth. Tiburce is at first afraid to pursue Christianity for fear of the earthly consequences:

'And while we seken thilke divinitee
That is yhid in hevene pryvely,
Algate ybrend in this world shal we be!'   316–18

Material fire however cannot touch Cecilia, who has been described in the Prologue as burning in charity. Tiburce's fear of the flames here is part of the limitation of his vision, transcended after his baptism.

The search for divinity hidden in heaven transmutes earthly fire into spiritual burning. The alchemists that the Canon's Yeoman talks of are seeking 'the secree of secrees', and the search is illegitimate:

Unto Crist it is so lief and deere
That he wol nat that it discovered bee.   1467–8

The fire that Tiburce dreads is the way to salvation; the fire that the alchemists work with is never transmuted into anything spiritual, nor will it so much as transmute their materials.

We blondren evere and pouren in the fir,
And for al that we faille of oure desire,
For evere we lakken oure conclusioun.   670–2

If Cecilia is associated with lilies for her 'whitnesse ... of honestee', the Yeoman's face is 'wan and of a leden hewe' from constant blowing on the fire in the cause of illegitimate gain, whether by transmutation of metals or, more successfully, by trickery and *illusioun*. When fire in this tale is used metaphorically, it stands for worldly and spiritual danger:

> O! fy, for shame! they that han been brent,
> Allas! kan they nat flee the fires heete? 1407–8

There are even undertones of the threat of the fires of hell: one must avoid the danger lest worse befall:

> Withdraweth the fir, lest it to faste brenne. 1423

Muscatine pointed out that the reason that the Canon was not one of the original pilgrims was because he is not in any sense involved in the spiritual journey towards Canterbury or the celestial city.[68] The Yeoman claims

> That al this ground on which we been ridyng,
> Til that we come to Caunterbury toun,
> He koude al clene turne it up-so-doun,
> And pave it al of silver and of gold. 623–6

He could not, of course; but the fact that he would like to is a measure of his substitution of gold for God. His spiritual way would be transmuted to material wealth. The Yeoman's tale leaves no doubt as to where such a path would ultimately lead.

The raw materials of the Cecilia story are spiritual: the guardian angel, spiritual vision, fire of charity, salvation. The materials of the Canon Yeoman's Tale are devilish. The alchemists are out for their own gain, and are continually identified with the devil. The canon of the second part of the tale is

> roote of al trecherie,
> That everemoore delit hath and gladnesse –
> Swiche feendly thoghtes in his herte impresse –
> How Cristes peple he may to meschief brynge. 1069–72

They arrogate to themselves the 'pryvetee' that is truly God's. They fail not only by religious standards but by secular ones too. 'Trouthe' in the Second Nun's Tale is divine truth, opposed to the dream of the

---

[68] Muscatine p. 220.

real world (262–4). The canon of the second part of the Yeoman's tale debases even the secular meaning of the word:

> 'Trouthe is a thyng that I wol evere kepe,'　　1044

he declares as he sets out to hoodwink his latest victim. Arveragus had seen the keeping of *trouthe* as man's noblest activity, and his response had led to the contest in *gentillesse* between the men of the tale; the canon repays the *gentillesse* shown him not by releasing the money owed him, as the Franklin's clerk does, but by absconding with money entrusted to him.[69]

If the Christians of the Second Nun's Tale can see to the truth beyond the dream of life, the victims of the Canon's Yeoman's Tale are taken in by 'illusioun' because of their blindness. The Yeoman himself has damaged his sight through his work; and, as with the image of fire, the notion is given a moral and metaphorical as well as a literal sense.

> O sely innocent!
> With coveitise anon thou shalt be blent!
> O gracelees, ful blynd is thy conceite,
> No thyng ne artow war of the deceite
> Which that this fox yshapen hath to thee!　　1076–80

If the image is a reminder of Daun Russell persuading Chauntecleer to crow with his eyes shut, the implications here are much more apocalyptic: not only death but damnation will ensue. Finally, however, it is not so much the dupes who are blind as the alchemists themselves, skilled though they may be in science and cunning:

> Ye been as boold as is Bayard the blynde,
> That blondreth forth, and peril casteth noon.
> He is as boold to renne agayn a stoon
> As for to goon bisides in the weye.
> So faren ye that multiplie, I seye.
> If that youre eyen kan nat seen aright,
> Looke that youre mynde lakke noght his sight.　　1413–19

Spiritual vision is the only remedy for such mental blindness. The pursuit of riches has brought the Canon nothing but poverty; and in addition he has made God his adversary. The rioters of the Pardoner's Tale died in their lust for wealth, but Chaucer did not follow them beyond death. The Canon is a man riding towards Hell. For the one

---

[69] VIII 1044–58.

time in the whole *Canterbury Tales*, the blessing conferred on the company at the end is selective:

> God sende every trewe man boote of his bale! 1481

It is a formulation that contains a disturbing reminder of its opposite: that the untrue man, the man committed to *falshede*, will find no remedy for eternal suffering.

Fragments IX and X (H and I): Manciple and Parson

The separation of the Manciple's and Parson's Tales into different fragments is unsupported by the manuscripts. There are discrepancies between their prologues that suggest that Chaucer may not originally have written them as a pair;[70] but their juxtaposition apparently goes back to the earliest exemplars, and almost certainly represents his own arrangement.

The question is of more than textual importance, because although the two tales have on the surface very little in common, there are certain elements in the Manciple's Tale – elements to do with the whole notion of story-telling – that are given much greater prominence by their juxtaposition with the Parson's Prologue. The implications of the tale are much more far-reaching if that juxtaposition is intentional; and it looks as if it is. There is certainly a concern with story-telling present in the Manciple's Tale whatever its placing, and to read it in isolation does not affect that; but as it stands, and as it seems Chaucer placed them, this is a crescendo rising to the great chord – or perhaps discord – of the Parson's Prologue. The effect of both tales together is first to question and then to destroy the whole foundation on which imaginative literature is built.

The tale looks innocuous enough at first glance, a long way from any such considerations. It is preceded by a quarrel between the Manciple and the drunken Cook which seems as if it might lead to another exchange of mutually insulting stories of the Friar-Summoner kind; but instead the disputants are reconciled with wine. The Host points out to the Manciple the dangers of insulting a professional acquaintance such as the Cook, who might get to know too much about his practices for comfort. The Manciple swiftly withdraws his words:

> That what I spak, I seyde it in my bourde. IX 81

The ensuing tale has nothing to do with the Cook, but a great deal to do with the dangers of speech.

---

[70] See pp. 61–2 and note 14.

It is the tale of Phoebus and the crow, taken from the *Metamorphoses*. The god keeps in a cage a snow-white crow that he has taught to speak; but it uses its powers to inform him that his wife has been unfaithful. In his fury he shoots her with an arrow from his bow; but he immediately repents, breaks his weapons and his instruments of music, and deprives the crow of speech and turns it black. At its simplest the tale is a just-so story, a *pourquoi*, as are so many of the stories in the *Metamorphoses*:

> And for this caas been alle crowes blake.   308

There is more to it than this, however. The tale is punctuated by three long digressions: one on how 'flessh is so newefangel' that men cannot hold to virtue for any length of time; one on the nature of words; and, as a conclusion, fifty lines on the dangers of talking too much. Most of this additional material is proverbial; but it is through these digressions that the tale ceases to be a harmless story about crows and turns into something more disturbing.

Even before one looks at the implications of the story for poetic activity as a whole, the Manciple's Tale is a slippery affair. Unsettling gaps keep opening up between the tenor of the narrative and the interpretation given to it. Phoebus is not only a god; he is the most handsome man on earth, and

> was therwith fulfild of gentillesse,
> Of honour, and of parfit worthynesse.   123–4

In taking a lover, therefore, his wife is showing a falling off from the highest standards. The images used to describe this process are progressively more degrading. The first is of a caged bird that would prefer freedom with worms to gold bars and 'deyntees'. The second is of a cat that will leave its milk and meat to chase a mouse, and which ends in the unreasonably harsh *moralitas*

> Lo, heere hath lust his dominacioun,
> And appetit fleemeth discrecioun.   181–2

Such an interpretation has no applicability to the animal world, and little enough to any other. The third and nastiest parallel is with a she-wolf, who, we are told,

> hath also a vileyns kynde.
> The lewedeste wolf that she may fynde,
> Or leest of reputacioun, wol she take,
> In tyme when hir lust to han a make.   183–6

This has a clear relevance to Phoebus' wife, who loves

> A man of litel reputacioun,
> Nat worth to Phebus in comparisoun;   199–200

but it is a relevance that is vigorously denied:

> Alle thise ensamples speke I by thise men
> That been untrewe, and nothyng by wommen.
> For men han evere a likerous appetit
> On lower thyng to parfourne hire delit
> Than on hir wyves.   187–91

If the examples lose touch with a naturalistic perspective on the animals' action, the application of them loses touch with the story itself.

Something similar happens after Phoebus has killed his wife. In Ovid, Coronis, the woman, reproaches him before she dies with killing their child as well as herself; and Apollo repents of his hasty action, too late to save the mother though he rescues the baby. In Chaucer, and in Gower's version of the same story, there is no mention of a child. Only in the Manciple's Tale does Phoebus repent not only the anger that made him kill her, but his very belief in the crow's story.

> O trouble wit, o ire recchelees,
> That unavysed smyteth gilteles!   279–80

There has been plenty in the *Canterbury Tales* before this about the sufferings of the innocent, and Phoebus wants to fit his wife into the same category; but she will not fit. The crow informs him that his eye has been 'blered' by his wife's adultery, but he is equally blind in abandoning his conviction that she has been unfaithful – as blind as January in a similar situation. Again, the moral being drawn within the narrative does not quite fit the story itself.

Many other apparent echoes of earlier parts of the *Canterbury Tales* are similarly misleading. Phoebus' wife is not the guiltless victim; and although she desires 'libertee', as women are acknowledged to do in the Franklin's Tale, the liberty she wants is licence to seek her sexual pleasure where she pleases. The falcon's image for 'newefangelnesse' in the Squire's Tale, of the bird leaving its cage, is criticised by the Franklin with his image of caged love beating its wings to escape; the image is repeated here, but Phoebus' wife will escape without ever having been caged. Her husband is 'jalous', but he has tried to keep her by kindness. The gods are given significant rôles in solving the plot dilemma in the Knight's and Merchant's Tale; here, the fact that Phoebus is a god is obliquely referred to in the first line, but the only supernatural power he shows is in punishing the crow. Apart from that, he could be any deceived husband. The conclusion to the tale is a lengthy and repetitive excursus on the theme summed up by Daun Russell the fox in three lines:

> God yeve hym meschaunce,
> That is so undiscreet of governaunce
> That jangleth whan he sholde hold his pees.   VII 3433–5

To devote fifty lines to a prolix insistence on keeping one's mouth shut is paradoxical, to say the least.

The Manciple's Tale is an Aaron's rod of a story: what looks fixed and rigid one moment wriggles away as soon as you let go of it and turn your eyes from a particular line to its context. The only theme in it to maintain any consistency of meaning is the idea that 'mynstralcie' is inadequate as a response to life, that the ability to tell tales is dangerous, and that the mouth exists to be kept shut. Phoebus may sing celestially, but that does not stop him killing his wife in anger and breaking his instruments in grief; and the crow's powers of speech are its downfall. The crow tells the truth; but it gets no thanks for it. Phoebus's response is,

> I wol thee quite anon thy false tale.   293

It had been common for one fictional tale to 'quite' another, but now the truth will be repaid with punishment – not only with blackness, but with the loss of song and speech.

Literary writing, in the Middle Ages, was defined by the use of rhetoric. Poetry was the art of employing words and syntax in ways other than the everyday. The Manciple's Tale, however, rejects the art in favour of an unadorned truth that makes no such artificial distinctions.

> If men shal telle proprely a thyng,
> The word moot cosyn be to the werkyng.   209–10

The only difference between a *lady* and a *wench* is one of social class, and the use of distinct terms blurs the fact of their moral, or immoral, equality. Likewise, a tyrant or a captain is only a stronger and more successful outlaw. On this basis, the generic differentiation of the *Tales* threatens to collapse. Romance with its ladies and *tragedie* with its tyrants are merely false ways of disguising fabliau and crime story.

Here too, however, there are paradoxes at work if one extends the Manciple's observations to the *Tales* as a whole. Chaucer does observe moral as well as social differentiation in his stories, and where he does not, as in the courtly language of the Miller's and Merchant's Tales, he forces a sense of its incongruity on his audience. The attack on tale-telling is, moreover, contained in a story. That particular inconsistency is smoothed out by the Parson, who firmly rejects the whole idea of fiction in the Prologue that follows:

> Thou gettest fable noon ytoold for me.   31

The Manciple's Tale questions the activity of story-telling within a fiction; the Parson destroys the whole principle on which the *Canterbury Tales* is based.

It is interesting, in this context, that the Manciple's Tale not only refers internally to the *Canterbury Tales*, but has a wider reference to story-collections at large. The tale itself is derived from Ovid's great Classical story-collection; and it is the one occasion when Chaucer keeps the metamorphosis as a climax to the story, with the crow turning from white to black. The retention of the motif makes the debt to the *Metamorphoses* all the more overt, without Chaucer having to compromise his general principle of avoiding turning men into beasts. The story is also of course contained in the *Ovide moralisé*; and analogous stories occur in two other story-collections, the *Seven Sages of Rome* and, more distantly, the *Directorium Vitae Humanae* (though it is not so likely that Chaucer would know of this parallel). It is also told by Gower in the *Confessio Amantis*; and while the general chronological relationship of the two works is uncertain, it is hard to believe that Chaucer's formula of 'My son –', used in the final excursus on tale-telling, is not a deliberate echo of the confessor's formula to the penitent in the *Confessio*. Chaucer introduces a wholly unnecessary character, the Manciple's mother, for no apparent reason but to make the phrase plausible. Such a width of reference outwards to story-collections beyond the *Canterbury Tales* – a width unparalleled elsewhere in the work – strengthens the suspicion that the tale-telling referred to so persistently in the story is indeed literature as well as gossip.

I referred earlier to the possibility that the *House of Fame* is in some ways a theoretical working out of the principles Chaucer puts into practice in the *Canterbury Tales*. If the poet can never reach the truth behind the traditional stories, he must turn instead to the *tidynges* told by travellers and pilgrims. The Manciple's Tale repeats the idea,[71] though it finally leaves the poet no function at all. Book III of the *House of Fame*, which is the section in which the poet-dreamer visits Fame's palace and the house of *tidynges*, opens with an invocation to Apollo as god of poetry. He denies that he wishes to show off any 'art poetical', but he prays for help in revealing his 'sentence'. The

---

[71] See also the discussion in Donald R. Howard, *The Idea of the Canterbury Tales* (Berkeley and Los Angeles, 1976) pp. 330–2.

dreamer, with his privileged insight, can see, as the earthly poet cannot, which of the groups who come before Fame deserve the reputation they have. In the Manciple's Tale, however, Apollo himself cannot distinguish false from true. The crow knows, but he is not believed; and the excursus on keeping quiet ends with an admonition – whether to the Manciple, to the penitent, to mankind, perhaps to poets in general or to Chaucer – against all stories, whether true or not:

> My sone, be war, and be noon auctor newe
> Of tidynges, wheither they been false or trewe.
> Whereso thou come, amonges hye or lowe,
> Kepe wel thy tonge, and thenk upon the crowe.   359–62

It is one of the few tales to end not with a blessing but with a warning.

The Manciple's Tale attacks story-telling for a practical reason based on a theoretical principle: the teller may get into trouble because truth and falsehood are indistinguishable. The Parson refuses to tell a 'fable' for exactly the opposite principle: fables are fictional, and it is truth that matters.

> Why sholde I sowen draf out of my fest,
> Whan I may sowen whete, if that me lest?   X 35–6

He will tell 'moralitee and vertuous mateere', all doctrine and no mirth: 'I take but the sentence.' He promises the pilgrims only lawful pleasure, 'pleasaunce leefull', and his description of what is to come as a 'myrie tale' is one of the most incongruous phrases in the whole collection.

The Parson rejects not only fiction but poetry too, whether alliterative or rhymed.

> I kan nat geeste 'rum, ram, ruf,' by lettre,
> Ne, God woot, rym holde I but litel bettre.   43–4

The prose that forms the medium of the tract is essentially functional, with little of the synonymy or other rhetorical patterning of *Melibee*. Nobody, to my knowledge, has argued that the Parson's Tale is written in *style clergial*, and such elaboration would indeed be inappropriate. The principles of decorum demanded plain style for preaching, and although the Parson's Tale is formally a penitential tract rather than a sermon, its contents require the same clarity of exposition. It does however differ from other tracts in one significant respect. Most of those (including at least one used by Chaucer as a source for the tale)[72]

---

[72] Siegfried Wenzel, 'The source for the "Remedia" of the Parson's Tale', *Traditio* XXVII (1971) 433–53, esp. p. 436.

contain *exempla* that lighten the tone and illustrate their didactic points, like the stories of *Handlyng Synne*. The Parson's Tale makes no such concessions to listeners who might wish for a pleasant fable: the message it expounds is too important, and too complex, for any narrative disguise. The imaginative and verbal skill Chaucer has shown in the other tales has no place here. The function of style in the Parson's Tale is bare communication, and the play of imagination could only detract from the relentless instruction.

The Parson's Tale represents a notorious critical problem in studying the *Canterbury Tales*. In many respects it is hard to see why this should be so. It is more appropriate to its teller than are many tales. It adds another genre to the encyclopaedia; and although by its nature this one rejects all ideas of quality such as would make it a candidate in the story competition, it is still a good pentitential tract as these things go, however alien the form may be to modern sensibilities. There was clearly no barrier to the acceptance of such tracts in the Middle Ages; Chaucer is giving an example of a well-recognised and widespread genre.

Many critics have been concerned with the question of the relationship of the Parson's Tale to the Canterbury pilgrimage. It has generally been taken as being told as the pilgrims approach their goal; and there has been some debate about whether it is the end of the work or only a half-way stage, with Chaucer intending more tales to be told on the homeward journey, and so on. Such questions arise, I suspect, from a misreading of the *Canterbury Tales* as a whole. It is not a novel about a pilgrimage, any more than it is a record of an actual pilgrimage. Unfinished as the work is, the Parson's Tale completes it in several ways. First, it alters the meaning of pilgrimage itself from the narrative or literal to the spiritual or allegorical: the Parson will

> shewe yow the wey, in this viage,
> Of thilke parfit glorious pilgrymage
> That highte Jerusalem celestial. 49–51

Donaldson sums up what is happening with these words:

> When, with the sun nine-and-twenty degrees from the horizon, the twenty-nine pilgrims come to a certain – unnamed – *thropes ende* (I (X) 12), then the pilgrimage no longer seems to have Canterbury as its destination, but rather, I suspect, the Celestial City of which the Parson speaks.[73]

[73] E. T. Donaldson, 'Chaucer the pilgrim', in *Speaking of Chaucer* (London, 1970) p. 10.

The Parson's Tale leaves behind the story of the pilgrimage just as it leaves specified location. It is an end rather than a conclusion; there is no reason why the narrative of the journey and the story-competition should stop here. The debate on the nature of literature, however, which has increasingly occupied Chaucer in the later sections of the *Canterbury Tales*, reaches in the Parson's Tale a point where it cannot continue. The tract denies the legitimacy of imagination and art; and the Retractions follow inevitably from that. If the setting up of the competition invites the readers and listeners to judge the tales by aesthetic standards, the Retractions recognise only the criterion of morality as endowing value.

The Parson's Tale ends the work; but it is not the last word on the subject. If in the Retractions Chaucer drops all pretence that the Parson's Tale was told by the Parson, he still attaches the tract to the *Canterbury Tales*. Read sequentially, the final story only adds one more voice to the twenty-two we have already heard. At least one critic, John Finlayson, believes that 'Chaucer creates a style deliberately and peculiarly appropriate to the Parson', not least in its dogmatism and its tendency to generalisation[74] – both distinctly un-Chaucerian characteristics. If many critics see the Parson's Tale as the ultimate revelation of Truth, Finlayson urges a reading that takes the whole work into account:

> The 'key' to *The Canterbury Tales*, if one is needed, lies in the dominant comic-satiric mode of the presentation, in which no one character or set of statements is the Truth, but all characters and statements qualify and modify each other and provide a comprehensive complex which, in its *wholeness*, may be a sort of truth.

There is, I think, deeper seriousness in the work than this quotation suggests; but it is an interpretation that more honestly faces what we have in the *Tales* than does the orthodox moralism that substitutes the Parson's Tale and the Retractions for all the rest.

It ought to be possible to settle the matter by looking at the text in detail. It is not. This is partly the result of its sheer length: it is shorter than many similar treatises, certainly – the *Remedia* sections constitute only one fortieth of their likely original – but it is still almost twice as long as *Melibee* or the Knight's Tale, and it feels even longer. There is plenty in it that relates back to the other tales, but given its encyclopaedic survey of every kind of human sinfulness this could hardly be otherwise. Every analysis of sin is based on the observation of human behaviour, and Chaucer's own observation of human behaviour makes an overlap inevitable. The tract, for instance,

---

[74] 'The satiric mode and the *Parson's Tale*', *Chaucer Review* VI (1971–2) 94–116; quotations from pp. 116, 111, and see also p. 112.

insists that God, reason, sensuality and the body should each dominate the other in due hierarchy, and this order is 'turned up-so-doun' by sin (260–3). One can relate this to the life of St. Cecilia, as a correct model, or to the Miller's Tale, as an incorrect one; but either comparison shows the limitations of the generalised reading. The saint's legend is scarcely concerned with sin: the spiritual sight of the Christians enables them to see directly the things of God, a vision that never gets a mention in the tract. The fabliau accepts that human beings may well be more concerned with the body than with the soul, and portrays the sheer vitality of life completely missing from the Parson's Tale. When statements are made that support the drift of the other tales, they do so either at the level of common platitude (such as that great men fall),[75] or else they are bloodless and unmemorable by comparison: the constant insistence that true *gentillesse* is independent of birth becomes the drab

Ofte tyme the gentrie of the body binymeth the gentrie of the soule. 461

There are times when identical phrasing is used in the tract and the earlier tales. January, for instance, declares

A man may do no synne with his wyf,
Ne hurte hymselven with his owene knyf;   IV 1839–40

the Parson disposes of the fallacy:

And for that many men weneth that he may nat synne, for no likerousnesse that he dooth with his wyf, certes, that opinion is fals. God woot, a man may sleen hymself with his owene knyf, and make hymselve dronken of his owene tonne.   859

The parallel would carry more weight if it were given more prominence; as it stands, it is buried in a mass of equally dogmatic assertions on the dangers of sin, and of lechery in particular (lechery seems, indeed, to be the Parson's favourite subject). In any case, the fallacy scarcely needs to be shown up: it is immediately obvious from January's formulation. Other assertions made in the tract receive rather less support from the rest of the tales. The most chaste wife, from the penitential angle, is the one who

[75] X 741. The platitudinousness of the observation has been made abundantly clear not only by Chaucer's treatment of it in the Monk's Tale but also by the Nun's Priest's reference to it, VII 3205–9; see p. 183 above.

yeldeth to hire housbonde the dette of hir body, ye, though it be agayn
hir likynge and the lust of hire herte.[76]   941

On this premise May becomes a model of virtue, at least before her
affair with Damian. There are times when the orthodox and moralistic
perspective can be not only inadequate but wrong.

An interpretation of the Parson's Tale that sees it as the ultimate
revelation of Truth has to ignore the text. Truth is finally identifiable
with God: Langland makes the terms effectively interchangeable, and
Chaucer does something similar in his *Balade de Bon Conseyl*, generally known as *Truth*. For Langland, the opposite of Truth is Falsehood: in effect, sin – and this is the main pre-occupation of the Parson's
Tale. Its derivation from treatises on the sins ensures such an emphasis. It has been estimated that the Parson has fourteen times as much
to say about sin as about grace.[77] It is quite clear from his analysis
that scarcely any human action is free from sin. Mediaeval writers
concerned with the Truth which is God, however, give their work a
very different emphasis. The author of the *Cloud of Unknowing*, who
warns his followers against analysing their sins, is perhaps unusual,
and intentionally so, since he is giving instruction in mysticism; but
Langland's dreamer, who is much more specifically representative of
the common man, has to move beyond the study of sin to the study of
well-doing and perfection, and to his vision of the Passion and Har-
rowing of Hell. Dante, too, does not spend all his time in Hell with
the sinful. Even in terms of religious literature, there is more to be
said; and the world has legitimate claims of its own as well.

The very last word of the Parson's Tale is 'sin': one purchases eternal
life through 'deeth and mortificacion of synne'. By contrast, the last
word we hear from the secular world of the pilgrimage, at the end of
the Parson's headlink, is 'grace'. The point is obscured in most modern
editions as the editors have rearranged the manuscript order of the
lines to tidy up what seems to be an awkward bit of syntax. What the
manuscripts read, and therefore presumably what Chaucer wrote, is
this:

> Oure Hoost hadde the wordes for us alle:
> 'Sire preest,' quod he, 'now faire yow bifalle!
> Sey what yow list, and we wol gladly heere.'
> And with that word he seyde in this manere,
> 'Telleth,' quod he, 'youre meditacioun.

[76] See the discussion by Carol V. Kaske, 'Getting around the Parson's Tale: an alternative to allegory and irony', in *Chaucer at Albany* ed. Russell Hope Robbins (New York,
1975) pp. 147–77.

[77] Emerson Brown, jr., 'The poet's last words; text and meaning at the end of the
Parson's prologue', *Chaucer Review* X (1975–6) 236–42.

But hasteth yow, the sonne wole adoun;
Beth fructuous, and that in litel space,
And to do wel God sende yow his grace!'[78]

It is hard to avoid the belief that more things are going on in this speech than Harry Bailey intends. Chaucer knows, as the Host does not, that the Parson in a *fructuous* mood is not going to limit himself to 'litel' space; but not all the further meanings are ironic in the deflationary sense. As far as the whole work is concerned, the sunset marks not only the end of the day but the move from one pilgrimage to the other, to the celestial Jerusalem that can only be reached through death. The Host wishes the Parson well in his tale-telling; but the formula he uses, 'to do wel God sende yow his grace!', has a deeper appropriateness in view of the treatise that follows. Harry Bailey embodies the secular side of the work; he is landlord of the Tabard Inn, which provides an alternative final venue to Canterbury. The Parson speaks of doing ill through sin; the worldly Host speaks of doing well through grace. In the final collocation of shrine and pub, Canterbury does not get everything its own way.

It is customary for mediaeval works to end with a prayer, as do most of the individual tales. It is also common for a writer to list the canon of his works, often at the start of a poem; and many authors who write a religious work after a number of secular ones will pray for forgiveness for what is past. In all these respects, the Retractions are entirely conventional.[79] The only difference lies in the fact that some of these motifs would normally appear at the beginning rather than the end of the work; the opening of the *Canterbury Tales*, however, is clearly inappropriate for them, and Chaucer gathers them together here. The deep conventionality of the piece greatly reduces the likelihood that it represents any profound personal spiritual upheaval, senile penitence, or deathbed confession, on Chaucer's part. The care with which the worldly books are named is suspicious when contrasted with the vagueness of the unspecified 'omelies, and moralitee, and devocioun', genres not foremost among his known works. Even the formulaic confessional phrase requesting absolution for sins both remembered and unremembered is brought in with less than perfect appropriateness:[80] Chaucer asks forgiveness for all his well-

---

[78] X 67–74, re-arranged; see Brown's article cited above. Robinson and others move the second couplet to the end to avoid the repetition of 'he seyde – quod he' in successive lines, so that 'he seyde' becomes a reference to the Parson. Similar constructions are however found at e.g. I 837–9; II 1172–3 (the epilogue, possibly cancelled); III 1269–70 (a very close parallel); etc.

[79] The question is discussed at length in a most interesting article by Olive Sayce, 'Chaucer's "Retractions": the conclusion of the *Canterbury Tales* and its place in literary tradition', *Medium Aevum* XL (1971) 230–48.

[80] Sayce pp. 241–2.

known works, and for 'many another book, if they were in my remembrance'. One can commit a sin thoughtlessly; one can hardly write a book unwittingly. Moreover, within the Retractions themselves he is urging the value of the very works for which he is asking forgiveness.

> For oure book seith, 'All that is writen is writen for oure doctrine,' and
> that is myn entente.   1083

The sentence acts as a pivot between the opening reference to the 'litel tretys', presumably the Parson's Tale, and the list of his works; but there is no indication that Chaucer is limiting the application of the maxim he quotes to religious works. The last time we heard the formulation was in the overtly secular context of the Nun's Priest's Tale:

> Seint Paul seith that al that writen is,
> To oure doctrine it is ywrite, ywis.   VII 3441–2

It was certainly in widespread use in the Middle Ages as a justification for the study of secular literature.[81] After making such a claim for his own 'entente', Chaucer has little need to acknowledge guilt in his writings.

All this does not prove that the Retractions are satiric, or that Chaucer did not mean what he said. It does indicate that one should not put too much weight on them as a deeply felt personal statement where every word is to be taken at its full face value. The ending is not inappropriate for the *Canterbury Tales* as we have them. Chaucer, like the Parson, rejects the worlds of imagination and art and chooses instead the way of 'verray penitence, confessioun and satisfaccioun'. He attaches the words, however, not only to the Parson's Tale but to the whole story-collection, his finest exposition of the worlds of imagination and art, where it is shown abundantly that there are things in life other than penitence, and where we are taught that the homiletic and didactic are not always enough.

In one sense, the Retractions are very important; they show that, in Larry Benson's words,

> We have the work in what Chaucer regarded as its final state; unfinished, unrevised, and imperfect as *The Canterbury Tales* may be, Chaucer had finished with it.[82]

It is not impossible that he returned to the work at a later date after

---

[81] Sayce pp. 237, 245; and cf. the use of the tag by the author of the *Ovide moralisé* to justify the reading of a pagan author (see above, p. 18).
[82] Benson p. 81.

writing the Retractions, but there is no evidence that he did so. Any speculation about what Chaucer would have made of the work if he had finished it is therefore not only hypothetical but illegitimately so. Chaucer had no intention of making any more of it: for him, the Parson's Tale and the Retractions were the end. Such an ending involves a change of plan from that outlined by the Host at the beginning; but it is not without justification from the way the work has developed. Chaucer's very faithfulness to his survey of literary kinds, the integrity with which he adopts each new perspective, finally leaves him no way to continue. That is why ultimately the Parson's Tale is a blind alley.

just the opposite

6

Themes and Variations

Chaucer, as Muscatine notes, 'has a passion for relationship',[1] and in the story-collection of the *Canterbury Tales* he found the form that could give the fullest expression to this passion. To write in a single genre demands the adoption of a single perspective; one can vary or modify this by refusing to fulfil generic conventions, or by mingling genres, but the most such methods can achieve is the setting up of an instability within fixed points. *Sir Gawain and the Green Knight* qualifies its hero's success on the quest, the Knight's Tale counterbalances romance with tragedy, but they both still function within the assumptions of chivalric idealism. The juxtaposition of different genres in the *Canterbury Tales*, and the assignment of the tales to a series of fallible narrators, allows for a potentially infinite series of perspectives and qualifications. The tales can suggest criticism of their own genre; adjacent tales qualify or parody particular elements in each other; the choice of a particular narrator can mean the abuse of story for personal insult, or personal gain, so that a tale is not allowed to express its own meaning but is slanted away by the circumstances of its telling from any inner 'truth' it might contain.

Chaucer's own choice of persona with the *Tales*, as a bumbling and not very intelligent reporter always prepared to take things at face value, eliminates any possibility of an authoritative or trustworthy voice within the work itself. The questions raised by the telling of the tales are therefore not resolved within the work, just as the explicit questions remain unanswered: who is worse off, Palamon in prison or Arcite in exile? who is the most generous, husband, squire or clerk? The entire work is framed as a question: which is the best tale? – and not only is no answer given, but each successive tale serves to unsettle one's estimate of the one before, to call for a re-appraisal of its values and to question its assumptions and perspectives. Language itself is subject to the same uncertainty. 'Wench' and 'lady' are not so far

---

[1] Muscatine p. 223.

apart, when it comes to the point; the language of the Song of Songs can express mystic vision or be degraded to stale eroticism; *Sir Thopas* is damned in the Host's ears, and saved in ours, by its adherence to crude provincial poeticisms.

A potentially infinite series of perspectives, designed to raise questions, and expressed through manipulable language put in the mouths of fallible speakers, sounds like a recipe for chaos. In fact, the *Canterbury Tales* is a finely ordered work, and Chaucer's control is everywhere apparent. The most detailed reflections between tales occur within the completed fragments; but the separate groups of stories are all part of the same larger pattern. Many themes and motifs are repeated throughout the work, recurring in different forms in different genres, but still all recognisably related to each other. Generic relativity, the various interpretations of the world (or of poetry) implied by different perspectives, can only be expressed on this larger scale. Relativity can be demonstrated in many ways; and Chaucer uses all kinds of methods, not only to hold different readings of the world in balance, but to draw the tales together into a cohesive pattern.

Many of the motifs found throughout the work have already been touched on in the discussion of the linked tales; this chapter attempts to bring into single focus some of the matters discussed disparately there. It makes no claim whatever to be exhaustive, and every reader of the *Tales* will find more examples. I have tried to choose a selection representative of Chaucer's variety of method. Some philosophical ideas are treated at large over the whole work; so are certain patterns of human behaviour. There are repeated plot motifs, and patterns of imagery. This chapter is intended to suggest how all-pervasive such interrelations are.

Fortune, Providence and suffering

> What governance is in this prescience,
> That giltelees tormenteth innocence?   I 1313–14

Palamon's question raises one of the key issues of the whole *Canterbury Tales*. There are few stories that do not touch on it in some way, and its prominence as one of the major themes of the opening tale helps to establish its importance. Discussion of the issue comes in two forms, both found in the Knight's Tale. First is the debate on the metaphysical context for human action, on the nature of Fortune, Providence, predestination, free will and so on. Second, the lack (or apparent lack) of justice in the ordering of the world is discussed from the point of view of particular suffering individuals. Palamon's question indicates how closely the two issues are interwoven.

Boethius' *Consolation of Philosophy*, which Chaucer translated and on which he drew in a number of his poems, concerns itself with these same questions, and the figure of Philosophy provides answers. The prisoner Boethius can only perceive Fortune, the haphazard ordering of the world in which all one can be sure of is mutability and in which merit and reward bear no relation to each other. Philosophy herself insists on the supremacy of Providence, God's just ordering of all things for good. She reconciles the apparent contradiction between them by asserting that Fortune or Fate is merely a man's-eye view of Providence;[2] it is only the inadequacies of human sight that create the contradiction. The trouble with this formulation is that one only has human eyes to see with: the assertion of any other vision must be an act of faith. Chaucer is keenly aware of this problem. The Knight's Tale is a profoundly Boethian work, but it qualifies the Boethian conclusion. The affirmation of faith is there in Theseus' insistence on the order created by the First Mover, but his assertion does not meet the objections raised earlier in the tale. That He allots every man a certain span of days merely restates Arcite's

> What is this world? what asketh men to have?
> Now with his love, now in his colde grave,   I 2777–8

and Arcite's passionate questioning lodges in the mind as Theseus' detached generalisation does not. Answers such as Theseus' will only work at a safe distance from individual examples; they do not begin to answer the questions raised by the deaths of Hugelyn's innocent children or the virtuous Virginia.

That the Knight's Tale has a pagan setting affects the validity of its conclusions singularly little. Its gods can be placed within a Christian scheme through their astrological functions, but that does not lessen their malevolence; and the characters can express an awareness of God when Chaucer requires. Theseus' First Mover is not an exclusively pagan concept, and Arcite's phrase about 'purveiaunce of God, or of Fortune' (1252) suggests an awareness of the Christian answer in theory even if human sight cannot distinguish it in practice. Overtly Christian tales, such as the Man of Law's (though not the exclusively religious ones, such as the Second Nun's), generally share this bewilderment before the order of things. 'Crueel Mars' brings Custance's first marriage to an end, and her husband's fall is ascribed to the 'firste moevyng, crueel firmament' (II 295–305). The Clerk's Tale, with its closing invitation to compare Walter's capricious infliction of suffering with the operations of God's Providence, intensifies the bewilderment. The opening tragedy of the Monk's Tale, the story of Lucifer,

---

[2] *Boece* IV pr.6. Boethius asks an initial question similar to Palamon's in I met.5.

acknowledges the lack of connection between earthly fortune and just reward, for it is only in the heavenly order that punishment and desert are matched:

> Though Fortune may noon angel dere,
> From heigh degree yet fel he for his synne.   VII 2001–2

Such an assertion undermines the easy moralistic conclusions given elsewhere. The Monk's Antiochus receives 'swich gerdoun as bilongeth unto pryde' (2630), but this means very little when Hugelyn's children receive a similar 'guerdon'. When the wicked Apius kills himself, the Physician asserts,

> Heere may men seen how synne hath his merite;   VI 277

but the concept of just punishment is counterbalanced by the fact that the virtuous Virginia has also been killed, even though

> nevere thou deservedest wherfore
> To dyen with a swerd or with a knyf.   216–17

The only response to such a state of affairs that commands the agreement of all the pilgrims is that Fortune is untrustworthy, a platitude repeated in one form or another at frequent intervals throughout the *Tales*.

The rôle ascribed to God in all this varies considerably. There are a number of assertions matching Theseus': that everything really happens according to a providential ordering. The Parson sees any resistance to such faith as a form of envy, when men complain

> that shrewes han prosperitee, or elles for that good men han adversitee./
> And alle thise thynges sholde man suffre paciently, for they comen by
> the rightful juggement and ordinaunce of God.   X 500–1

He has nothing to say about the point raised in other tales, that God's standards of 'rightful juggement' and man's may differ irreconcilably. A number of times in the *Tales* the most awkward theological questions are referred to 'divines' (even the Parson does this on one occasion), in a frank admission that ordinary human reason cannot encompass them.[3] The Nun's Priest refers his hearers to Augustine, Boethius and Bradwardine as authorities who could 'bulte it to the bren', but Fathers, philosophers and theologians have alike failed to come up with any single or simple answer. Only in the tales that

---

[3] E.g. Knight's Tale I 1323, 2811–2; Franklin's Tale V 885–90; Nun's Priest's Tale VII 3234–52; Parson's Tale X 957.

approximate most closely to God's perspective on human affairs, the saints' lives and related genres, does the problem cease to be problematic. There, there is a straightforward equation between virtue and reward, even if the reward happens beyond death. The *litel clergeon* of the Prioress's Tale may be murdered, but he is assured of his place in the Lamb's procession. The fire will not harm Cecilia, and she is assured of her everlasting crown of life however unpleasant her martyrdom may be. She can therefore speak of God as a 'rightful Juge' (VIII 389) with more conviction than less saintly mortals, for she looks beyond the perspective of earthly fortune. She has no fear of Almachius' earthly power, for that is no more than a 'bladdre ful of wynd' (439). The Man of Law's Tale, despite its moments of questioning, asserts an equally simple answer, and this time brings the operation of God's justice forward to within this life instead of postponing it till after death. Custance is under the protection of the 'Lord of Fortune' (II 448), and so her apparently desperate adventures in open boats become overt demonstrations of Providence.[4] The constable asks a question very similar to Palamon's:

> O myghty God, if that it be thy wille,
> Sith thou are rightful juge, how may it be
> That thou wolt suffren innocentz to spille,
> And wikked folk regne in prosperitee?   II 813–16

The answer, in this tale, is straightforward: He does not. He ensures that wicked mothers-in-law are punished and rapists drowned; and He lays on a miracle to assert Custance's innocence of murder. If life were really like that, there would be no problem.

One of the most interesting answers as to why God's Providence should take such apparently perverse courses is given in the Franklin's Tale. The perspective here remains consistently secular, but the workings of Providence are none the less justified. The problem is raised by Dorigen when she contemplates the rocks that threaten to wreck her husband's ship on his return, and which seem to her the antithesis of what God's 'purveiaunce' ought to provide.[5] They are a 'foul confusioun', a 'werk unresonable', that 'do no good, but evere anoyen'. She finds the orthodox answer – the answer given later by the Parson – totally unsatisfying:

> I woot wel clerkes wol seyn as hem leste,
> By argumentz, that al is for the beste,
> Though I ne kan the causes nat yknowe.   V 885–7

---

[4] See the extensive discussion in Kean pp. 114–22.
[5] VI 865–90.

The course of the story does not exactly endorse the clerks' point of view, but it does suggest something closely parallel. Dorigen wishes the rocks away, but it is their removal, by a magic that while not sorcery is still not exactly Christian, that threatens the stable order of her marriage. Neither Providence nor Fortune wrecks Arveragus' ship, but she herself very nearly succeeds in wrecking their love. Her attempt to interfere with the apparently confused order of creation produces only worse confusion. Dorigen speaks a long complaint against Fortune when she discovers what has happened; but Fortune in fact plays very little part in this story. The emphasis is on the human, not the metaphysical – or the supernatural. The tale does not attempt to give a generalised answer to the nature of Providence and Fortune: it relocates the problem in particular circumstances with particular individuals, and they must work things out themselves. In the end virtue is rewarded; and it is rewarded not with material wealth, but with happiness. The tale is an exemplification of Boethius' insistence that virtue brings its own reward, and that true felicity is inseparable from goodness, with a romance happy ending to prove it. The story does not guarantee such a happy ending; but it could not be brought about by anything less than the good action of everyone concerned.

'I cannot praise a fugitive and cloister'd vertue, unexercis'd and unbreath'd . . . That which purifies us is triall, and triall is by what is contrary.'[6] Milton's words touch the centre of human experience in a fallen world. They sum up the essence of mediaeval romance, in which the knight sets out to test his virtue in a hostile environment; and they also come close to defining Chaucer's less dogmatic but no less firm stand. Virtue in a sense cannot exist without evil or suffering. Some of the most powerful tales in the Canterbury series are those that insist on the suffering of the virtuous, and so admit the apparent disorder of a world that provides no guarantee of reward. The Knight's and Clerk's Tales lay particular stress on this; so does the Franklin's Tale, in a quieter way. The tales that polarise good and evil too sharply, however, like the Man of Law's, the Physician's and the Prioress's, weaken their point through their lack of full humanity of treatment or significance. The Monk's tragedies are also inadequate because they leave aside all questions of virtue and trial and substitute an image of man as passive victim. The tales in which evil men are brought to a moment of trial and are not purified by it but damned – the Pardoner's and the Friar's – do however have a power of their own.

One of the most explicit discussions outside the Knight's Tale of the issues of Fortune, free will and predestination occurs in the Nun's

[6] *Areopagitica* (*The Works of John Milton* Vol. IV (New York, 1931) p. 311 8–14).

Priest's Tale, despite the ludicrous disproportion between such matters and the subject in hand. The lowering of literary level to the farmyard lends a welcome irony to the discussion after the seriousness of the other tales on the subject (not least the Monk's). One of Chauntecleer's miniature fables takes up the issue presented at large in the Knight's Tale, of two people of apparently equal moral desert who come to very different ends. One of the two sworn brothers of the Knight's Tale dies; so does one of the two travelling-companions in the *exemplum* of a prophetic dream. The Nun's Priest, however, explicitly avoids getting entangled in metaphysical speculation. None of the morals at the end of the tale has anything to do with Fortune. Instead, they call for virtuous action: Chauntecleer and the fox both make resolutions about their future behaviour; and the final blessing takes the form of a prayer that we may all be made 'goode men'. Once again, virtue is given precedence over Fortune.

Chaucer does not provide any final answer to the problems of Providence and the suffering of the good. He could hardly be expected to succeed in finding one where St. Augustine had failed. Rather, his very use of stories, with their emphasis on the individual case and not the detached generalisation, highlights the fact that the problem is rationally unanswerable. The saints' lives and miracles posit a simplified world that leaves ordinary existence aside; in the secular tales, supernatural intervention may take the form not of providential miracle but of violent disruption, as when Arcite's horse stumbles. Theseus' answer, that one must make virtue of necessity, does not resolve the problem, but it does provide a way to go on living. One may not be able to alter Fortune, but that is no excuse for inaction. However great the gulf may be between desert and reward, Chaucer insists on the necessity of attempting to live by the standards of ideal virtue. Whatever rôle is played by Fortune, men must still bear moral responsibility for their actions. Walter's cruelty is no reason for Griselda to cease to act virtuously, nor is Arcite's death a reason for Palamon to hold back from adding his own link to the 'faire cheyne of love' by marrying Emily. The turning of Fortune's wheel may crush the carter, obliterate the Monk's victims or trick the fox out of his prey, but Chaucer will never let that be an excuse for acting, or writing, with less than full humanity.

Felicity and vision

> We witen nat what thing we preyen heere . . .
> We seken fast after felicitee,
> But we goon wrong ful often, trewely.   I 1260, 1266–7

Arcite's comment on men's inability to perceive true good is as basic

to the *Canterbury Tales* as is Palamon's question about the sufferings
of the innocent. He longs for release from prison and finds exile; he
prays for victory and receives death. He is not the only character to
confuse ends and means. Absolon gets his kiss, but it is not what he
wants. Dorigen believes she wants the rocks removed, but her true
desire is to preserve her husband and her marriage. The Pardoner's
rioters believe they have found 'heigh felicitee' in the treasure; in fact,
as the Old Man had told them, they have found Death, and an agon-
izing death at that.

The dying Arcite repeats his question with still greater intensity:
'What asketh men to have?' The felicity men seek can never be fulfilled
in anything earthly, for everything mortal is mutable. This at least
was the Boethian, and the religious, answer; but the *Canterbury Tales*
do not quite say that only felicity beyond the world is worth having.
Heaven offers unending bliss, as the saint's life and the tracts point
out; but some of the secular tales end in a bliss that is no less genuine
for being rooted in human values.

Some kinds of felicity are unquestionably true, others equally certainly false. Virtue is no bulwark against suffering, but it can offer a
direct way to salvation. The ultimate good that Cecilia seeks is
Heaven, and her way to achieve it is chastity for God's sake. The
Prioress's *litel clergeon* adores the Virgin, and his setting his heart on
heavenly things again ensures that he reaches celestial bliss. The
search for material wealth, by contrast, is damnable. The summoner
of the Friar's Tale is out for what he can get; all he in fact attains is
damnation. The Pardoner's rioters come to a particularly nasty end
through their lust to have all the treasure to themselves. The Canon's
Yeoman's alchemists seek the philosopher's stone to turn everything
to gold, but for ever

> We faille of that which that we wolden have.   VIII 958

Ends and means part company, with even more disastrous results
than they do for Arcite. His search for *felicitee* proved a hollow mockery; their pursuit of material good means a turning away from God to
play into the hands of the Devil.   *No*

Martyrdom is always good; the substitution of Mammon for God is
always bad. Sexual relationships are much more interesting, because
the same physical facts never have the same interpretation. Sex can
be good, bad, or anything in between, as the Temple of Venus illustrates (though the emphasis there, much more than in the *Canterbury
Tales* as a whole, is on the bad aspects). Sex, unlike martyrdom or
murder, cannot be given instant moral categorisation; there are too
many variables. That may be why theologians have had such trouble
with it, and why it is such an inexhaustible subject of literature. We

know instantly that the rioters' treasure does not represent the felicity they fondly imagine; but when Chaucer speaks of the bliss of marriage, he is – sometimes – speaking entirely without irony.

The *blisse* that Palamon and Emily enjoy at the end of the Knight's Tale is given a metaphysical context in Theseus' exposition of the providential 'faire cheyne of love': earthly felicity reflects the divine order for good. Dorigen and Arveragus end their tale 'in sovereyn blisse', and one believes in such a state all the more for the testing their love has undergone. The knight of the Wife of Bath's Tale is married in the belief that he is entering a matrimonial hell:

> 'My love?' quod he, 'nay, my dampnacioun!'   III 1067

He ends up none the less in 'parfit joye'. The Merchant's Tale goes through the reverse process, describing marriage first as the highest bliss and then showing it as the Fall. The tale even contains an ironic proof that a wife is a gift of God (and therefore represents true felicity), and not of Fortune (representing mutable, and therefore false, felicity), for while the gifts of Fortune 'passen as a shadwe upon a wal',[7]

> A wyf wol laste, and in thyn hous endure,
> Wel lenger than thee list, paraventure.   IV 1317–18

By entering into the *paradys* of marriage, January is also letting in the serpent. Like Arcite, he is pursuing a *parfit felicitee* that proves to be a phantom – though he never realises its hollowness, and ends the tale in a state of self-congratulation.

The equation of marriage with felicity is far from straightforward even in earthly terms; but Chaucer's readiness to admit that they need not be the same thing lends weight to the occasions when they are. The hagiographical perspective of St. Cecilia, or the ascetic theology of the Parson, may condemn all sex as sinful and regard virginity alone as virtuous, but the care with which Chaucer discriminates between different kinds of marital relationships shows how far he is from adopting any such simplistic viewpoint.

There is a general correlation in the *Canterbury Tales* between the kind of sovereign good valued by the individual pilgrims – what they are described as loving most – and the kind of bliss envisaged in the tales they tell. Often this is no more than a moral equivalence, with the virtuous pilgrims telling of virtuous ends, but it can become more specific. The correlation is never over-schematised (it is not even consistent) but there are a few cases where Chaucer demonstrates a single concept of felicity, true or false, in both teller and tale.

---

[7] The simile is used again by the Parson, X 1068.

The Wife of Bath is one of the most interesting instances. She leaves us in no doubt as to what women, represented by herself, most desire, and she devotes much of her Prologue and Tale to expounding the doctrine of female *maistrie*. Neither her autobiography nor her story is however as straightforward as this might suggest. The husband she loved best was the one who was least amenable to her domination; and the knight and his newly beautiful bride end up by obeying each other, to their mutual pleasure. In both cases, the *maistrie* so eagerly sought turns into something different. The Wife finishes up 'kynde' and 'trewe' to Jankyn, and the 'parfit joye' in which the knight and his bride end leaves an impression of something very different from the monstrous regiment of women that the Wife advocates in theory.

The tales of evil are the clearest example of false felicity carried over from their tellers. The Pardoner's rioters, the Friar's summoner and the alchemists all set their hearts on earthly treasure, and are all on their way to Hell. The implications of this extend back into the 'real' world of the pilgrimage. The Canon's Yeoman extricates himself from evil practices; not so the Friar or the Pardoner. That they are themselves so adept at extracting worldly wealth from their victims is presented in the General Prologue as a sign of professional expertise, but their tales leave no room for any ironic moral equivocation. Their vision is of a world devoid of good – a godless world, in effect. The Pardoner boasts of the paradox that he can tell a moral tale despite himself being 'vicious', but the fit between teller and tale is all too close.

One more tale deserves mention in this context: *Sir Thopas*. The object of Sir Thopas's quest, and the felicity on which he sets his heart, is an elf-queen. This felicity is neither heavenly nor earthly, but other-worldly, and hopelessly impractical. It is perceived moreover only in dream, and dreams are notoriously fallacious. Chaucer the poet-pilgrim not only produces the worst poetry; he also inhabits a moral world in which the highest bliss that can be envisaged is a product of irrelevant fantasy. That the popular romance he tells so consistently refuses to go beyond the superficial level of narrative action is of a piece with his presentation of himself as both physically and morally short-sighted, always gazing at the ground (VII 697) and always ready to take things at face value.

Chaucer uses imagery of sight and blindness extensively throughout the *Tales*, and it is closely related to the question of the nature of felicity. Those with clear sight can distinguish true felicity; those who are morally blind seek the wrong things. This set of imagery reaches its climax in the fragment comprising the Second Nun's Tale, of the clear-sighted Cecilia with her spiritual perception of heavenly things, and the Canon's Yeoman's Tale, of the alchemists half-blinded by their

work, hoodwinking their victims, and, like 'Bayard the blynde' (VIII
1413), unable to see the true way they should be following.

The imagery of true and false sight is closely connected with another
image series, of drunkenness. The two come together most clearly in
the Summoner's Tale, in the *exemplum* of Cambises.[8] One of his lords,
who loves 'vertuous moralitee', warns him against the debilitating
effects of strong drink. Cambises responds by shooting dead the lord's
son, asking,

> Hath wyn bireved me myn eyen sight?   III 2071

The question is the climax of the story. It is a rhetorical question,
with no answer given; but the audience are none the less expected to
supply one. Cambises' physical sight may be intact, but his spiritual
insight – like that of Almachius in the Second Nun's Tale – is non-
existent.

Drunkenness is frequently associated with sin in the *Canterbury
Tales*: the drinking habits of the Pardoner's rioters are contrasted
with the virtuous Virginia's abstinence; and the connections between
strong drink and gluttony, lust, quarrelling and murder are pointed
out on a number of occasions.[9] Chaucer has the Miller blame the ale
of Southwark for his tale, with its obscenity and its lack of moral
insight. In the Knight's Tale, metaphorical drunkenness is used in an
image parallel to the Canon's Yeoman's of blind Bayard, for mankind
unable to distinguish false felicity from true or to find the way to it:

> A dronke man woot wel he hath an hous,
> But he noot which the righte wey is thider,
> And to a dronke man the wey is slider.   I 1262–4

There is no moral condemnation here of the kind attached to literal
drunkenness: the image is associated more with the limited vision of
man, who can only see Fortune and fate, where God's clear sight sees
a providential ordering. Dame Prudence, in *Melibee*, insists on a mor-
alised interpretation of a similar image. The name Melibee, she declares, means 'a man that drynketh hony'; her husband is so drunk
with the delights of the world that he has turned away from Christ.[10]

Drunkenness is often literal in the first instance; blindness is most
often metaphorical. There are two exceptions to this: the blind man
who is healed through Custance's agency, and January. The blind
man is a Christian, and can see with 'thilke eyen of his mynde' despite

---

[8] III 2043–73.
[9] See e.g. III 852, V 782, VI 484–588, VII 2491, 2644, X 822. The Wife of Bath takes
a less moralistic line on the connection between wine and Venus, III 457–68.
[10] VII 1410–15.

his physical blindness (II 552). January is also cured of literal blindness, but he remains metaphorically as much in the dark as ever:

> As good is blynd deceyved be
> As to be deceyved whan a man may se.   IV 2109–10

That 'love is blynd alday', and that January chooses his wife by reference to her visible surface, as if by looking in a mirror, are part of the same image sequence. His continuing moral blindness at the end of the tale is of a piece with his conviction that his marriage will be 'parfit felicitee'.

January is tricked into believing that what he has seen (his wife and Damian making love in the pear-tree) is mere illusion.

> Ful many a man weneth to seen a thyng,
> And it is al another than it semeth.   IV 2408–9

Illusion is another motif that occurs several times in the *Tales*. It is closely connected with the image sequence of inadequate sight, but where blindness correlates with sin, *illusioun* is contrasted with *trouthe*. *Illusioun* gives a pretence of true felicity but in fact falls short. Symkyn the miller mocks the students by claiming that they can make their cramped quarters appear vast 'by argumentes' (I 4123); other clerks are able to put such *apparences* into practice. The clerk of Orleans in the Franklin's Tale is the most notable of these. He can give Aurelius the illusion of what he wants, dancing with his lady and so on; and he can make the rocks *seem* to vanish. Dorigen's *trouthe*, however, did not take illusion into account:

> Hir trouthe she swoor thurgh innocence.
> She nevere erst hadde herd speke of apparence.   V 1601–2

In the end, *trouthe* wins the day over illusion. In the Canon's Yeoman's Tale, the alchemists live by creating false appearances:

> To muchel folk we doon illusioun;   VIII 673

and they also have no intention of keeping *trouthe* (1044). Illusion here is a very dangerous matter indeed. It is a way of creating blindness, of turning men away from the true perception of the good.

Illusion in the *Canterbury Tales* is closely connected with dreaming. Chauntecleer may cite *exempla* of true dreams – and even have a prophetic dream himself, although he blindly refuses to act by it – but the other dreams of the *Tales* are all misleading or false. Worldly felicity is dream, illusion, when compared with the true bliss, the *trouthe*, of the perception of God:

'In dremes,' quod Valerian, 'han we be
Unto this tyme, brother myn, ywis.
But now at erst in trouthe oure dwellynge is.'   VIII 262–4

Actual dreams are equally illusory. Arcite dreams of Mercury promising an end to his woe, but the end is in fact death. Absolon dreams of being at a feast, but he gets a mouthful of something he doesn't expect. Croesus dreams of being washed by Jupiter and dried by Phoebus, but this is prophetic not, as he imagines, of high honour, but of being hanged and his corpse exposed to the weather.[11] Drunken dreams are totally insignificant and have nothing of 'visioun'.[12] Some dreams are outright false, not in the sense of being misleading or wrong but because they are invented. The friar of the Summoner's Tale claims to have seen a vision of Thomas's wife's dead child being 'born to blisse' (III 1857). Alisoun of Bath informs her fifth-husband-to-be that she has had a symbolically prophetic dream of prosperous marriage,

And al was fals; I dremed of it right naught.   III 582

Both the friar and the Wife are using dreams to further their own desires. The friar sees them as a way of extracting money, the Wife as a way of catching her next man. The means the friar pursues, however, do not produce the desired result: he seeks felicity in the form of donations, but goes about it by what proves to be the wrong way. The Wife's machinations are entirely successful, even if Jankyn resists conforming to her expectations of meekness. The friar's false dream shows how far he is from *trouthe* in any of its meanings; the Wife, having caught Jankyn with her invented dream, ends up by insisting on how *trewe* she was to him. Once again, love and sex resist the easy moral categorisations implied elsewhere.

Physical blindness is under the control of Fortune, as the Merchant's Tale points out. It therefore says nothing about the moral status of the sufferer, any more than Arcite can be morally distinguished from Palamon on the strength of their different fates. Mental blindness, on the other hand, is a condition of the will. The Canon's Yeoman warns,

If that youre eyen kan nat seen aright,
Looke that youre mynde lakke noght his sight. VIII 1418–19

The context here makes the reference primarily to spiritual matters. Worldly wisdom also depends on clear sight, however, and, as Chauntecleer points out, to shut one's eyes is wilful, stupid, and a short way

[11] VII 2740–56.
[12] V 357–9, 372.

to disaster. Clear sight, a clear head, clear reason and virtue all belong together; so do blindness, drunkenness, folly and sin. As always, however, Chaucer refuses to schematise such relationships. It is Arcite's pagan virtue that enables him to realise his own short-sightedness. After all the sermons against drunken quarrelling, the row between the Manciple and the Cook is reconciled with wine. The Wife of Bath, fond as she is of alcohol and sex, still tells a tale of Christian *gentil-lesse*. The further away one moves from the simple perspective of hagiography, the more confused such schemes become. Moral tales and saints' lives operate in a world of light and darkness, black and white. The Wife of Bath with her red stockings does not fit easily into such a pattern.

Female saints and wikked wyves

The 'marriage group', with its discussion of sovereignty in marriage, has been endlessly analysed,[13] and there seems no need to repeat the analysis here. The debate is itself, however, part of a larger issue running throughout the *Tales*: an issue one might call the Woman Question. The woman most in question is of course the Wife of Bath, with her estates function as archetypal female. She is backed up by a number of others within the tales: by Alisoun and May on one side, by Custance, Griselda and Cecilia on the other. Somewhere behind them all, and glimpsed from time to time through allusion or overt reference, are the even more archetypal figures of Eve and the Virgin.

Again, it is fatally easy to schematise: to divide Chaucer's women into sheep and goats, and condemn or applaud the moral examples they set. But the *Canterbury Tales* is not a moral allegory. Its insistence on relativism and variety of perspective never narrows down to a single vision; the Parson may come last, but he does not have everything his own way. Moreover, if the *Canterbury Tales* really had been written from such a perspective, Chaucer would never have been acknowledged as a great poet. The Parson's Tale is unsatisfactory, not primarily because of its style and length, but because it substitutes dogmatic generalisation for individual humanity. Chaucer's characters, both within the pilgrimage and within the tales, are always treated as people first and personifications second, if at all. They do not exist in a moral vacuum — the act of judgment from Chaucer or from the reader in the *Canterbury Tales* is always important — but neither do they exist primarily to be assigned an anagogical classifi-

[13] The inspiration was given by George Lyman Kittredge in 'Chaucer's discussion of marriage', *Modern Philology* IX (1911–12) 435–67; for a bibliography, see note 1 to the reprint in *Chaucer Criticism* Vol. I: *The Canterbury Tales* ed. Richard J. Schoeck and Jerome Taylor (Notre Dame, 1960), p. 158.

cation. Dante can afford to show human sympathy for his characters because God has already adjudged their ultimate destinies. Chaucer tends to give the least developed treatment to figures whose ultimate salvation or damnation is clear. His most fully realised characters are those who are most fully involved with life in the world – not the 'world' of the world, the flesh and the devil, but the world as a place of common experience, where people have to get on with the business of living without either meeting serpents in the garden or seeing guardian angels beside the marriage-bed.

Eve and May both come to their sexual fall in a garden; the Virgin and Cecilia both live in married chastity. That Cecilia's angel is literal, while May's serpent takes the form of her husband's amorous squire, is a measure of the difference in texture and treatment between the tales. That May is in a sense another Eve re-enacting the Fall is made clear: the creation of Eve to be Adam's *helpe* is cited early in the Merchant's Tale, with the comment that their marriage proves that a wife is man's *paradys terrestre* (IV 1332). The garden, the misapplication of the mystic language of the Song of Songs, and the pear-tree all continue the level of allusion. But while May's goings-on may be the result of living in a postlapsarian world, Chaucer holds back from presenting her actions in simple theological terms. Pluto and Proserpina rule this world, and their presence turns the whole tale into a just-so story of a different kind. Instead of its moral being that Eve fell and woman will always fall again, it claims that this particular tale will explain why women always have a ready answer. The story thus becomes not only an individual example of a theological archetype, but a human archetype of all the instances where a woman's tongue has got her out of trouble. There is more going on in the tale besides all this, of course, but the change of emphasis is still significant; and to ignore it, or to insist that the moral and exemplary level is all that matters, is to make Chaucer indistinguishable from the Parson.

The Woman Question in the Middle Ages was a literal question: were women a good thing, or not? In the debate poem *The Thrush and the Nightingale*, the birds' lengthy argument is brought to an instant end when the Nightingale cites the example of the Blessed Virgin.[14] The opposition on the matter not only referred back to Eve, but also cited the endless miseries of married life. The point of view is consistently masculine: the arguments are conducted from the perspective of Adam or the husband. The Virgin is the ideal for similar reasons, for she promised total humility and obedience to her Lord's will. The theoretical nature of such an argument is revealed as soon as it is

[14] In *English Lyrics of the XIIIth Century* ed. Carleton Brown (Oxford, 1932) pp. 101–7.

placed in a human rather than an abstract context, as happens when the subject is dramatised. In many of the mystery cycles, Mary's earthly husband, Joseph, does not have such an easy time of it: he becomes dangerously close to being identified with any henpecked and cuckolded husband, in a way that stands the pro- and anti-feminist arguments on their heads.

Chaucer's placing of his debate on the nature of woman in a naturalistic rather than theoretical context has a similar effect. The clearest paradigms of good and evil are those furthest removed from the practical realities of everyday living. The villainously wicked stepmothers of the Man of Law's Tale are compared to 'the serpent depe in helle y-bounde' who betrayed Eve (II 361–8) and a 'feendlych spirit' (783); Custance is continually likened to the Virgin. All this belongs to the overtly fictional world of pious romance. Cecilia too lives on a spiritual plane found only in hagiography. The Wife of Bath, on the other hand, is firmly rooted in the everyday world, even though the 'experience' she talks of can be paralleled abundantly from anti-feminist literature, including Jankyn's own 'book of wikked wyves' (which starts with Eve). Her entire Prologue is devoted to the Woman Question; but it is impossible to define quite what answer to derive from it. She gives a thorough exposition of conventional anti-feminism – she is in herself an epitome of it – but she expounds it from the woman's angle, and no fewer than five husbands have fallen victim to her.

Her Prologue promises orthodoxy: she will 'speke of wo that is in mariage'. Within a few lines, however, it turns into a defence of marriage, specifically of as many marriages as possible. Solomon is the ideal in her eyes:

> Which yifte of God hadde he for alle his wyvys!   III 39

The Merchant is less convinced that wives are God's gift.[15] She goes on to defend marriage against virginity, with an abundance of scriptural citations and *exempla* and the unanswerable pragmatic argument,

> If ther were no seed ysowe,
> Virginitee, thanne wherof sholde it growe?   71–2

If the Christian saint Cecilia and the pagan martyr Virginia remain chaste, Chaucer's other most holy women find no incompatibility between marriage and perfection. Custance must 'leye a lite hir hoolynesse aside' (II 713) on her wedding night, but the line is not without irony; and Griselda's virtue is most rigorously tested through her

---

[15] See IV 1311 ff. and p. 216 above.

children. Chaucer will certainly not make any division between sin and perfection along the line between marriage and virginity. His refusal to do so is entirely orthodox in religious terms, but not altogether usual in practice: there is more than a little truth in the Wife of Bath's accusation that clerks have nothing good to say about wives. The Clerk's Griselda refutes her both on that point and on the stand she takes on the place of women, but his tale is disturbing partly because of the clash it contains between the archetypal handling of Griselda as a reflection of the Virgin and its treatment of secular marriage. Custance and Cecilia inhabit a world where divine intervention is the order of the day. The events of the Clerk's Tale are all the more unnerving for being within the bounds of possibility, as the fairy-tale world of the Man of Law's Tale or the divine order of the Second Nun's are not. Griselda's virtue must exist with no such supernatural endorsement, and she suffers the 'wo that is in mariage' far more acutely than the Wife or January. Chaucer's sympathy for women extends not only to giving the Clerk a tale in praise of a wife, but in giving the feminine point of view on marital suffering.

The woman question in the *Canterbury Tales* appears in several forms. The most functional is the marshalling of arguments and *exempla* on each side, as happens in the Introduction to the Man of Law's Tale, the Wife's Prologue, the early sections of the Merchant's Tale, and Dorigen's complaint, in which she lists numerous chaste or faithful wives and maidens. The question of whether women are good or bad generally resolves itself into three more specific questions. There is the issue of sex *versus* chastity, which I have discussed briefly above; there is the question of sovereignty; and there is the related question of 'wommenes conseils'.

The issue of sovereignty has generally been discussed in relation to the 'marriage group', and it is indeed centrally important there.[16] The Wife's insistence on female *maistrie*, the Clerk's demonstration of an obedience so extreme as to be *inportable*, the Merchant's ironic insistence on the theory of women's humility and the very different results of experience, and the Franklin's urging of mutual respect, are clearly all closely related. While all four tales look at the subject from very different angles, they do not differ so widely in their conclusions: the mutual obedience at the end of the Wife's tale, Walter's cruelty and January's wilful self-delusion all point towards the Franklin's conclusion. The theme of sovereignty however extends much more widely than these four tales. It is probably no accident, even though Chaucer chooses not to stress the fact, that the very first action we hear of in the world of the story-telling is that Theseus 'conquered al the regne

---

[16] I keep my discussion of the matter short since it has been so extensively debated: see n. 13 above. One of the best of the more recent discussions is in Kean pp. 139–64.

of Femenye'; and in the final tale too we hear from the Parson of the right relationship between husband and wife, a relationship based on love and respect as well as wifely obedience.[17] The Parson may not be quite as generous as the Franklin, but he does not fall far short.

The Knight's Tale sets up a model for the later debates on women as on so many other issues. Sex *versus* chastity is touched on briefly in the incident of Emily at Diana's temple. *Maistrie* is hinted at in Theseus' defeat of the Amazons and marriage to Hippolyta; and it overlaps into the question of women's counsel. Twice in the tale the women make appeals to Theseus: once the widows plead for help, the second time the court ladies beg for mercy for the lovers. Theseus responds to both appeals, but he does not merely give in. He acts with authority, keeping control of events himself. The Wife of Bath's Tale shows the other side of the coin, when King Arthur not only reprieves the rapist knight but hands him over to the ladies to do with as they please. Theseus keeps judgment in his own hands.

The issue of sovereignty, of marital relationships and of Biblical archetypes surfaces again in a number of tales. The archetype for the Miller's Alisoun is Noah's wife;[18] and if Bible commentaries remain comparatively silent on the matter, the human development of drama in the mystery cycles, and in Nicholas' version of the story, makes it abundantly clear that Noah is a henpecked husband. The Man of Law insists that wives are 'bounden under subjeccioun' of their husbands,[19] which after the preceding fabliaux is less platitudinous than it might appear. The Franklin's Tale insists that a husband's trust and a wife's freedom create love and faithfulness, but other tales do not bear this out. Inset within the 'marriage group' is the Squire's Tale, with the falcon's warning that an apparently good and equal relationship is no guarantee of faithfulness. The point is made again in one of the other bird stories of the *Tales*, the Manciple's, when Phoebus' attempts to treat his wife well are repaid with adultery; and the husband in the Shipman's Tale is also good to his wife. That trust, in the form of absence of jealousy, is no answer, is given heavily ironic emphasis in the Pardoner's claim to possess some holy water that will make a husband believe in his wife's faithfulness in the teeth of all evidence

---

[17] X 918–38.

[18]
    'Hastou nat herd,' quod Nicholas, 'also
    The sorwe of Noe with his felaweshipe,
    Er that he myghte gete his wyf to shipe?
    Hym hadde be levere, I dar wel undertake
    At thilke tyme, than alle his wetheres blake,
    That she hadde had a ship hirself allone'   I 3538–43

– the moral of which is that Alisoun too must have a ship to herself.
[19] II 270–3.

to the contrary. The Merchant's Tale shows that such a belief does not require a miracle.

The Merchant's Tale also treats the question of women's counsel with heavy irony, by demonstrating why it is that women are never stuck for an answer. The narrator urges,

> If thou wolt werken as the wyse,
> Do alwey so as wommen wol thee rede,   IV 1360–1

but Proserpina shows why men are 'as lewed as gees' when faced with a smooth-tongued woman. Proserpina curiously also counterbalances her own actions with an insistence that there are many virtuous women, and that Solomon's declaration that he never found a good woman in fact expresses the *sentence*

> that in sovereyn bontee
> Nis noon but God, but neither he ne she.   2289–90

Her other ruder remarks about Solomon (that he was a 'lecchour' and so on) derive point from their dramatic and argumentative contrast with the Wife of Bath's idealisation of him. It is surprising, however, to find Proserpina and Dame Prudence arguing on the same side. Melibee quotes Solomon to the effect that 'alle wommen been wikke', and Prudence rebuts the charge at her usual inordinate length. Even if Solomon found no good women, she says, other men have;

> Or elles, per aventure, the entente of Salomon was this, that, as in sovereyn bounte, he foond no womman;/ this is to seyn, that ther is no wight that hath sovereyn bountee save God allone.   VII 1078–9

Prudence is the literal embodiment of *wommennes conseils*, and in arguing for their value she has the justification of allegory on her side. Personify Prudence as a wife, and she is overruled at one's peril.

The Nun's Priest's Tale brilliantly parodies most of these issues. Chastity can have no place in the farmyard; Chauntecleer stands in for Solomon as the ideal man of many wives. The Wife of Bath advocates octogamy (III 33), Chauntecleer practises heptagamy. Even worse, he does not limit his sexual activities to the function of pro-creation: he acts

> More for delit than world to multiplye.   VII 3345

He follows his wife's advice in ignoring his dream, and lands in serious trouble – a fact which sends the narrator off into colossal moralistic generalisations:

Wommennes conseils been ful ofte colde;
Wommannes conseil broghte us first to wo,   3256–7

even though he denies it all a few lines later. It is Chauntecleer, too, who is given the decisive words on the greater Woman Question – words which I make no apology for quoting again.

In principio,
Mulier est hominis confusio, –
Madame, the sentence of this Latyn is,
'Womman is mannes joye and al his blis.'   3163–6

The girl with two lovers

It is generally the larger themes that lend themselves best to discussion over the whole range of the *Canterbury Tales*: themes such as Fortune, the suffering of the good, or the nature of women. Specific plot motifs are most often contrasted in adjacent tales. There are exceptions, however, and one of the most striking of these is the motif of the love-triangle, of the girl with two lovers.[20] It is the basis of the plot in the Knight's Tale and is parodied in detail in both the juxtaposed Miller's Tale and the more distant Merchant's;[21] and the Franklin's Tale in turn picks up closely from the Merchant's.

In terms of their placing in the *Canterbury Tales*, the four tales fall into two groups – Knight's and Miller's, and Merchant's and Franklin's. The division by genre works across this spatial arrangement. The Miller's Tale is a fabliau; and so too, for all its disguise as a romance, is the Merchant's. One would expect the handling of abstract issues to vary with the generic perspective of a particular tale: hagiography and fabliau will give very different estimates of such matters as Fortune and chastity. The more specific contrasting of narrative detail in these four tales shows how subtle such differentiation can become. The later pair of tales do not merely repeat the genres of the first pair, and their handling of plot motifs carries the distinctions beyond surface texture into the meaning borne by the stories. As a Breton lai, the Franklin's Tale emphasises human reaction and emotion more than narrative action and outward event; the rhetorical elaboration of an unsavoury story in the Merchant's Tale differentiates it at a moral as well as a stylistic level from the Miller's.

The essential similarity of plot in the four tales is immediately obvious. Palamon and Arcite are rivals for Emily's favours, Nicholas

---

[20] An earlier form of this discussion is found in the author's 'The girl with two lovers: four Canterbury tales', in Heyworth pp. 65–79.
[21] For the possibility that Chaucer may once have considered a closer relationship between the Knight's and Merchant's Tales, see pp. 67–8 above.

Only for a moment

and Absolon for Alisoun's, January and Damian for May's, Arveragus and Aurelius for Dorigen's. The variations in that basic pattern follow the generic implications of the stories. In the Knight's Tale the lovers' aim is marriage: the tale of courtship, with the idealised lady as the ultimate reward, is the most idealistic form of romance. That Palamon, who is prepared to worship Emily in the belief that she is a goddess, eventually gets her hand in preference to Arcite, who is never in any doubt that she is flesh and blood, emphasises how far the tale is from simply equating love and sex. In the Miller's Tale, the lovers' aim is adultery. Alisoun is married already; and although her elderly husband is clearly fond of her, he is so outclassed in the sexual stakes as to cease to be a contestant. He does not constitute a third rival, though the proliferation of men in the tale certainly contributes to its effect. January, the other elderly husband of the four stories, most definitely is a contestant, though sexually he is even more clearly outclassed. In the Franklin's Tale the characters are all young, and therefore, like Palamon and Arcite, act appropriately for their age in loving; but Arveragus and Aurelius parallel January and Damian socially and in plot function as husband and amorous squire. For both husband and wooer, however, there is more in their love for Dorigen than mere physical lust, whereas January and Damian never think of anything else. The Knight's Tale stands out from all the others in having an unmarried heroine – the lady who is all the more unattainable for never having been attained. This too helps to make Emily more of a symbol than a character, and contributes to the high idealism of the romance.

The imagery of the four tales shows similar interrelations and variations. The love-garden had been a traditional motif of courtly romance long before Guillaume de Lorris institutionalised it in the *Roman de la Rose*, and the two romances and the tale with romance pretensions all make use of it. The absence of the garden from the Miller's Tale is of a piece with its unequivocal nature as a fabliau. In the Knight's Tale, the garden provides the idealised courtly background against which the cousins glimpse the idealised courtly lady. The beauty of the setting, the season and the heroine are all intermingled, and all contrast with the dark tower where the lovers are imprisoned. They cannot get into the garden, and it becomes a part of Emily's unattainableness – a *hortus conclusus*. The love-garden in the Merchant's Tale is all too vulnerable, and the heroine all too accessible, in spite of January's care with walls and locks, and in spite of the Song of Songs imagery that associates it with spiritual love. It is compared explicitly with the mystic garden, and with the garden of the *Roman de la Rose*; but nothing spiritual, or even courtly, goes on here. It is a secularised Eden, with Damian as the serpent, and the traditional apple tree replaced by a pear-tree, with all its sexual

connotations (Alisoun too is like a 'pere-jonette tree'). The garden in
the Franklin's Tale is also described hyperbolically, even as 'the verray
paradys'; but in this tale, the Fall never happens. The analogues to
the tale in Boccaccio have the heroine set the squire the task of
making the garden bloom in midwinter; Chaucer's garden remains
subject to the processes of the natural cycle. It is not a spurious image
of a seasonless Eden, but remains within the providential ordering of
the world. The adulterous tryst in this garden is forestalled by the
operation of human virtue.

The season is as important as the setting in the same three tales.
Love and Maytime are inseparable, in Chaucer as in Malory or endless
mediaeval lyrics. The main events of the Knight's Tale – the vision of
Emily, the meeting in the woods, and the tournament – all take place
in May, as does Aurelius' declaration of love in the Franklin's Tale.
The pear-tree episode in the Merchant's Tale happens when the sun
is about to enter Cancer, in late May or early June, perhaps with the
implication of more heat and less freshness. In the Miller's Tale, as
befits a fabliau, the season is of supreme unimportance: all the events
of any significance take place indoors, and it is the mundane days of
the week rather than the connotation-laden months that are stressed.

The season is all but inseparable from the heroine in the Knight's,
Miller's and Merchant's Tales. There is no formal description of
Dorigen, except for a passing reference to her beauty, and by way of
variation it is Aurelius who is compared to May. In the Knight's Tale
Emily and the month of May come to be almost interchangeable, and
their close association is impressed sufficiently firmly to reflect on the
heroine of the Merchant's Tale. For Emily the connotations are of deep
symbolic import; for May, the constant repetition of '*fresshe* May'
becomes increasingly sarcastic as the tale progresses. The courtly
associations of love with the month, as with the garden, are disas-
trously undermined. Alisoun too is described through an abundance
of spring imagery, even though the season is never explicitly mentioned; but the choice of imagery – kid, calf, swallow, 'newe pere-
jonette tree' – is ludicrously different from the seasonal associations
given to Emily. Emily's lily associates her with purity; Alisoun is all
animal sex.

The ways in which the plots are worked out continue the generic
differentiation of the tales. The gods intervene to bring about the final
resolution in both the Knight's and Merchant's Tales. The Knight's
planetary deities have a metaphysical function in the world and are
a serious force to be reckoned with; the questions raised in the Tale
about the ordering of the universe are focused through them. The
Merchant's gods are doubly debased, as gods of the underworld and as
bickering fairies, and they play an active part in the sexual deception
of the tale. Rhetorically they belong with the elevated style of rom-

ance, but here Chaucer turns even deities into fabliau characters. In the Miller's Tale there are no gods at all. Nicholas claims to know all about divine plans through his astrological learning, but the supernatural plane in the tale is pure invention, and the plot is in fact worked out at the level of the commonplace and everyday. The marvellous here never actually materialises. In the Franklin's Tale, the gods are invited to help, but they do not: Aurelius prays to Apollo for aid, but there is no way out through divine intervention. Even the magic removal of the rocks is kept strictly subordinate in terms of the plot to human virtue. They may 'seem' to have disappeared, but that turns out to be irrelevant. The supernatural here acts only as a catalyst to, and a measure of, individual *gentillesse*.

The selection of a motif such as the girl with two lovers might appear too arbitrary, and the motif itself too widespread, to be of much critical use. It could be argued that it appears in other places even within the *Canterbury Tales*: in the wife's adulterous affair in the Shipman's Tale, for instance, or in Custance's two husbands, or even, perhaps, in Cecilia's earthly and heavenly spouses. The distance of such tales from the four I have discussed in detail is itself perhaps sufficient to indicate how very precisely Chaucer works out the motif there. A collection of their sources – the *Teseida*, the *Filocolo* or *Decameron*, the analogous fabliaux of the Miller's and Merchant's Tales – would also show few or none of these correlations. The relationships among the four tales show particularly clearly Chaucer's concern to create a tightly-knit, centripetal structure for his story-collection, with none of the jumble or the monotony associated with other varieties of the form. The unconventional diversity of the tales he tells itself becomes a principle for coherence, as the same plot, with similar embellishments of motif and imagery, can go through a series of shape-shiftings that put the hag of the Wife of Bath's Tale in the shade. The diversity implies relativity; and what one sees in the plot of the girl with two lovers changes with the generic viewpoint. But the shifts do not take place in a moral vacuum. The effect of 'now you see it – now you don't' may apply within the tales to January's experiences under the pear-tree or to the disappearing rocks, but the four tales do not add up to illusion alone. The Knight's Tale, as so often, opens up the questions; the Franklin's Tale, as so often, gives a kind of answer. Beyond illusion there is *trouthe*, which is also the principle of a stable Providence and of marital fidelity.

Brotherhood and friendship

Friendship between men has never attracted the same intense literary or moral interest as relations between the sexes, but it was a subject of debate in the Middle Ages, and it provides another recurrent theme of the *Canterbury Tales*. Like heterosexual relationships, it can take both good and bad forms, though Chaucer does not define these in terms of their distance from homosexuality. The one homosexual relationship of the work is hinted at in the General Prologue, in the friendship of the Summoner and the Pardoner; and that is not developed further. Within the *Tales*, male fellowship is defined as good by its affiliation to God, evil by its affiliation to the Devil; though, as with sexual love, there is also a large area of secular reference where the stark polarities of religious testing do not apply.

The discussion of friendship goes beyond the question of mere liking. The words Chaucer uses most often are 'felaw' or 'brother', implying a formal recognition of the relationship – the swearing of brotherhood, or the kind of social and professional companionship suggested by the modern usage of 'fellowship' for a society or college. 'Felawe' can also have the more suspicious idiomatic sense of a drinking-companion, and the double meaning opens up some telling ironies in the ease with which some of the characters speak of fellowship.

The range of possible implications of fellowship and brotherhood is sketched in the General Prologue. On the good side are the literal brothers, Parson and Ploughman, with their common ideal of service to God and their fellow-men. The epithet 'good felawe' is however always ironic: it is used of the piratical Shipman, and the drunken and corruptible Summoner. The Pardoner, another highly suspicious character, is his 'freend and his compeer'. The whole company of pilgrims also constitute a 'felaweshipe', with none of the moral overtones, for good or ill, attached to the term elsewhere.

Friendship is a major issue in the first tale, the Knight's. Palamon and Arcite owe each other a double duty, as blood-relations and as sworn brothers. They will only appeal to their sworn brotherhood, however, when it suits their own purposes. Palamon accuses Arcite of treachery when he too falls in love with Emily, and Arcite responds with brutal directness:

> At the kynges court, my brother,
> Ech man for hymself, ther is noon oother.　　　　I 1181–2

The inadequacy of such an attitude is shown up by the immediate introduction of Perotheus and Chaucer's summary of his friendship with Theseus:

> So wel they lovede, as old bookes sayn,
> That when that oon was deed, soothly to telle,
> His felawe wente and soughte hym doun in helle. 1198–200

This is an unusual version of the legend (derived from the *Roman de la Rose*), but it pointedly contrasts an ideal friendship with the less than perfect brotherhood of the lovers. The skill with which he avoids specifying which of the two, Theseus or Perotheus, sought the other, has the effect of affirming the mutual strength of their love for each other.

Friendship may be stronger than death; it is not stronger than love.

> Ful sooth is seyd that love ne lordshipe
> Wol noght, his thankes, have no felaweshipe.   1625–6

It is not until Arcite is dying that he is willing to release Emily to Palamon. Before that they are quite prepared to fight to the death over her – even if they arm each other 'as freendly as he were his owene brother', which they indeed are; and Palamon even urges Theseus to put him to death just so long as he will execute his 'felawe' as well. The example of Theseus and Perotheus could hardly be further removed from this. Their friendship is however restored at the end, when Arcite acknowledges the 'strif and rancour' he has had with Palamon, now referred to as his 'cosyn deere', and commends him to Emily with a generous acknowledgement of his virtues.

The lovers each 'leyd his feith to borwe' that they would meet for their mortal combat in the wood. The pledging of one's word is repeated many time in the *Tales* as an aspect of sworn brotherhood or fellowship. It is especially clear in the Friar's Tale, where the summoner and the devil swear 'to be sworne bretheren til they deye' (III 1405), and whose fellowship indeed lasts beyond death; and in the Pardoner's Tale, where the three rioters, already 'felawes' in vice, swear

> To lyve and dyen ech of hem for oother,
> As though he were his owene ybore brother.   VI 703–4

These three, however, are prepared to betray their oath for self-interest in a manner far more horrifying than Palamon and Arcite. The youngest is despatched to the town to fetch bread and wine, for refreshment while they wait for nightfall but with the implication of an unholy sacrament. Meantime the others, in the name of their sworn brotherhood, agree to kill their *felawe* and part the money between the two of them. The youngest in his turn decides to murder his *felawes*. Their pledge to keep fellowship until they find Death is ironically fulfilled.

Other tales touch on the theme of friendship or pledged brotherhood more lightly. Nicholas plans to set up a *felaweship* like Noah's, but the story is a cover for his own nefarious purposes. John and Aleyn are friends, but not in a way that becomes thematically significant – unless the Reeve's Tale is seen as a delightfully easy way round the dilemma of two friends loving a single lady, by doubling the number of women available. Perkin of the Cook's Tale moves in with a 'compeer', a fellow in crime, after his master has shown him out, but the theme remains undeveloped. The Man of Law's Prologue notes that poverty too can disrupt friendship and brotherhood, so associating them, as in the Knight's Tale, with the mutable order of earthly Fortune. After the Friar's Tale, the Summoner picks up the notion of brotherhood and applies it to the practice of lay fraternities; but although the friar and Thomas are brothers in a religious fellowship, the ecclesiastical context is no guarantee against self-seeking. The 'cosynage' of the Shipman's Tale continues the theme; and the Canon's Yeoman's Tale too stresses how professed friendship can be used as a cover for extracting money.

There are two stories, one secular and one religious, that present the opposite image of fellowship, as a matter not of self-seeking but of generosity. One is the Franklin's Tale; the other, the Second Nun's. Neither makes friendship the crucial concept in its *sentence*, but in both the good relationship contributes to the strong statement of positive virtue they contain.

The Second Nun's Tale contains images of both blood-brotherhood and male fellowship, but the ultimate form of friendship is religious. The Christians become associates as 'Cristes owene knyghtes': the ideal of human fellowship here is a kind of heavenly Round Table. Tiburce is Valerian's brother, and therefore also Cecilia's; the earthly relationship of fellow-Christians is embodied in the relationship of brother and sister, just as the Christian Parson and Ploughman are brothers. A third Christian convert, Maximus, is introduced, to make a trinity of martyrs contrasting with the unholy trinity of the Pardoner's rioters, and Cecilia buries his body beside those of her husband and brother-in-law. She herself is finally buried with Urban's 'othere seintes', in a reminder of the company of the Church triumphant that completes the fellowship of 'Cristen folk' on earth.

Given the precision of many of the links between the two tales of the fragment, where the Second Nun's Tale gives the celestial version of what the Canon's Yeoman echoes in infernal terms, the account of Christian brotherhood may perhaps explain one of the more puzzling sections of the Yeoman's tale. As the story draws to its close, the apocalyptic final chords are clearly heard; but in the middle of them all is an obscure alchemical passage that seems to bear little relation to the urgent didacticism of its immediate context. Arnoldus de Villa Nova and 'Hermes Trismegistus' are quoted:

> 'Ther may no man mercurie mortifie
> But it be with his brother knowlechyng' . . .
> He seith how that the dragon, doutelees,

Ne dyeth nat, but if that he be slayn
With his brother; and that is for to sayn,
By the dragon, Mercurie, and noon other
He understood, and brymstoon by his brother. VIII 1431–2, 1435–9

The chemical process being described is apparently the reaction of
mercury with sulphur ('brymstoon'). Skeat comments testily on the
first couplet, 'The dictum is, I suppose, as worthless as it is obscure',[22]
and so it is if it is confined to its alchemical meaning. If it is taken as
an infernal counterpart to the Second Nun's image of brotherhood, it
makes much more sense, and its emphatic placing becomes logical.
The Christian brothers accepted fleshly mortification and death to
achieve everlasting life. The dragon and brimstone both have hellish
associations. They are associated as 'brothers' in the alchemical jargon
for sulphur and mercury, and their chemical operation on each other
is an image of spiritual death. The quotation continues,

> 'And therefore,' seyde he, – taak heede to my sawe –
> 'Lat no man bisye hym this art for to seche,
> But if that he th'entencioun and speche
> Of philosophres understonde kan.'   1441–4

Taken at face value, this is bathetic nonsense: after all the Canon's
Yeoman's warning of imminent damnation, he is not weakly going to
urge learning the jargon before one starts on the downward path. It
is rather a plea that those who have ears to hear should 'taak heede
to my sawe' and interpret it at a deeper level than the literal, understanding the *entencioun* behind the *speche*: and that is a warning of
death and hell.

The Franklin's Tale uses the concept of brotherhood neither in a
celestial nor in an infernal sense, but to help to define its concept of
secular *gentillesse*. The story generally subordinates the idea of fellowship to ideas of love, but it is fellowship and brotherhood that have
the last word. When all other sources of help fail him, it is Aurelius'
brother who comes to his rescue: blood-brotherhood here brings with
it natural affection and concern. He determines to find an old 'felawe'
of his, and the term at first carries only the most functional meaning;
but the brother connects the term with friends as well as associates,
and weeps for those *felawes* of his who have died. The clerk of Orleans
is at first described as a 'maister'; and the pledge he makes with
Aurelius is a financial bargain, of money in return for services ren-

---

[22] *The Complete Works of Geoffrey Chaucer* ed. W. W. Skeat Vol. V (Oxford, 1900), note
to G 1432. His explication of this passage, or that of A. V. C. Schmidt (in his edition of
*The General Prologue to the Canterbury Tales and the Canon's Yeoman's Prologue and
Tale* (London, 1974)), is essential to supplement Robinson's notes at this point.

dered. When Aurelius comes to him to ask for time in which to pay, he addresses the magician as 'maister'; but the clerk substitutes a new relationship:

> 'Leeve brother,
> Everich of yow dide gentilly til oother.
> Thou art a squier, and he is knyght;
> But God forbede, for his blisful myght,
> But if a clerk koude doon a gentil dede
> As wel as any of yow, it is no drede!'   V 1607–12

He posits a new definition of brotherhood based on equality of moral worth, overriding difference of social rank; and it is with that image that the tale ends.

Chaucer's treatment of friendship follows a pattern similar to his treatment of love. Just as women and heterosexual relationships can be seen as following the model of Eve (leading to the Fall), or the Virgin (leading to chastity and salvation), so male fellowship can lead to Death beneath the tree or to heaven 'with aungels ful of cleernesse and of light'. But these are not the only alternatives. The Knight's Tale portrays sworn brotherhood disrupted and then healed by a dying act of generosity; the Franklin's Tale makes a claim for the equality endowed by virtue. Both present a secular ideal of fellowship, just as they both present marriage as the source of deep human happiness.

Tidings, tales and voices

In the *House of Fame*, Chaucer ended in the wickerwork house of rumour, full of 'tidynges' told by shipmen, pilgrims, pardoners and travellers of every kind. He sees 'a man of gret auctorite', who appears to be about to still the racket of multiple voices with an authoritative speech of his own. Instead, the poem breaks off. The *Canterbury Tales* are also full of such multiple voices, not only of the various pilgrims telling their tales, but within the stories too.

In the least complex tales these background voices serve the least complex rôle, as chorus to the action. The bystanders mock John the carpenter; they weep at the moments of most intense pathos in the Man of Law's Tale. In the Squire's Tale, the 'prees that swarmeth to and fro' come to wonder aloud at the magic gifts. These voices can represent good and bad counsel, as the advisers in *Melibee* do; Justinus and Placebo are single representatives of the same thing. Generally, however, the more voices the worse:

The trouthe of thynges and the profit been rather founden in fewe folk that been wise and ful of resoun, than by greet multitude of folk ther

every man crieth and clatereth what that hym liketh. Soothly swich
multitude is nat honest.　　　　　　　　　　　　　　　　　　VII 1069

Like all Dame Prudence's generalisations, this may be true or it may
not. In the Physician's Tale, it is 'the peple' who intervene to reveal
Apius' lust and save Virginius: truth is finally rescued from Apius'
distortion of it by the multitude.

In the more complex stories these choric voices are used to express
emotions or ideas oblique to the main thrust of the tale, or so over-
simplified as to force the reader to reassess the real meaning of the
story. This is what seems to be happening in the women's laments
over Arcite's death in the Knight's Tale:

> 'Why woldestow be deed,' thise wommen crye,
> 'And haddest gold ynough, and Emelye?'　　　　　　I 2835–6

In the Clerk's Tale Walter persists in deliberately misrepresenting
the people's voices to provide an excuse to Griselda for his cruelty;
their true feelings are only brought into line with the events of the
story at the end, when she embraces her children and the onlookers
weep for pity. This is the moment of the supposedly happy ending:
that their reaction is tears is an indication of the inadequacy of the
comic structure to express the meaning of the tale. The Nun's Priest's
Tale picks up this idea of multiple voices and amplifies them into an
anarchic clamour. The hens shriek, the widow and her daughters run
out,

> And cryden, 'Out! harrow! and weylaway!
> Ha! ha! the fox!' and after hym they ran,
> And eek with staves many another man.
> Ran Colle oure dogge, and Talbot and Gerland,
> And Malkyn, with a dystaf in hir hand;
> Ran cow and calf, and eek the verray hogges,
> So fered for the berkyng of the dogges
> And shoutyng of the men and wommen eeke,
> They ronne so hem thoughte hir herte breeke.
> They yolleden as feendes doon in helle;
> The dokes cryden as men wolde hem quelle;
> The gees for feere flowen over the trees;
> Out of the hyve cam the swarm of bees.
> So hydous was the noyse, a, *benedicitee*!
> Certes, he Jakke Straw and his meynee
> Ne made nevere shoutes half so shrille
> Whan that they wolden any Flemyng kille,
> As thilke day was maad upon the fox.
> Of bras they broghten bemes, and of box,
> Of horn, of boon, in which they blewe and powped,

And therwithal they skriked and they howped.
It semed as that hevene sholde falle.   VII 3380–401

Human and animal voices are alike overwhelmed in the din. There is
no meaning to be perceived in such noise, 'the trouthe of thynges and
the profit' are drowned out, and so it can serve as an image of civil
and cosmic disorder. The Nun's Priest's voice breaks in with a quiet
authority reminiscent of the man at the end of the *House of Fame*:

> Now, goode men, I prey yow herkneth alle:
> Lo, how Fortune turneth sodeynly
> The hope and pryde eek of hir enemy!   3402–4

There is at last something for the audience to 'herken' to apart from
sheer din. The. *moralitates* of the tale are mostly concentrated in the
concluding lines that follow. They may not be any final answer, but
they do at least indicate that meaning is not to be found in multiplicity
of voices alone.

The *House of Fame* and the Nun's Priest's Tale reduce the clamour
to a single voice at the end. Occasionally in the *Canterbury Tales*
Chaucer glances at the opposite process, of one person's voice being
amplified into rumour or tidings. This is the theme of one of his
stories-within-stories, when the Wife of Bath breaks off her tale to tell
the story of Midas' wife whispering the secret of her husband's ass's
ears to the water (III 951–82). The tale is told as an *exemplum* of
women's inability to keep secrets, so the theme has implications beyond the confines of the tale. The Manciple's Tale picks up the idea
again, when the dame warns her son against being the 'auctour newe/
Of tidynges'. Tale-telling and gossip are dangerously close, when one
man's words can be echoed by the multitude.

The multiple voices of the *Canterbury Tales* are primarily those of
the various pilgrims. The voices within the tales are secondary to
those. Chaucer will often use choric voices within the tales to reinforce
meaning; in the case of the pilgrims, he adopts each voice in turn. It
is interesting, in this context, that two tales concern themselves explicitly with the dangers of imitating other people's voices. In the
Nun's Priest's Tale this remains an incidental theme, but it comes to
the fore in the Manciple's. Daun Russell flatters the cock into shutting
his eyes to crow by describing his father's angelic voice; and, he urges,

> Save yow, I herde nevere man so synge
> As dide youre fader in the morwenynge . . .
> Lat se, konne ye youre fader countrefete?   VII 3301–2, 3321

The immediate cause of Chauntecleer's downfall is his attempt to rival
or surpass his father's voice. The Middle English *countrefete* meant

not only 'imitate' or 'forge' but also 'fashion', artistically or poetically.[23]
Nemesis catches up with the cock, not only when he assumes another
voice, but when he takes part in a singing-contest. This is doubly
appropriate, to a tale in which the narrator attempts to equal high
rhetoric by quoting the textbook,[24] and to a work which is built on the
poet's imitation of others' rival excellence of speech.

The crow in the Manciple's Tale is the best of all singing-birds,
singing a hundred thousandfold more 'myrily and weel' than a nightingale. It is taught by Phoebus, god of poetry, to speak; and

> countrefete the speche of every man
> He koude, whan he sholde telle a tale.   IX 134–5

One could scarcely find a better way of summing up Chaucer's own
method in the *Tales*. The crow makes the mistake of imitating the
cuckoo – he sings 'Cokkow! cokkow! cokkow!' – but the moral drawn
from the story is that tale-telling of every kind is a dangerous activity.
The finest singer ends up hoarse, slung out of doors by the god of
poetry.

If the Manciple's Tale shows the dangers of 'counterfeiting', artistically fashioning other people's voices, the Parson's Tale takes the
theme to its conclusion. Here there are no voices beside the Parson's.
The only direct speech in it consists of quotations from Christ's words,
or St. Paul's or St. Augustine's, and they serve simply to reinforce his
own message and his own tone. Multiplicity of voices is here reduced
to a single authoritative statement; by the time the Tale concludes
 and the Retractions begin, even the distinction between the Parson's
voice and Chaucer's has been lost. There is no more counterfeiting in
any of the senses of the word: no imitation, no fashioning. There is
only a single narrow and unadorned morality.

It is of the essence of the Parson's Tale that it will not admit to
being only one more perspective to set beside the others, one more
 voice to add to the rest. Chaucer, none the less, put it into the *Canterbury Tales*. Its claim to absolute authority is undermined by its
context. It may be the last of the voices we hear, but it is still only
one of many; its claim to unique privilege is denied by the rest of the
work. Its rejection of fiction and art may make a continuation of the

---

[23] See *Middle English Dictionary, countrefet* (n.)1(a) 'a likeness, a representation, an
image'; *countrefeten* (v.)2(b) 'to represent (sth.) by sculpture or painting'; 2(c) 'to pattern
(sth.) after something else'; (d) '? to devise, invent, make'. The Latin term *contrafactum*
was used to describe a set of words (usually religious) substituted for the original
(usually secular) text to fit a given tune. See also *OED counterfeit* A (ppl.) 2 'fashioned,
wrought'; 4 'represented by a picture or image'; B (adj.) 5 'represented in a picture or
image (or *transf.* in writing or literary art)'; verb, 9b, 'To represent, portray, or reproduce
in writing or by literary art'.
[24] VII 3347 ff.

work impossible, but its refusal to counterfeit does not finally bring one much nearer to truth.

7

A Multiple Conclusion

Al that is writen is writen for oure doctrine.

Chaucer uses this maxim twice, once in the Nun's Priest's Tale, once in the Retractions. St. Paul meant it to apply to the Scriptures; but it was commonly given a wider application in the Middle Ages, as justifying the study of pagan authors in order to extract the moral kernel, by allegorisation if necessary. This is the sense in which the author of the *Ovide moralisé* uses the words. Whether it is applied in a scriptural or a wider literary context, the meaning of the dictum would seem to be clear; but Chaucer manages to make both its occurrences in the *Canterbury Tales* remarkably equivocal. The problem at the end of the Nun's Priest's Tale is that it is impossible to discover quite what *doctrine* one is supposed to be extracting. The problem in the Retractions is that as soon as Chaucer has insisted that his intention in all his works is instructional, in the very next sentence he revokes the greater part of them as being sinful.

The appeal to *doctrine* in itself suggests that there is some inner truth to be found – the fruit within the chaff of the story. The insistent relativity of the structuring of the *Canterbury Tales*, however, serves to undermine the notion of literature as a vehicle for some fixed and accessible truth. The whole concept takes a considerable battering in the course of the work; but it would be too simple to say that this happens because Chaucer does not believe in it. He is not attacking the notion of truth as such, any more than he, or the Gawain-poet, or, in later years, Spenser, is attacking idealism when they show the attainment of absolute virtue to be an impossibility in a fallen world. Within the world, the most one can achieve is a series of partial and contingent truths, expressed in fallible language – human truths, not divine. Divine truth, as the Prioress points out, lies beyond the reach of human language.[1] Chaucer's refusal to adopt any authoritative

---

[1] VII 481–7.

level of discourse in the *Tales* means that he can keep open as many questions as possible. The storytelling competition remains unadjudicated within the work; and the criteria for judgment are subjected to a radical review in the course of the *Tales* in a way that makes a judgment by the reader equally impossible. 'Best sentence and most solaas' is a formula as incapable of covering the virtuoso performance of *Sir Thopas* or the subversive Pardoner's Tale as the resolutely anti-artistic Parson's Tale. The *Canterbury Tales* is one of the clearest examples of the kind of discourse recently described as the interrogative text.[2] It does not set out to impart knowledge or adopt stances, but remains open to different human or generic perspectives with their different ideologies expressed through different levels of language and imagery. The removal of a fixed basis for judgment makes the singling out of any tale impossible. Any attempt to select one tale as the best would also imply that it should be taken as the norm; and the *Canterbury Tales* insists that in human experience, and in poetry and language, nothing can be regarded as normative.

The work is not, however, amoral. By tradition, the story-collection is particularly closely associated with the notion of *doctrine*. Its commonest forms, as anthologies for preachers, aesopic fables, legendaries and so on, all lay overt emphasis on the didactic function of the tales, and often accompany each story with its own moralisation. Where Chaucer provides his tales with such apparently clear-cut meanings, they are always countered by contradictory elements within the tale, or by a contradictory moral in an adjacent tale. The presence of the Monk's Tale shows how far he is from accepting any simple moral pattern. He is none the less finely aware of moral distinctions, so that, for instance, we recognise the villains in the General Prologue despite his use of superlatives. He emphasises the *doctrine* of the work; but the *Canterbury Tales* calls for a re-evaluation of the nature of literary meaning at a deeper level than the conventional formulation suggests. If it is indeed written for our doctrine, we must try to come to terms with what that might be.

Earlier attempts that have been made to give answers – about spiritual pilgrimage, or the sinfulness of the world, or even human comedy – have tended to operate too far from the text to be acceptable. They work by way of distant generalisation, or by the substitution of a fixed and authoritative perspective for Chaucer's multiplicity. If there is any answer, it must be one that takes into account the tales as well as the framework, Chaucer as well as the pilgrims, the poetry as well as the themes. No straightforward formula will be able to encompass all of these.

There is indeed no shortage of morals within the work. Different

---

[2] Catherine Belsey, *Critical Practice* (London, 1980) pp. 90–1.

genres conventionally use different ways to express meaning, and Chaucer uses all such ways in the separate tales. Morality can be found all the way through a work, as in the discursively didactic tracts of *Melibee* and the Parson's Tale, or, in different and more surprising ways, the Wife of Bath's Prologue and the Cook's Tale. There can be a separable *moralitas* appended to the end of a tale: this happens in more or less conventional fashion with the individual tragedies of the Monk, which repeat the same moral formula with minimal verbal variation, and also in the Physician's and Canon's Yeoman's tales. The Manciple expands the final moral disproportionately and turns it into a sub-narrative of advice from his mother. The Reeve ends with the shortest moral possible. The Nun's Priest's Tale ends, as a beast-fable conventionally should, with a *moralitas*, or rather two, and implies a good many more. The Clerk's Tale offers a *moralitas* of the kind associated with works such as the *Gesta Romanorum* or Holcot's *Moralitates*, where the whole tale is read allegorically or at least parabolically; but it also goes strongly against the convention in withdrawing the moral as soon as it is given, not only in the Envoy to the Wife of Bath, but in the warning that wives should not model themselves on Griselda, and in the implication that divine testing may be as irrational as Walter's.

The meaning of a tale need not be spelled out: as with saints' lives, the moral import may be carried by the exemplary nature of the narrative. This happens in those tales that approximate most closely to hagiography, the Man of Law's, Prioress's and Second Nun's. The Man of Law and the Second Nun add something resembling an overt *moralitas* as a prologue, and the Prioress and the Nun also add an invocation to the Virgin at the beginning. If saints are exemplars of piety and virtue, Chaucer also gives exemplary tales of wickedness, in the Friar's, Pardoner's and Canon's Yeoman's tales.

Meaning in the romance is less easily defined. *Sens* there is incarnated in the narrative, it is not a premise or an appended moral. The three major romances of the *Canterbury Tales*, the Knight's, Wife of Bath's and Franklin's, all project their meanings in this way, though they all use other means as well. The Knight's contains a good deal of discursive philosophical comment on the progress of the action; and Theseus' final speech could be seen as a kind of concluding *moralitas*, except for the fact that it is not a moral exposition of the preceding story, nor a generalisation drawn from it, so much as a way of getting round it. The Wife of Bath's Tale also concludes with some overtly feminist sentiments, but these are counterbalanced by the long speech earlier on the nature of true *gentillesse*. In the Franklin's Tale, as befits a Breton lai, action and meaning are particularly closely interrelated, but two unequivocal morals do emerge: at the beginning, the insistence on the need for liberty in love; and at the end, the demonstration of human virtue.

There are, too, a number of tales where further meaning is quite simply absent. The Miller's Tale portrays a world of frenzied activity and comic situation where deeper meanings are irrelevant. The Summoner's Tale has the potential for being exemplary in the way the Friar's is, but its sermon against anger is undermined by irony, and the final fate of the friars is more farcical than didactic. The Shipman's Tale is more subversively amoral than the other fabliaux. The Squire's Tale makes free with moral apophthegms, but they notably fail to add up to anything; and the utter lack of moral import or significance in *Sir Thopas* is part of its undoing.

There remains the Merchant's Tale, which does not fall easily into any of these categories, not because its handling of morals is the answer to all larger Chaucerian problems of meaning, but because it so persistently subverts the categories it sets up. The opening discourse on marriage would align it with the tales of pervasive didacticism if it were not for the blatant irony. It is in a sense exemplary, but the narrative structure is too highly particularised for it to act as a paradigm. It could be said to have a *sens*, in keeping with its romance pretensions, but the meaning that emerges is so anti-courtly as to parody the whole notion. Also, even more strikingly than with most of the tales, its meaning is not complete in isolation. It needs its multiple context – of love and May, cosmic and supernatural controls on human action, Eve *versus* the Virgin, the Wife of Bath *versus* Griselda, physical and spiritual blindness, authority and experience, the true nature of secular virtue, even its setting in the storytelling contest – if its full import is to emerge.

As with the Merchant's Tale, so with the rest. The formal concluding *moralitates* always seem inadequate, not only by contrast with the richness of the story that leads up to them, but because the context for the story points to so many other possibilities extending far beyond the narrowing focus of the pat little final maxims. The juxtaposition of the exemplary tales with others that give a more complex view of characterisation and action alters our perspective on them: they may offer one way of reading the world, but it is not the only one. The rigid moral generalisations of the Parson or Dame Prudence are shaken loose by their contrast with individual people and situations that refuse to fit the orthodox stereotype. The tales that lack meaning in themselves have that lack highlighted by their proximity to others that are brim full with significance – the Miller's beside the Knight's, the Squire's beside the Franklin's, *Sir Thopas* beside *Melibee* and not too far from the Nun's Priest's. The romances are some of the most satisfying tales in themselves, but they too are still completed by their context: there is a sense in which the Knight's Tale requires the

Miller's, or the Merchant's, or even the Second Nun's, just as the Wife of Bath's requires the Friar's and the Franklin's.

The Nun's Priest's Tale brings all the others together most completely. It is brilliant in itself, and needs nothing beyond; but its levels of richness increase manyfold the more one looks at the other tales. Just as it gives a structural model of a Chinese box of a story-collection, so it brings together most of the themes and styles found sequentially in the rest of the work. The only unequivocal message of the Nun's Priest's Tale is the one at the very centre, with the dream guide who utters a single, stylistically neutral, sentence of warning and adds, 'My tale is at an ende' (VII 3082). Morality, language and meaning become increasingly complex and indefinable as one moves outwards, through Chauntecleer and the Nun's Priest to Chaucer himself. The simplifying perspectives of prophetic dream, *exemplum* and beast-fable become increasingly inadequate as one draws closer to the multifariousness of the 'real' world of the pilgrimage and to the poet who can present so many different ways of reading human experience and hold them all in balance.

' "Al that is writen is writen for oure doctrine", and that is myn entente.' Some of what is written may still 'sownen into synne', and therefore, from the fixed univocal perspective of the Parson's Tale and the Retractions, be worthy of revocation. But we should perhaps put a different emphasis on the words.

Al that writen is,
To oure doctrine it is ywrite, ywis.   VII 3441–2

The appended *moralitas* of the *Canterbury Tales*, the Retractions, is, like so many of the concluding morals within the work, inadequate because it does not take enough into account. The *Canterbury Tales* demands to be looked at whole; anything less will yield only partial and restricted results. Its meaning finally cannot be separated from 'al that writen is'.

She comes right to the edge of seeing the Parson's Tale as independent treatise, without quite making it.

Bibliography

Abraham, David H. 'Cosyn and Cosynage: pun and structure in the Shipman's Tale.' Chaucer Review XI (1976–7) 319–27.

Alfonsi, Petrus. Die Disciplina Clericalis des Petrus Alfonsi ed. Alfons Hilka and Werner Söderhjelm. Sammlung mittellateinischer Texte 1. Heidelberg, 1911.

Alfonsi, Petrus. The 'Disciplina Clericalis' of Petrus Alfonsi trans. and ed. Eberhard Hermes, trans. into English by P. R. Quarrie. London, 1977.

Allen, Judson Boyce, and Theresa Anne Moritz. A Distinction of Stories: The Medieval Unity of Chaucer's Fair Chain of Narratives for Canterbury. Columbus, Ohio, 1981.

An Alphabet of Tales ed. Mary Macleod Banks. EETS O.S. 126–7, 1904–5.

The Auchinleck Manuscript. Facsimile intro. Derek Pearsall and I. C. Cunningham. Ilkley and London, 1979.

Baldwin, Ralph. The Unity of the Canterbury Tales. Anglistica 5. Copenhagen, 1955.

Bastin, Julia, ed. Recueil Général des Isopets Vol. I. Société des Anciens Textes Français. Paris, 1929.

Baugh, A. C. 'The original teller of the Merchant's Tale.' Modern Philology XXXV (1937) 15–26.

Beidler, Peter G. 'The pairing of the Franklin's Tale and the Physician's Tale.' Chaucer Review III (1968–9) 275–9.

Belsey, Catherine. Critical Practice. London, 1980.

Bennett, J. A. W. Chaucer at Oxford and at Cambridge. Oxford, 1974.

Bennett, J. A. W. Chaucer's Book of Fame. Oxford, 1968.

Bennett, J. A. W. 'Chaucer's contemporary.' In Piers Plowman: Critical Approaches ed. S. S. Hussey. London, 1969. Pp. 310–24.

Benson, Larry. 'The order of the Canterbury Tales.' Studies in the Age of Chaucer III (1981) 77–120.

Berger, Harry. 'The F-Fragment of the Canterbury Tales.' Chaucer Review I (1966–7) 88–102, 135–56.

Bishop, Ian. 'The narrative art of The Pardoner's Tale.' Medium Ævum XXXVI (1967) 15–24.

Blake, N. F. 'On editing the Canterbury Tales.' In Heyworth pp. 101–20.

Bloomfield, Morton W. Essays and Explorations. Cambridge, Mass., 1970.

Bloomfield, Morton W. 'The Miller's Tale – an unBoethian interpretation.' In Mandel and Rosenberg pp. 205–11.

Bloomfield, Morton W. 'The wisdom of the Nun's Priest's Tale.' In Vasta and Thundy pp. 70–8.

Boccaccio, Giovanni. *Boccaccio on Poetry* trans. Charles G. Osgood. 1930, repr. Indianapolis, 1956.

Boccaccio, Giovanni. *Decameron, Filocolo, Ameto, Fiammetta* ed. Enrico Bianchi, Carlo Salinari and Natalino Sapegno. La Letteratura Italiana 8. Milan, 1952.

Boccaccio, Giovanni. *Decameron* trans. G. H. McWilliam. Harmondsworth, 1972.

Boccaccio, Giovanni. [*Filocolo*]. *Thirteene most Pleasaunt and Delectable Questions . . . englished anno 1566 by H.G.* intro. Edward Hutton. London, 1927.

Boccaccio, Giovanni. *De Casibus Illustrium Virorum.* Facsimile intro. Louis Brewer Hall. Gainesville, Florida, 1962.

Boccaccio, Giovanni. *De Claris Mulieribus.* Berne, 1539.

Boccaccio, Giovanni. *Concerning Famous Women* trans. Guido A. Guarini. New Brunswick, N.J., 1963.

Boccaccio, Giovanni. *Die Mittelenglische Umdichtung von Boccaccios De Claris Mulieribus* ed. Gustav Schleich. Palaestra 144. Leipzig, 1924.

Boitani, Piero. *English Medieval Narrative in the Thirteenth and Fourteenth Centuries* trans. Joan Krakover Hall. Cambridge, 1982.

Bokenham, Osbern. *Legendys of Hooly Wummen* ed. M. S. Serjeantson. EETS O.S. 206, 1938 for 1936.

Born, Lester K. 'Ovid and allegory.' *Speculum* IX (1934) 362–79.

Bornstein, Diane. 'Chaucer's *Tale of Melibee* as an example of the *style clergial*.' *Chaucer Review* XII (1977–8) 236–54.

Bovill, Moira F. *The Decameron and the Canterbury Tales: A Comparative Study.* Unpublished B.Litt. thesis. Oxford, 1966.

Branca, Vittore. *Boccaccio: The Man and his Works* trans. Richard Monges. New York, 1976.

Brewer, Derek. 'The arming of the warrior in European literature and Chaucer.' In Vasta and Thundy pp. 221–43.

Brewer, Derek. *Towards a Chaucerian Poetic.* Sir Israel Gollancz Memorial Lecture. British Academy. London, 1974.

Brewer, Derek, ed. *Chaucer and Chaucerians: Critical Studies in Middle English Literature.* London, 1966.

Brewer, Derek, ed. *Writers and their Background: Geoffrey Chaucer.* London, 1974.

Brooks, Douglas, and Alastair Fowler. 'The meaning of Chaucer's *Knight's Tale.' Medium Aevum* XXXIX (1970) 123–46.

Brown, Carleton. 'The Man of Law's head-link and the Prologue of the *Canterbury Tales.' Studies in Philology* XXXIV (1937) 8–35.

Brown, Emerson. 'The *Merchant's Tale*: why is May called "Mayus"?' *Chaucer Review* II (1967–8) 273–7.

Brown, Emerson. 'The poet's last words: text and meaning at the end of the Parson's Prologue.' *Chaucer Review* X (1975–6) 236–42.

Bryan, W. F., and Germaine Dempster, eds. *Sources and Analogues of Chaucer's Canterbury Tales.* 1941, repr. New York, 1958.

Burrow, John. *Medieval Writers and their Work*. Oxford, 1982.

Burrow, John. *Ricardian Poetry*. London, 1971.

Chaucer, Geoffrey. *The Works of Geoffrey Chaucer* ed. F. N. Robinson. 2nd ed., London, 1957.

Chaucer, Geoffrey. *The Works of Geoffrey Chaucer* ed. W. W. Skeat. 6 vols, Oxford, 1894–1900.

Chaucer, Geoffrey. *The Poetical Works of Geoffrey Chaucer: A Facsimile of Cambridge University Library MS Gg.4.27* intro. M. B. Parkes and Richard Beadle. 3 vols, Cambridge, 1979–80.

Chaucer, Geoffrey. *The Canterbury Tales* ed. John M. Manly. New York, 1928.

Chaucer, Geoffrey. *The Text of the Canterbury Tales* ed. John M. Manly and Edith Rickert. 8 vols, Chicago, 1940.

Chaucer, Geoffrey. *The Canterbury Tales by Geoffrey Chaucer edited from the Hengwrt Manuscript* ed. N. F. Blake. London, 1980.

Chaucer, Geoffrey. *The Canterbury Tales: A Facsimile and Transcription of the Hengwrt Manuscript* ed. Paul G. Ruggiers. Norman, Oklahoma, 1979.

Chaucer, Geoffrey. *The Ellesmere Chaucer reproduced in Facsimile*. 2 vols, Manchester, 1911.

Chaucer, Geoffrey. *The General Prologue to the Canterbury Tales and the Canon's Yeoman's Prologue and Tale* ed. A. V. C. Schmidt. London, 1974.

Chaucer, Geoffrey. *The Knight's Tale* ed. J. A. W. Bennett. 2nd ed., London, 1958.

Cooper, Helen. 'The girl with two lovers: four Canterbury tales.' In Heyworth pp. 65–79.

Cox, Lee Sheridan. 'A question of order in the *Canterbury Tales*.' *Chaucer Review* I (1966–7) 228–52.

Crampton, Georgia Ronan. *The Condition of Creatures: Suffering and Action in Chaucer and Spenser*. New Haven, 1974.

Crow, Martin M., and Clair C. Olson, eds. *Chaucer Life-Records*. Oxford, 1966.

Donaldson, E. T. 'The ordering of the *Canterbury Tales*.' In Mandel and Rosenberg pp. 193–204.

Donaldson, E. T. *Speaking of Chaucer*. London, 1970.

Doyle, A. I., and Malcolm B. Parkes. 'A paleographical introduction.' In *The Canterbury Tales: A Facsimile and Transcription of the Hengwrt Manuscript* ed. Paul G. Ruggiers. Norman, Oklahoma, 1979.

Doyle, A. I., 'The production of the *Canterbury Tales* and the *Confessio Amantis* in the early fifteenth century.' In *Medieval Scribes, Manuscripts and Libraries: Essays presented to N. R. Ker* ed. M. B. Parkes and Andrew G. Watson. London, 1978. Pp. 163–210.

East, W. G. 'By preeve which that is demonstratif.' *Chaucer Review* XII (1977–8) 78–82.

Eisner, Sigmund. 'Chaucer's use of Nicholas of Lynn's calendar.' *Essays and Studies* XXIX (1976) 1–22.

Finlayson, John. 'The satiric mode and the *Parson's Tale*.' *Chaucer Review* VI (1971–2) 94–116.

Fisher, John H. *John Gower: Moral Philosopher and Friend of Chaucer*. London, 1956.

Frank, Robert Worth. *Chaucer and the Legend of Good Women*. Cambridge, Mass., 1972.

Frye, Northrop. *Anatomy of Criticism: Four Essays.* Princeton, 1957, repr. 1971.

Frye, Northrop. *The Secular Scripture: A Study of the Structure of Romance.* Cambridge, Mass., 1976.

Gaylord, Alan T. 'The promises in *The Franklin's Tale.' ELH* XXXI (1964) 331–65.

Gaylord, Alan T. '*Sentence* and *Solaas* in Fragment VII of the *Canterbury Tales*: Harry Bailey as horseback editor.' *PMLA* LXXXII (1967) 226–35.

Geoffrey of Monmouth. *Historia Regum Britanniae* ed. Jacob Hammer. Cambridge, Mass., 1951.

Geoffrey of Monmouth. *The History of the Kings of Britain* trans. Lewis Thorpe. Harmondsworth, 1966.

Geoffrey de la Tour-Landry. *The Book of the Knight of la Tour-Landry* ed. Thomas Wright. EETS O.S. 33, 1868.

Geoffrey de la Tour-Landry. *The Book of the Knight of the Tower* trans. William Caxton, ed. M. Y. Offord. EETS S.S. 2, 1971.

Gesta Romanorum ed. Hermann Oesterley. Berlin, 1872.

Gesta Romanorum ed. Sidney J. H. Herrtage. EETS E.S. 33, 1879.

Gesta Romanorum trans. Rev. Charles Swan, revised by Wynnard Hooper. London, 1905.

Ghisalberti, Fausto. 'Mediaeval biographies of Ovid.' *Journal of the Warburg and Courtauld Institutes* IX (1946) 10–59.

Godfrey of Viterbo. *Gotifredi Viterbiensis Opera* ed. G. Waitz. Monumenta Germaniae Historica: Scriptorum 22. Hanover, 1872.

Gower, John. *The Complete Works of John Gower* ed. G. C. Macaulay. 4 vols, Oxford, 1899–1902.

Gower, John. *The English Works of John Gower* ed. G. C. Macaulay. 2 vols, EETS E.S. 81–2, 1900–01.

Grennen, Joseph E. 'Saint Cecilia's "chemical wedding": the unity of the *Canterbury Tales*, Fragment VIII.' *JEGP* LXV (1966) 466–81.

Grubmüller, Klaus. *Meister Esopus: Untersuchungen zu Geschichte und Funktion der Fabel im Mittelalter.* Münchener Texte und Untersuchungen zur Deutschen Literatur des Mittelalters 56. Munich, 1977.

Haines, R. Michael. 'Fortune, nature, and grace in Fragment C.' *Chaucer Review* X (1975–6) 220–35.

Haller, Robert S. 'The *Knight's Tale* and the epic tradition.' *Chaucer Review* I (1966–7) 67–84.

Hamel, Mary. 'And now for something completely different: the relationship between the *Prioress's Tale* and the *Rime of Sir Thopas.' Chaucer Review* XIV (1979–80) 251–9.

Hammond, Eleanor Prescott. *Chaucer: A Bibliographical Manual.* New York, 1908.

Hervieux, Léopold, ed. *Les Fabulistes Latins depuis le Siècle d'Auguste jusqu'à la Fin du Moyen Age.* 5 vols, Paris, 1884–99.

Heyworth, P. L., ed. *Medieval Studies for J. A. W. Bennett.* Oxford, 1981.

Hibbard (Loomis), Laura A. *Mediaeval Romance in England.* 2nd ed., New York, 1960.

Hirsh, John. 'Why does the Miller's Tale take place on a Monday?' *English Language Notes* XIII (1975) 86–90.

Holcot, Robert. *In Librum Sapientiae Regis Salomonis Praelectiones CCXIII.* Bâle, 1586.

Howard, Donald R. *The Idea of the Canterbury Tales.* Berkeley and Los Angeles, 1976.

Huizinga, Johan. *Homo Ludens.* 1949, repr. London, 1970.

Hume, Kathryn. 'Why Chaucer calls the *Franklin's Tale* a Breton lai.' *Philological Quarterly* LI (1972) 365–79.

Jacobus a Voragine. *Legenda Aurea* ed. Th. Graesse. 2nd ed., Leipzig, 1850.

John of Capua. *Johannis de Capua Directorium Vitae Humanae* ed. Joseph Derenbourg. Bibliothèque de l'École des Hautes Études 72. Paris, 1887–9.

John of Capua. *The Morall Philosophie of Doni* trans. Sir Thomas North (1570), ed. Joseph Jacobs as *The Fables of Bidpai.* London, 1888.

Jones, Terry. *Chaucer's Knight: The Portrait of a Medieval Mercenary.* London, 1980.

Joseph, Gerhard. 'The gifts of nature, fortune, and grace in the *Physician's, Pardoner's,* and *Parson's Tales.' Chaucer Review* IX (1974–5) 237–45.

Josipovici, Gabriel. *The World and the Book.* 2nd ed., London, 1979.

Kalila and Dimna: Selected Fables of Bidpai retold by Ramsay Wood. London, 1982.

Kaske, Carol V. 'Getting around the Parson's Tale: an alternative to allegory and irony.' In *Chaucer at Albany* ed. Rossell Hope Robbins. New York, 1975. Pp. 147–77.

Kaske, R. E. 'The *Canticum Canticorum* in the Miller's Tale.' *Studies in Philology* LIX (1962) 479–500.

Kaske, R. E. 'The Knight's interruption of the Monk's Tale.' *ELH* XXIV (1957) 249–68.

Kean, P. M. *Chaucer and the Making of English Poetry* Vol. II: *The Art of Narrative.* London, 1972.

Kellogg, Alfred L. *Chaucer, Langland, Arthur: Essays in Middle English Literature.* New Jersey, 1972.

Kiernan, Kevin S. 'The art of the descending catalogue, and a fresh look at Alisoun.' *Chaucer Review* X (1975–6) 1–16.

Kittredge, George Lyman. 'Chaucer's discussion of marriage.' 1911; repr. in Schoeck and Taylor I 130–59.

Langland, William. *The Vision of William concerning Piers the Plowman* ed. Walter W. Skeat. 2 vols, 1886, repr. London, 1965.

Lenaghan, R. T. 'The Nun's Priest's fable.' *PMLA* LXXVII (1963) 300–7.

Loomis, Laura Hibbard. *Adventures in the Middle Ages.* New York, 1962.

Lydgate, John. *Lydgate's Siege of Thebes* ed. Axel Erdmann. Part I, EETS E.S. 108, 1911.

McGrady, Donald. 'Chaucer and the *Decameron* reconsidered.' *Chaucer Review* XII (1977–8) 1–26.

Mandel, Jerome, and Bruce A. Rosenberg, eds. *Medieval Literature and Folklore Studies: Essays in Honor of Francis Lee Utley.* New Jersey, 1970.

Manly, John M., and Edith Rickert. *The Text of the Canterbury Tales.* 8 vols, Chicago, 1940.

Mann, Jill. *Chaucer and Medieval Estates Satire: The Literature of Social Classes and the General Prologue to the Canterbury Tales.* Cambridge, 1973.

Mann, Jill. 'The *Speculum Stultorum* and the *Nun's Priest's Tale.*' *Chaucer Review* IX (1974–5) 262–82.

Manning, Stephen. 'The Nun's Priest's morality and the mediaeval attitude toward fables.' *JEGP* LIX (1960) 403–16.

Mannyng, Robert. *Robert of Brunne's 'Handlyng Synne'* ed. Frederick J. Furnivall. EETS O.S. 119, 123; 1901, 1903.

Mannyng, Robert. *The Story of England* ed. F. J. Furnivall. Rolls Series, 2 vols, 1887.

Marie de France. *Die Fabeln der Marie de France* ed. Karl Warnke. Bibliotheca Normannica 6. Halle, 1898.

Marie de France. *Lais* ed. A. Ewert. 1944, repr. Oxford, 1963.

Minor Poems of the Vernon MS Vol. I ed. Carl Horstmann. EETS O.S. 98, 1892.

Morsbach, Lorenz. 'Chaucer's Plan der *Canterbury Tales* und Boccaccios *Decamerone.*' *Englische Studien* XLII (1910) 43–52.

Muscatine, Charles. *Chaucer and the French Tradition*. Berkeley and Los Angeles, 1957.

Neville, Marie. 'The function of the Squire's Tale in the Canterbury scheme.' *JEGP* L (1951) 167–79.

Nykrog, Per. *Les Fabliaux*. 1957; repr. Publications Romanes et Françaises 123. Geneva, 1973.

Ovid. *Metamorphoses* ed. and trans. Frank Justus Miller. Loeb Classical Library, 2 vols, London, 1958–60.

Ovide Moralisé ed. C. de Boer. Verhandelingen der Koninklijke Akademie van Wettenschappen te Amsterdam: Adfeeling Letterkunde, Nieuwe Reeks, vols 15, 21, 30, 37, 43. 1915–38.

Owen, Charles A. *Pilgrimage and Storytelling in the Canterbury Tales*. Norman, Oklahoma, 1977.

Palomo, Dolores. 'What Chaucer really did to *Le Livre de Melibee.*' *Philological Quarterly* LIII (1974) 304–20.

Payne, F. Anne. *Chaucer and Menippean Satire*. Madison, Wis., 1981.

Payne, Robert O. *The Key of Remembrance: A Study of Chaucer's Poetics*. New Haven, 1963.

Pearcy, Roy J. 'Chaucer's Franklin and the literary Vavasour.' *Chaucer Review* VIII (1973–4) 33–59.

Pearsall, D. A. 'The Squire as story-teller.' *University of Toronto Quarterly* XXXIV (1964–5) 82–92.

Petrarca, Francesco. *De Viris Illustribus Vitae* ed. Luigi Razzolini. 2 vols, Bologna, 1874.

Praz, Mario. 'Chaucer and the great Italian writers of the Trecento.' *Monthly Criterion* VI (1927) 18–39, 131–57, 238–42.

Richardson, Janette. *Blameth Nat Me: A Study of Imagery in Chaucer's Fabliaux*. Mouton Studies in English Literature 58. The Hague, 1970.

Robertson, D. W. *Essays in Medieval Culture*. Princeton, 1980.

Root, R. K. 'Chaucer and the Decameron.' *Englische Studien* XLIV (1911) 1–7.

Rosenberg, Bruce A. 'The contrary tales of the Second Nun and the Canon's Yeoman.' *Chaucer Review* II (1967–8) 278–91.

Rowland, Beryl. *Blind Beasts: Chaucer's Animal World*. Kent, Ohio, 1971.

Ruggiers, Paul G. *The Art of the Canterbury Tales*. Madison, Wis., 1965.

Ruggiers, Paul G. 'Serious Chaucer: The *Tale of Melibeus* and the Parson's Tale.' In Vasta and Thundy pp. 83–94.

Sayce, Olive. 'Chaucer's "Retractions": the conclusion of the *Canterbury Tales* and its place in literary tradition.' *Medium Ævum* XL (1971) 230–48.

Scattergood, V. J. 'The originality of the *Shipman's Tale.*' *Chaucer Review* XI (1976–7) 210–31.

Schlauch, Margaret. 'The art of Chaucer's prose.' In Brewer, *Chaucer and Chaucerians* pp. 140–63.

Schoeck, Richard J., and Jerome Taylor, eds. *Chaucer Criticism* Vol. I: *The Canterbury Tales*. Notre Dame, 1960.

Sercambi, Giovanni. *Novelle Inedite di Giovanni Sercambi* ed. R. Renier. Turin, 1889.

The Seven Sages of Rome ed. Killis Campbell. Boston, 1907.

The Seven Sages of Rome ed. Karl Brunner. EETS O.S. 191, 1933.

Singleton, Charles S. 'On meaning in the Decameron.' *Italica* XXI (1944) 117–24.

Smalley, Beryl. *English Friars and Antiquity in the Early Fourteenth Century*. Oxford, 1960.

The South English Legendary ed. Charlotte d'Evelyn and Anna J. Mill. Vol. I, EETS O.S. 235, 1956 for 1952.

Spearing, A. C. *Criticism and Medieval Poetry*. 2nd ed., London, 1972.

Sullivan, S. A. *Handlyng Synne in its Tradition*. Unpublished Ph.D. thesis. Cambridge, 1979.

Szittya, Penn R. 'The Green Yeoman as Loathly Lady: the Friar's parody of the Wife of Bath's Tale.' *PMLA* XC (1975) 386–94.

Tatlock, John S. P. 'Boccaccio and the plan of Chaucer's *Canterbury Tales.*' *Anglia* XXXVII (1913) 69–117.

Tuve, Rosemond. *Allegorical Imagery: Some Mediaeval Books and their Posterity*. Princeton, 1966.

Utley, Francis Lee. 'Five genres in the *Clerk's Tale.*' *Chaucer Review* VI (1971–2) 198–228.

Vasta, Edward, and Zacharias P. Thundy, eds. *Chaucerian Problems and Perspectives: Essays presented to Paul E. Beichner*. Notre Dame, 1979.

Vinaver, Eugène. *The Rise of Romance*. Oxford, 1971.

Vincent of Beauvais. *Bibliotheca Mundi (Speculum Maius)*: Vol. II, *Speculum Doctrinale*. Douai, 1624.

Wenzel, Siegfried. 'The source for the "remedia" of the Parson's Tale.' *Traditio* XXVII (1971) 433–53.

Wetherbee, Winthrop. *Platonism and Poetry in the Twelfth Century*. Princeton, 1972.

Whittock, Trevor. *A Reading of the Canterbury Tales*. Cambridge, 1968.

Wilkinson, L. P. *Ovid Recalled*. Cambridge, 1955.

Young, Karl. *The Origin and Development of the Story of Criseyde*. Chaucer Society 1908, repr. New York, 1968.

Zacher, Christian K. *Curiosity and Pilgrimage: The Literature of Discovery in Fourteenth-Century England*. Baltimore, 1976.

Index